Children of Paradise

Children
of
Paradise

Successful Parenting
for Prosperous Families

Lee Hausner, Ph.D.

PLAZA PRESS

Library of Congress Cataloging-in-Publication Data
Hausner, Lee
  Children of Paradise: Successful Parenting for Prosperous Families /
Lee Hausner, Ph.D.
      p. cm.
Includes bibliographical references.
ISBN 0-9769948-0-1
1. Child rearing—United States. 2. Children of the rich—United States
3. Parent and child—United States. I. Title
HQ769.H397 1990
649'.1—dc20

Second Edition 2005 Lee Hausner, Ph.D., Copyright © 2005

Plaza Press
Two Park Plaza, Suite 1245
Irvine, CA 92614

Distributed by Sheridan Books, Inc., Ann Arbor, MI

Manufactured in the United States of America
10 9 8 7 6 5 4 3 2 1

To my husband, Murray,
for his support and encouragement
on all my endeavors

To my children, Bryan and Carrie,
who have given me great joy and pleasure
in meeting my personal challenges
in parenting.

To my parents, Ernestine and Leon Blum,
whose wisdom and love enabled them to create
an enriched family system in which each
member could grow and flourish.

Contents

Acknowledgement

A book represents many years of accumulated knowledge, experience and the input of clients, friends, and colleagues. I am grateful for all these enriching associations in my life.

My special thanks to Rick Benzel for his professionalism and commitment to this project as well as his willingness to help me increase my skills as a writer; Norman Brokaw for his constant encouragement to undertake this writing project; the Beverly Hills Unified School District staff, whose sensitivity to the education and emotional needs of each student is noteworthy; the Special Services Department of the Beverly Hills Unified School District, my colleagues, who have always given me friendship, knowledge, support and the freedom to grow professionally; all the parents who have participated in my parents classes and come to my programs and have shared so honestly and worked so diligently to increase their parenting effectiveness; and to my colleagues at IFF Advisors, Doug Freeman for the constancy and quality of his advice, professionalism, and friendship, Ken Neisser for his ever-sharpened pencil and wit, and Carrie Huntley for her organizational genius.

Finally, a special thanks to all the multi-generational families over the years who have given me the opportunity to observe the inner workings of the family in all its wondrous complexity through my participation in their family meetings and retreats.

Preface

In the fourteen years since this book was first published, there are many new books on the issues of wealth and children. But few have really provided the step-by-step process in parenting their "children of paradise." It is a well known cliché that money does not buy family happiness. Less universally acknowledged, however, is the fact that a life of privilege can bring with it problems that are far from enviable for both parents and children.

Over the past forty years, I have lectured and taught parenting workshops, counseled and coached thousands of the world's wealthiest and most successful people. For nineteen of those years, I was the senior psychologist for the Beverly Hills School district. Through this close and intimate contact with affluent parents from wide and varying backgrounds, including business, finance, politics, entertainment, and notable heirs, I became aware of many common and serious childrearing problems among this population group. Since that time, I have worked with parents and families throughout the United States and on five continents. To no one's surprise, the issues of parenting are the same and so are the steps to effective parenting.

The parents with whom I have worked are frequently confused, disappointed, and in pain over their children. They want to learn why their children are underachievers in school, seem to lack motivation and drive, appear unhappy and depressed, behave in a dependent and irresponsible manner, and are sometimes involved in various forms of delinquency or substance abuse. Some parents relate to me that they are still financially supporting their offspring when they become adults because their youngsters simply cannot manage their own responsibilities on their income.

Such affluent family situations are both ironic and sad. I find myself working with parents who genuinely love their children and are trying to provide them the very best to ensure a happy childhood and maturation to an equally happy and successful adulthood. Sometimes this necessitates great personal sacrifice on the part of the parents. And yet, from the point of view of these parents, their children appear not to appreciate this life of privilege and, in fact, sometimes abuse their wealth in counter-productive ways.

The problems of these affluent families have led me to some provocative questions. Is the financial success of parents detrimental to the development of emotionally healthy, productive children? Does high parental achievement put children "at risk"? Do the hard-won advantages that affluent parents are rightfully proud to provide their children automatically create problems that outweigh the benefits? What happens to the basics of good parenting when we add the advantages and disadvantages of wealth and power that come with affluence? Do the personality characteristics of economically successful parents—the Type A, driven professional, or the ambitious entrepreneur—get in the way of good parenting? My work in the field has taught me that these are all extremely valid questions.

The purpose of this book is therefore two-fold. Initially, I will identify a number of factors that, indeed, appear to place advantaged families at risk. Awareness of these issues is an important first step in changing your parenting behavior. I firmly believe that many of the problems I have observed in affluent families have occurred because the parents were genuinely unaware of the deleterious effects of their own actions and attitudes on their children.

But awareness of these dangers is only the first step in becoming an effective parent. Corrective actions must also take place if you are to be truly successful in avoiding the pitfalls and challenges frequently encountered in affluent families. The second goal of this book is therefore to provide a nine-step action plan that you can follow to increase your effectiveness.

In the second chapter, we will examine the heart and soul of good parenting: building your child's self-esteem. This first step identifies two important actions you can take to enhance your child's sense pf personal worth, as well as pointing out what you might unknowingly be doing that creates in your child a negative self-image, perhaps the most destructive force in preventing a child from maturing into a happy, productive adult.

One of the prices many affluent parents pay for their success is loss of time and energy for the family. Step two therefore presents an analysis of three extremely important areas in which time spent with your children is crucial to their development. There are also suggestions for reducing your personal stress level and for transforming the time you spend with your children into quality time. Additionally, since many affluent parents must frequently travel on business, we will examine how to hire and train responsible caregivers to help raise your children and maintain your value system while being your surrogates.

Realistic expectations will be the focus of step three. Many affluent children fail to live up to their potential, but the reason is often the unrealistic pressure and standards parents apply to make their children achieve. It is therefore important that you understand how to shift your focus from recognizing only a specific end product, which your children often cannot achieve, to acknowledging the effort and small steps they take each day. By learning how to encourage your children to excel in those areas they enjoy, you can remove the pressure and build your child's internal motivation—the only motivation that truly lasts.

Step four will help parents make the shift from being a "good" to a "responsible" parent. This difference is crucial. Whereas the former kind of parent is excessively involved in his child's life, the latter kind of parent learns to create a balance in his involvement that permits a child to develop independence and competency skills, both of which are critical to positive self-esteem.

Steps five and six address the ever problematic issue of communication between parents and children. In step five, you will initially learn how to increase your listening skills so that you can better understand who your children are—their fears, hopes and dreams. When parents cannot listen to their children, they have created one of the most serious blocks to effective parenting.

Step six will then examine techniques for talking to your child in a supportive and respectful manner. Many affluent parents have told me that they are the last to know what is happening in their children's lives. Unfortunately, the reason for this is too often that they do not know how to talk to their children, or how to develop a close and comfortable communication style in which problems can be calmly discussed and resolved in mutually satisfying ways.

The spoiled brat is often the first picture that comes to mind when people think about rich children. Materially overindulging your child will seriously interfere with healthy psychological and emotional development. Step seven therefore addresses this issue, and provides several guidelines for avoiding overindulgence and for giving your children a healthy perspective on possessions.

All parents want their children to benefit from and enjoy the fruits of their hard work. But when your children grow into adulthood without understanding the value of a dollar, or how to save and invest, you are guaranteeing problems. Step eight will therefore look at methods for helping your child develop a practical understanding of finances and money management skills so that he will grow up with a realistic concept of money and how to manage it.

Finally, step nine will address methods of disciplining your children, when necessary, so that they will learn self-regulatory controls for successful functioning within the family as well as within society.

Throughout this book, I have used specific examples drawn from my clinical experience. These cases are based on actual family histories, although obviously the details have been changed to protect confidentiality. The children cited in these examples vary in age; however, the principles that each example illustrates have the same implications whether your child is a toddler or an adolescent.

Your children are a very precious resource. They have the capacity to provide great joy, or devastating pain and despair. I have seen the anguish on the faces of many affluent parents whose children are experiencing serious difficulties. They are deeply concerned; and when their child is in pain, they, too, are hurting. Their frustration with the lack of an immediate solution is usually clearly evident.

But, unfortunately, when we are dealing with human behavior, there is no quick fix or easy answer. This book does not offer an instant solution, nor does it present simplistic answers to the complex problems of parenting within an affluent environment. As you will see, in addition to the specific parenting techniques described here, your own attitudes, awareness, sensitivity and intuition can all make a difference.

The application of this program takes time, thought, practice, and patience. However, those parents who have followed the recommendations contained in these nine steps have seen their children utilize the advantages of affluence to become well-adjusted, productive young adults. Whether your child is a toddler or a teen, I encourage you to begin immediately utilizing these steps. You will guarantee that your beloved children will never become like the "disadvantaged advantaged" children of paradise I have too often seen.

Please note, if you are currently experiencing difficulties in your family, the techniques herein can improve your effectiveness in resolving many situations. However, if serious disturbances have already occurred, your ability to apply the methodology of this program may require the assistance of a well-qualified mental health professional, and I can only encourage you to take that step if needed.

I hope this fresh and updated look at an old and familiar challenge is helpful to new and not so new parents and families.

Lee Hausner, Ph.D.
Los Angeles, California
June 2005

ONE

How Affluence
Helps—and Hinders

WANTED: Two warm, patient, and selfless individuals with diverse abilities and talents to direct the development of a critical, long-range project, the outcome of which will have significant consequences on the general well-being of all involved. HOURS: Must be flexible. Job can, during crises, require maximum of twenty-four hours per day. Limited vacation time. SALARY RANGE: None. Compensation will be in the form of psychological and emotional satisfaction, which can be very high but is not at all guaranteed. Please note there are considerable *unreimbursed* monetary expenditures required in order to do the job adequately. Additional qualifications include:

- Strong managerial and organizational skills
- Ability to deal with stress and mood swings
- Crisis management expertise
- Purchasing agent
- Paramedical background
- Ability to demonstrate love and support regardless of the situation
- Skill in a variety of motivational techniques
- Outstanding listening skills and ability to draw conclusions from a minimal amount of shared information

- Ability to communicate in a calm, clear, concise manner even though responses may be inappropriate and hysterical
- Must be a tough but fair negotiator
- Ability to function as a team member of this project and negotiate necessary compromises with coworker regarding goals and strategies

Project Title: Parenting

Few would disagree with the proposition that parenting is one of the toughest, most challenging and overwhelming jobs around. If you put the above job description on the wall of an employment agency, it is doubtful that anyone would apply.

Perhaps you are even among those who would say, "If I knew what I was getting myself into I never would have become a parent." But that is the classic paradox. It is virtually impossible to comprehend the difficulties and challenges of parenthood without experiencing them, and by then it is too late to change your mind. You are already a parent, and children, unfortunately, don't come with a "satisfaction guaranteed or your money cheerfully refunded" warranty. You are committed to lifetime involvement.

Parenting should not be viewed as an overwhelming chore and a source of constant frustration. It can, in fact, be quite the opposite. Good parenting creates a happy family life and is perhaps the most meaningful and reliable source of ongoing pleasure and personal satisfaction human beings have. It is only when the process if not effective that it can seem a burden, or lead to pain and anguish for both parent and child.

The problem is, most people enter parenthood with little, if any, training—not even an apprenticeship period. There are no formalized educational programs for parents, no licensing requirements, and virtually no supervision (in-laws notwithstanding). Suddenly you have a child and the reality is that the manner in which you parent this baby will affect not only his or her life but *yours*, either positively or negatively, for as long as you live.

Because mothers and fathers have been around for so long, it is not surprising that many individuals feel that doing this job should come naturally. Everywhere we look we see children with their parents. But how many of these parents have committed themselves to any formalized course of study?

Affluence Adds a Different Set of Challenges

While effective parenting is an arduous task for all mothers and fathers, and some parenting pitfalls are universal, affluent parents and their offspring face a unique set of problems. Just as poverty has a profound influence, so too does affluence. It creates distinct opportunities as well as problems.

Some of these issues of the affluent are well known: spoiled children with obnoxious behavior and superior attitudes, unmotivated adolescents who care only for their stereos and clothes, reckless teenagers living delinquent and self-destructive lives.

Question the average person about the problems of the wealthy and he may sound like an expert on the subject, quoting the latest installment of VH1's "The Fabulous Life of . . . or "Inside Edition", or an article in a supermarket tabloid. With regularity the media chronicles the exploits and tragic disasters of privileged offspring. We can all recall, for example, the rape conviction of a grandson of the cosmetic baron, Max Factor, the heroin overdose death of a young Kennedy, the brutal and sordid Preppie murder in New York City's Central Park, and the murder and fraud case of the Billionaire Boys Club in Los Angeles, to name a few. Nor are these reports of affluent problems confined exclusively to the United States.

But the majority of affluent parents are neither famous nor royal, and their problems are not the material for tabloids. Today the effects of affluence upon a family are as much of a concern to successful professionals, entrepreneurs, and affluent, two-income couples as to celebrities and heirs to fortunes. And the concerns of these parents are normal and natural. They want their children to grow up healthy, happy, productive, and fulfilled, and they want their job of parenting to be satisfying, painless, and joyful.

Does having money in and of itself sabotage families and corrupt children? Absolutely not. It is definitely possible to have a happy and loving family life and to raise caring, motivated, responsible, and psychologically healthy children even when one has by most standards sizable wealth. This book will show how that can be accomplished.

An Overview of the Problems

Beyond the stereotypes and the media hype, there has been relatively little scientific study directed toward analyzing and evaluating the factors that produce problems for the affluent family. However, when we examine what limited research does exist, we clearly see evidence that all is not well in paradise, that the family problems of the affluent usually do not have monetary solutions (indeed, their money is part of the problem), and that the issues are as deep-rooted as the difficulties in any family. These studies are entirely consistent with the clinical evidence I have observed during my years of working with affluent families both in and outside of the United States.

Based upon this research and my own experience with this population, I have identified several important challenges facing affluent parents and their offspring. Being aware of and understanding these common pitfalls is the first step toward ensuring that your children grow up emotionally and intellectually prepared for successful, productive, and satisfied adult lives in a world that may be quite different from the one in which you were brought up.

The Challenge: Knowing What You Don't Know

The first challenge affluent parents face is based upon the psychology of success. Those who have achieved considerable riches in their professional and financial affairs can often feel invincible. The men and women who have bucked the odds in business, medicine, law, the arts, and other demanding professions, and have risen to the top, can have a hard time imagining that they do not already have what it takes to succeed in an endeavor so universal as parenting.

On one hand, the self-assurance of a successful parent can be a positive force. Children absorb and integrate many parental traits, and so a mother's or father's confidence and security can be infectious. But such self-assurance must be tempered with humility, or else it will be more harmful than beneficial.

I do not believe that anyone can be an effective parent unless he or she is open-minded, willing to question the correctness of his or her own attitudes, able to admit a mistake, and be receptive to new learning. In many cases, the very successful just don't operate from that point of view, or if they do professionally, they don't bring it home.

I recently encountered a father in one of my workshops who began dispensing his authoritative advice to all of the other parents in the group. "You cannot let your children push you around," he told them. "Children need to be put in their place. Make them *earn* your respect." These were just a few of the directives he blurted out throughout the evening. When I asked him later if he had taken prior parenting classes, he handed me his business card, stating, "I never felt it was necessary. I import precious metals, largest on the West Coast. Raising children is like running a business." In further conversation, I discovered that he was remarried, his two children from his first marriage were not on speaking terms with him, and he and his new wife were in constant disagreement over the handling of their two young children. However, his sad home reality did not dissuade this so-called expert from proudly proclaiming his child-rearing philosophy to the world.

Many of my affluent clients need to acknowledge that their attitudes have to be changed. Effective parenting involves a special set of skills, and a special orientation that cannot be taken from the board room, the office, or advice from around the country club poolside. You must acknowledge your vulnerabilities and be open to new learning. This is especially difficult for affluent parents who may feel that the success that has come to them will simply transfer into a problem-free family life.

The Challenge: Differentiating Home from Business

Many wealthy parents feel that by having successfully managed their professional destinies, they can exert the same degree of control with their children. How sadly mistaken they are.

Even those parents who would not openly state that they believe in total control as a child-rearing philosophy may unconsciously adopt it because it is the prevailing approach to so many other important things in their lives. This is especially true for entrepreneurs and executives who manage their own destinies and that of their employees through being both disciplined and highly controlling. They set high standards for themselves and others, constantly driving toward achievement. They have difficulty tolerating imperfections—both in themselves and in those around them. These are take-charge people, masters of achievement, accustomed to telling others what to do and how to do it. Their energy is so well-focused, generally toward the single goal that has created their success, that they have minimal amounts left over for developing a healthy relationship with their family. Frequently they are not very good at listening, especially to their children, whose thoughts and feelings seem trivial.

This management mentality, necessary as it may be in the professional jungle, is simply not conducive to effective parenting. Controlling parents can often become overly intrusive in their children's lives, seriously undermining their development of self-confidence and independence and ultimately causing a deep-seated resentment that destroys the family unit.

Philip, Sr., is an example of this type of parent. Having created and built a remarkably successful insurance business in Southern California through a single-minded determination, he was accustomed to being in control at all times with clients, employees—virtually everyone around him. Even when he displayed warmth and affection, he did it on his own terms. The problem was that

Phillip, Sr., carried over this working style from his business into his relationship with his children.

The predictable outcome was that Phillip, Jr., the oldest of three children, described growing up as a kind of tyranny. Nearly every time he tried to make a decision or express an idea or a feeling contrary to his father's opinion, he was rebuked. As a result, Phillip, Jr., vented his smoldering anger in asocial, illegal, and sometimes dangerous ways. During his adolescence, he participated in a number of pranks for which he was arrested, received grades vastly below his potential, and experimented with drugs in high school, nearly failing to graduate. His problems spilled over into his adulthood in the form of a failed marriage, career instability, and depression.

I worked with Phillip, Jr., when he was in high school and have stayed in touch with him. Now in his thirties, he still experiences rage at always having had to acquiesce to his father's demands and directives. In his mind, he feels punished for the crime of trying to be his own person. Through years of therapy, Phillip, Jr., has now begun to resolve the emotional scars of his childhood. Today, his relationship with his father is much less stormy, but there is still a great deal of tension and occasional clashes of will whenever they are together.

Phillip, Jr., is, ironically, the most well-adjusted member of his family. His brother is still struggling with addiction problems and has been unable to function in any kind of career—or even hold a job. His sister, he tells me, is in an abusive marriage which she refuses to leave. Her domineering husband has forcibly estranged her from her family.

Yet, Phillip, Sr. was truly not a malicious father. He was devoted to his family and always tried to be there for them. He loved his children, only wanting what he thought was best for them—a subject on which he considered himself an expert. Unfortunately, his love was too often expressed in a stifling manner that allowed for only one of two reactions: passivity or rebellion, neither of which is healthy for children.

Children need to be nurtured and encouraged, not managed or controlled by a domineering parent. They need tolerance when they make mistakes, and the willingness to allow them to make their own choices. They need to know that parents will listen and discuss their problems, not simply lecture or pontificate to them. Above all, they need opportunities to take charge of themselves and to assume personal responsibility if they are eventually to manage their own lives. If these skills are not part of your management style, it is clearly time to make a change in your parenting techniques.

The Challenge: Having Enough Time

Time is a limited commodity for many affluent parents. Their career and social commitments constantly compete with family needs, and mandatory business and social engagements can severely cut into evenings and eliminate free time on weekends. Professional cohorts, too, may add to the pressure, offering little understanding for a colleague's familial obligations.

As a result, many affluent children are raised by nannies or housekeepers, and see their parents only a few hours each day, or in some cases, each week. In such situations, these children may grow up lacking sufficient parental attention, strong role models, and a close-knit family.

I recently encountered a family consisting of a mother, father, three children, a nanny, and three others in household help. The parents, highly successful restaurateurs, spent the vast majority of their time traveling to their various restaurants all over the country. Their children were so conditioned to seeing their parents only rarely that it hardly seemed to faze them when Mom and Dad flew off to Chicago, Denver, or Palm Beach. Yet, when one of the nannies quit, the children were devastated and went through a period of mourning as if they had lost the parents themselves. The shock of this response forced these parents to reevaluate their lifestyle and make some dramatic changes so that they could reestablish closeness within their family.

Clearly, not all affluent families reach this extreme, but most do struggle with severely limited time and how they might enhance the little amount they have available for their children. The parents in my workshops are constantly looking for guidelines to establish what has been called quality time, shared moments that are special to both parent and child. Some busy parents are even looking for specific rules about what might be a minimum amount of time they need to devote to their children.

While it is not possible to create universal rules regarding time, learning effective parenting techniques can make the time you spend with your children meaningful, memorable, and special so that you are, in a sense, with them even when you are not. It is entirely possible to be an effective parent and role model for your children without giving up your active social life or feeling like you are semi-retired.

The Challenge: Learning New Motivational Techniques

The problem of motivating children to do their best and fulfill their true potential is a general parenting concern, but affluence adds several special considerations.

First, many affluent parents can be described as super achievers, a complimentary term for people who have mastered a field or profession with a level of excellence far beyond others. However, when these parents bring the super-achievement mentality to bear upon their children, expecting the same high levels of success from them at school and in their outside activities, they fail to realize that this attitude almost always has the opposite effect. When parents place too much pressure on a child to achieve at unrealistically high levels, they may give that child feelings of hopelessness and anxiety. If the child thinks, "How can I ever reach the exalted levels of Mom and Dad's success?" the end result may be that she does not try at all.

Even those overly pressured children who do try to put forth their best effort often discover that nothing is good enough to satisfy a perfection-oriented Mom and Dad. If they got a B, they should have gotten an A. If they got an A, they then must explain why they did not get all A's before, and so on. One child I know told of bringing home a report card with five A's only to be asked: "What's the matter, have they stopped giving out A+'s?" And this was from a parent who, although a highly successful business-woman in advertising, had been a very poor student in college. The perfectionism that might drive Mom or Dad to the pinnacle of success can create incapacitating frustration for their children and ultimately lead to burn out in a child who was initially trying his hardest.

Another reason that affluent children often have motivational problems is that they have little experience in learning the rela-tionship between effort and reward. One mental health profes-sional who deals with affluent youngsters and their parents recently illustrated this problem of motivation quite vividly when he told me of a mother who was buying her son a new BMW con-vertible for his high school graduation.

"You must be very proud of him," commented my colleague.

"Yes," said the mother, he didn't get any A's or B's, but since he didn't fail any of his classes and only got into trouble once, I think he deserves a little reward."

My colleague was appalled. What kind of message was this young man getting from his parents about the connection between effort and reward? My colleague recalled his own first car, and how hard he had worked and saved to achieve his desire. He was moti-vated because he knew that without his efforts, there would be no reward. Would our new high school graduate, driving his shiny BMW convertible, ever be able to make the connection between real effort and achievement?

Above all, many wealthy children lack internal motivation because they know that if they do not succeed, they will have a financial safety net to catch them. These children are usually not inherently lazy, but they lack the basic drive that necessity and hardship provide. Obviously, these conditions do not exist in the affluent family, and the message of creating them artificially is not believable.

In families of substantial inheritance there are special chal-lenges. In some cases, the parents do not appear to work on a regular basis, and so the children do not observe a diligent work ethic and, correspondingly, lack an achievement model to emulate.

Nelson Aldrich, in his book, *Old Money*, states:

> The inheritor is placed in the unique position of being able to choose whether to participate in purposeful activities or do nothing at all. Because they are not forced into participation, they often don't take risks, stretch themselves, connect in a meaningful and instructive way with others, and end up leading an isolated life, one which is lacking in the richness and complexity of experiences.

That is why so many young inheritors express a sense of emptiness, unhappiness, and depression. Their lives have no clear purpose.

All affluent parents must look for motivational techniques to stimulate their children to excel and to take responsibility for themselves. Furthermore, the choice of techniques is particularly important, since to be truly effective, they must not pressure the child or set up unrealistic expectations the child could never achieve.

The Challenge: Permitting Children to Be Personally Responsible

Many affluent families employ the services of outside help. From housekeeper to gardeners to butlers, the children often grow accustomed to having others do for them what they might otherwise do for themselves. One affluent child recently told me that when his mother asks him to clean his room he simply orders the maid to do it.

But this kind of environment can create in children an unhealthy dependence on others, and an inability or unwillingness to take care of themselves. This dependence often can continue throughout childhood and adolescence, and potentially cripple them as adults.

In his book, *Children of the Rich*, psychiatrist Burton Wixen elaborates on this problem. According to Wixen, children cared for by servants who immediately gratify all their needs on demand learn little about independent functioning or coping with frustration. Without an ability to tolerate the initial difficulty of a new situation, such children cannot stick with a task long enough to develop an absorbing interest or a sense of achievement. As a result, they are easily bored. Many psychiatric professionals see this type of boredom as a potential precursor to adolescent drug experimentation as well as other potentially disastrous risk-taking behaviors.

Clearly, using household help is necessary in many affluent families. However, you, as parents, must recognize the potential for the dependency syndrome and learn ways, through your parenting techniques, to mitigate it.

The Challenge: Avoiding Both Guilt and Entitlement

As wonderful as being an heir appears to many people, being the recipient of money without having had any part in achieving it can have two serious negative effects: guilt and entitlement.

Regarding the first, many children of the affluent feel undeserving of their parents' wealth, since they had no part in earning it. In some cases, the parents may even point this out to their children. In either case, the resulting emotion is guilt.

Affluent children often believe that they only way to relieve this guilt is to live up to the success of their parents or forefathers, yet they may feel inadequate or unable to do so. In his book, *Rich Kids*, John Sedgwick examines this dilemma.

> Hard as it must be to make a fortune, it is better than receiving one out of the blue. Earned money is clearly one's own, an affirmation of talent, energy, self. An inheritance is none of these things. Instead of being a source of pride, it is a subject of embarrassment; instead of rewarding accomplishment, it fosters sloth. Instead of belonging to you, you belong to it.

The guilt of the affluent child becomes a dark cloud hanging above his or her every moment. Mark exemplifies this situation. The son of a wealthy Beverly Hills family and now a parent himself, he still vividly recalls his mother's consistent response to any of his expressions of anger, disappointment, or frustration, or to any critical statement he might make concerning family matters. She would immediately remind him how lucky he was to have all the material advantages he enjoyed, telling him that rather than complain, he should feel grateful and appreciative.

Today, Mark is a brooding, withdrawn adult. While he acknowledges that he did, indeed, enjoy these benefits, and was appreciative of them all, it nevertheless troubled him that his mother constantly focused on their material advantages (for which he could take no credit), and invariably dismissed his emotions, making him think he was somehow wrong for feeling hurt or for questioning. Mark recalled:

> I would end my conversations with mother feeling very guilty and actually envying children from poor families whom I fantasized had the understanding of their parents. I remember thinking that, yes, we could afford to buy a new car every year and go on exotic vacations, but we couldn't afford to make each other feel good about ourselves.

While growing up amidst wealth can foster feelings of guilt, it can also create a somewhat opposite point of view: the feeling of entitlement. "Wealth does not corrupt, nor does it ennoble," writes Robert Coles in *Children of Crises, The Privileged Ones*. "But wealth can govern the minds of privileged children, giving them a unique identity which they never lose, whether they grow up to be stock brokers or dilettantes and whether they lead healthy or unstable lives." Coles found that virtually all wealthy families transmit an entitlement message to their children: I have the right to money and power by virtue of birth rather than achievement.

Author Ferdinand Lundberg describes a similar sense of specialness among the wealthy in *The Rich and the Super Rich*.

> What is problematic about the rich is more as follows: The possession of wealth, inherited or acquired, itself informs the possessor that he is special, that he holds the winning cards over most people

in most social situations and may so turn his head as to give him delusions of inherent superiority. Money is like a spirited horse in at least this respect: One must know how to ride it, which few really do.

Superficially, the attitude of entitlement may appear to be self-confidence, a trait all parents want their children to possess. But beneath the surface there can be serious psychological problems. If a child feels the world owes him, then he will have little motivation to achieve independently, waiting passively instead for life's "goodies" to be presented to him. In the most extreme cases, feelings of entitlement may result in a personality disorder called narcissistic entitlement. This type of individual is so totally absorbed in fulfilling his own needs that he lacks any sensitivity to the needs of others. Children with such an over-emphasis on self have tremendous difficult forming meaningful relationships or feeling empathy for others.

Robert Coles also noticed that the entitlement message can give children an exaggerated sense of class, superiority, and even power. These children may grow up believing rules are made for others, and their disregard for school or legal restrictions often brings them into serious conflict with authorities.

One client of mine, a student at a private prep school, told me the following story about her wealthy roommate, Megan, who saw her working hard on a term paper one day. Megan exclaimed with consternation, "What's the matter with you? Don't you know that everyone buys those silly papers? You don't have to waste your time writing these assignments yourself." Megan had completely lost sight of what an educational experience really involved. She felt *entitled* to a good grade with no effort other than writing a check. The challenge for affluent parents is to make their children appreciative of the special financial benefits in their lives without either the guilt trip or the passive "you-owe-me" complex.

The Challenge: Keeping Money in Its Place

Many affluent children fail to learn to understand their relationship to money or how to manage it effectively. Since money is plentiful, it is often difficult for these youngsters to associate its value with the work or effort that it represents on the part of the wealth creator. To them, it has always been there; it is a given.

If affluent parents do not actively instill within their children a sense of value and respect for money and the effort earning it requires, the result can be a child who not only believes there is an endless supply of capital, but who consequently abuses it as well. A case in point is the lost and found boxes in the schools of affluent neighborhoods—by year's end they could stock the most exclusive children's clothing store with unclaimed items.

Unfortunately, some affluent parents fail to see the issue of understanding money as a problem. They believe that their children shouldn't have to be concerned with mundane money matters since their needs will always be taken care of through allowances and inheritance.

But without a capacity to value money, children do not acquire the ability to *manage* it. As adults, their ignorance can lead to reckless spending, careless investing, and, in the most extreme cases, the squandering of an entire family fortune. "Shirt sleeves to shirt sleeves" is a universally accepted adage. Addtionally, research shows that, contrary to popular belief, family business empires are not passed down from generation to generation through the ages. On the average, by the third generation (second generation of inheritors) the fortune is greatly dissipated. One sad example of this is the once fabulously wealthy Vanderbilt family, whose great fortune is lost today.

The Challenge: Helping Your Child to a Self-Generated Identify

The process of creating an individual identify can become particularly problematic for children in affluent families.

Children of high-profile parents, such as celebrities or politicians, or even well-known business people or professionals, are prime examples of this. They often experience tremendous pressure to conform to an image the external world has created of their family, and, consequently, their own needs and interests are ignored. Family friends and business acquaintances, the media, and sometimes even their own friends, refuse to let them be themselves, or simply think of them as the son or daughter of "Joe or Jane Famous." Walter Cronkite's daughter Kathy, author of *In the Spotlight*, discovered this fact when she interviewed numerous children of celebrities. All of the individuals interviewed shared a common concern in their search for an identity of their own, distinct from that of their famous parents.

The children of the famous may also be painfully aware of the falseness between the outer image the family projects and the underlying reality of what goes on at home. As a result, they can develop an intense rage at having to perpetuate their parents' façade. This anger is most evident in such tell-all books as Christina Crawford's *Mommy Dearest*, and similarly disturbing autobiographies by the children of such immortals as Bing Crosby, Bette Davis, Debbie Reynolds and Eddie Fisher.

But problems of identity for the children of the affluent are not restricted to those who have famous parents. Dr. Michael Stone, professor of clinical psychiatry at Cornell University Medical School, points out that many upwardly mobile, affluent families are preoccupied with rules of etiquette, social façade and maintaining a happy appearance, thereby overemphasizing external matters rather than the internal needs of their children. Dr. Stone also found in his research that since wealthy parents often depend upon domestic employees to help raise their children, these youngsters may have limited time with the mother and father during periods when parental contact and role modeling are crucial for identity formation.

Many affluent children, from both high- or low-profile families, are also nagged by an internal doubt: Am I valued for who I am, or because of my family connections? This has a significant impact on their self-image. From an early age, they may be courted and befriended by people looking for favors: being invited on exotic vacations or to extravagant birthday parties, or meeting a famous parent.

As the affluent child grows older, he often develops defenses against these sorts of opportunists, but such defenses can lead to isolation, loneliness, fear of intimate relationships, and a general lack of confidence with regard to being valued as an independent individual.

In the course of his research reported in "Children of the Rich," noted psychiatrist Dr. Frank Pittman examined fifty wealthy families whose children were his patients. He discovered a sad paradox: If such children were raised with children of lesser (or no) affluence, they tended to lack trust because they were uncertain if they were liked for their money or themselves. Yet, if they were raised with other wealthy children, they lost their sense of identity under the intense pressure to compete. Rather than simply being a person, they felt only like a series of accomplishments and failures.

The positive development of your child's identity is a challenge for the affluent parent. It requires a profound understanding of your youngster's personality, strengths, and interests. This, too, requires parental education.

The Challenge: Developing Your Child's Financial Independence

Many young adults are tempted to live at home during summers and after college. For the affluent youngster, however, this can be an invitation hard to refuse. Between the beautiful room remaining unused, the extra car sitting in the garage, and food service equaling that of the best restaurant in town, many affluent youngsters are now spending months and even years with parents when their less advantaged peers have moved out on their own.

It is a frightening reality for these children to recognize that they cannot duplicate the privileged environment in which they were raised. However, even in today's economic climate where it can often take months to find a job, young adults cannot indefinitely avoid or delay taking the necessary steps to deal with life more realistically.

Many affluent parents today are finding themselves in an active parenting relationship long beyond the time when children should be establishing their own financial and emotional independence. This situation also requires special techniques regarding the when and how of cutting the umbilical cord without damaging their child's self-image, while at the same time providing the impetus for independence that he or she ultimately needs.

The Challenge: Recognizing a Different World

The last challenge facing affluent parents today is simply that childhood, and by extension, parenting, are no longer the same as they were years ago. Because of the rapid changes in our culture and advances in technology over the past twenty years, your own experience as a child no longer translates into automatically knowing, as a parent, the issues your children now face in their development to adulthood. Consider the following factors in our society that youngsters are forced to handle, often at a young age:

Values Confusion. Children today have a much greater sense of freedom and independence in thought and in expression. In school they are encouraged to participate actively in classroom discussions, question the teacher, and even express disagreement, not a common experience for children educated in the forties, fifties, and sixties. Today's children turn on the television set and are exposed to varied types of families—some realistic, some idealized—to which they compare their own, often unfairly. Affluent children in particular have many opportunities not available years ago, such as extensive national and international travel, specialized schools and summer programs, access to expensive cars and boats, and so on. And the effects on today's children of access to and exposure from the Internet, now a fixture in a substantial percentage of American homes, are only just beginning to be studied.

But too many choices can be confusing for a child. Children are, after all, just that: children. In a fast-changing world, they require guidance and informed parental advice in order to mature into responsible adults.

The World Is a Tougher Place. In the past generations, a growing and developing economy offered seemingly unlimited opportunities for all who sought them. Today, although our economy continues to expand, competition has become far more prevalent, making the changes of noteworthy success much less secure. At the same time, career options have become so specialized that it is hard for many young adults to establish a clear and directed goal.

Historically, affluent children have tended to grow up with less of awareness than other kids about the economic realities around them. Yet, in order to succeed in today's competitive market, our children will need that awareness—and they will also need to be assured that it is worth the effort to reach their optimal potential both emotionally and intellectually. While all parents must be concerned about this issue, this is an especially acute problem for the affluent, whose children so often lack the intrinsic ambition of those from poor and middle-class families, and who do not see themselves as able to obtain on their own a standard of living equal to the one in which they were brought up.

Pessimism. When you were growing up, it is likely that you felt optimistic about the future. This is no longer true; the majority of today's youth view their future with a keen awareness of its perils. They are, in many cases, pessimistic, sometimes even fatalistic. They worry about nuclear war, the ecological destruction of the planet, famine, the spread of AIDS, and other world problems that to them appear to have no resolution.

While it is certainly admirable for children to be concerned about important social issues, a lack of optimism about the future can undermine a child's motivation. If a child seriously questions the possibility that he world will not be around long enough for him to become an adult, how much energy will he be willing to invest in a long-range task, such as career preparation, that does not have an immediate payoff?

One manifestation of the hopelessness of today's youth is the rising suicide rate. Chicago psychiatrist Harold Visostsky, who has treated numerous children from the highly affluent North Shore suburbs of Chicago, has stated: "Whatever anger the poor experience may be acted out in anti-social ways—vandalism, homicide, riots. The affluent kid is more likely to take it out on himself, not society."

Drugs. The availability of alcohol and drugs is pervasive; and the age of children first experimenting with illegal substances has become increasingly younger. Drugs offer a quick escape from the realities of personal problems which, to the child, often seem unsolvable.

Affluent parents whose children may have the money to purchase drugs must be prepared to deal with the issue of drugs. They especially need to know how to communicate honestly with their children in order to prevent them from becoming at risk.

All of these new challenges require a different approach to parenting, one that cannot be based on your memory of being a child, or on the parenting models you learned from your parents. If you are thinking, as some parents participating in my workshops have commented, "My parents never knew anything about parenting theory or took classes, and they were able to raise three successful children," you need to recognize that many changes have occurred in your own lifetime and your parenting attitudes may be out of date. You must be prepared to handle these new developments forthrightly and directly. They will not go away.

It's Worth Your Effort

None of the above problems of parenting in affluence is insurmountable, no matter what your current circumstances are. But they require your attention and effort. Your children play a very important role in your life. Unlike a business, you can't cut your loses and sell out if you see your profit margin plummeting. You are always connected to your children, and even when they reach maturity, they remain your children.

The joys of parenting can be wonderful, but the heartbreaks can be devastating. Problems with children can create an intolerable strain on a marriage and a burden throughout your lifetime. I have seen the sullen look of disappointment on the faces of many of my clients. These parents care deeply and are working hard to provide a very special life for their children. "Where did I go wrong?" they painfully ask. The answer most generally lies in their own ignorance. The majority of these parents were simply not aware of the problems their own behavior and parenting style could cause.

But problems with children need not persist. I have seen family turnarounds that when recalled still bring a smile to my face. If any of the pitfalls I have described are causing you concern, you are headed in the right direction. Concern is an important catalyst, a motivator to encourage you to master the techniques that can increase your parental effectiveness and give your child the foundation essential for a productive, satisfying life. By understanding and dealing constructively with the pitfalls, you will find parenting to be a truly rewarding and satisfying experience. Only then can you guide your child toward success and happiness in his or her own life.

I am well aware of the fact that, although your desire may be great, making the necessary adjustments will not be easy for many of you. To the hard-charging entrepreneur or corporate executive, making what amounts to dramatic changes in his or her parenting style may not come naturally. Furthermore, you cannot expect change to occur instantly. But with proper education, practice, and persistence, you can learn and apply new parenting skills.

However, it is up to you as parents to take the leadership role in making these changes. You are the first responsible party, not your children. As you will see, your own parental attitudes and behavior are an important aspect of this book. In many of the issues we will cover, simply becoming aware of your own attitudes and values can greatly enhance your effectiveness. Of course, there are also specific techniques you must learn and practice, but if you, as parents, establish the right environment, your attitudes and actions will inspire your children, and take them out of the risk category.

The Family System

One important point to understand as you begin your transition to becoming an effective parent is the concept of the family system. A family is a dynamic group, made up of multiple interactions between all of its members: each parent toward each child, each child toward each parent, each child toward his or her siblings, and parents toward each other. In addition, mother and father make up a parental unit, which is an entity unto itself, but also a part of the larger family system.

The family system is a newborn child's entire world. His/her feeling about himself in relation to the world comes exclusively from that family system. How the parents respond to the child, their attitudes and values, all combine to create the environment in which a child matures and learns to function.

This family system is in a continual state of flux and reacts to pressures from external as well as internal crises. In the often changing world of the affluent family, such issues as financial difficulties, stress-related illness, divorce, frequent job changes and relocations can all have a significant effect on the interactions within the family system. Through all this, however, the family system assumes the primary responsibility for providing stability, role models, and nurturing for the child.

For this reason, developing a healthy family system is one of the primary goals of this book. Parents need to examine their daily actions in terms of the impact they have on the larger context of the family. The choice of parenting techniques to help your children grow up to be well-adjusted and productive will depend on your own circumstances. Nonetheless, it is important to keep the interactions of the entire system in mind as you begin to implement the principles of effective parenting.

The Apple Doesn't Fall Far from the Tree

Affluent parents must also consider the effects of their own family system. If you were fortunate enough to be raised in a family where your mother and father provided nurturing and encouragement throughout your important developmental years, where you felt loved and cherished because of who you were rather than what you did, where you were given the opportunity to prove your competency and were rewarded with respect and acknowledgement, where criticism was directed toward the unacceptable activity and not toward you personally, then you were lucky indeed to have such excellent role models for parenting within your own family system.

For many parents, however, this ideal picture may not seem familiar or even vaguely like the family in which they were raised. Today we are gaining a wide awareness of how relatively rare truly good parenting was and is, and consequently how much we all have to learn about this treasured skill. Few adults today grew up in perfect circumstances, so it is not so surprising that anger, stress, tension, anxiety, fear, and a general sense of unhappiness often permeate our memories.

Perhaps some of your drive to succeed is the product of these less-than-ideal circumstances. But when adults carry such early negative influences into their own families, the family system will often become dysfunctional. That is, the interaction between various family members will be destructive rather than supportive. In such situations, the children have a high risk of developing and suffering from serious emotional problems. If both parents grew up with dysfunctional family models, the risk for their children is even greater.

Overcoming the demons of one's own childhood is no simple task. Even exhaustive effort does not always yield success in shaking the effects of poor role models. Often I have had a mother in my office agitatedly telling me how she hated her own mother's continual nagging and criticism, how difficult it was to discuss anything without creating a new emotional upheaval, how she had promised herself that she would never do this to her own child. And to her horror, when faced with similar situations with her own daughter, she would hear words that closely imitated her mother's despised words. Or a father will sadly describe the distant, formal relationship he experienced with his own father, always trying to win his praise and affection. No matter what his accomplishments, his father would point out a shortcoming, continually raising the achievement standards to an impossible degree of perfection. Now an adult, this man will sadly admit that he is doing the same thing to his own sons.

The reality is that we learn parenting from our parents, and, sadly, some of us have to *un*learn what they have taught us and relearn a new way. It is up to each individual parent to decide how to best approach an examination of his or her own background. If you feel your own family history has a significant impact on your parenting style, you may wish to seek professional guidance in order to make changes.

Parenting With One Voice

A united parental unit is essential to effective parenting. Although two people enter into marriage with their own parenting models—positive or negative—they must still develop a unified parenting plan in a calm, objective manner so that important issues of child-rearing don't get mixed up with personal issues or those of the marital relationship. And since each parent spends individual time with children, mother and father should not be operating in a manner that directly contradicts each other. Otherwise, children will never be sure what is acceptable and what is not.

This is not to say that successful parents must agree about every aspect of parenting, but rather that when conflicts arise they must be resolved through compromise—and in private. Debate and ambiguity within the parental unit will be communicated to children in many different ways, non-verbally as well as verbally. Children spot such divisions between parents immediately and quickly learn how to use them to their advantage, especially around issues of rules and discipline.

One of the reasons I taught all my parenting programs in the evening rather than during the day is my uncompromising belief that both parents need to participate. Many times, though, I have received a variation of the following call from an apologetic spouse (usually the wife). "I'm looking forward to meeting with you tonight, Dr. Hausner. I was wondering, though . . . Bill has this meeting to prepare for and . . . well, is it really absolutely necessary for my husband to come with me?"

"Only if you want to make sure you both are as successful at parenting as Bill has been in his business," is my usual response.

It is all too easy to abdicate parenting responsibilities or justify prolonged absences from the family with career-related reasons. The influence of both mother and father are equally important in childrearing. You might do well to remember this: it has been stated that on his death bed, no man has ever cried, "I wish I had spent more time at the office."

When both parents receive information from a neutral third party, the issues of parenting are less likely to become mixed up with personal marital issues such as dominance and control. It is quite common for a mother or father in a parenting class to state, "I've said the same thing you are now saying a thousand times before and my husband [or wife] never listened. When you say it, it suddenly becomes gospel in our house!"

The reason for this is that in many marriages, control and power issues in the relationship remain a frequent source of conflict. These issues need to be resolved in order to parent as an effective unit. But before that can happen both partners must become open-minded, and often a neutral teacher is the only way to accomplish that. This book, I hope, can be that neutral teacher.

Educating yourself and planning well are the fundamental principles of creating a strategy for your family happiness. Having a plan means thinking through difficult situations before they occur. It means making the right choices, especially between competing demands.

Through long-range planning, every parent can become a more effective individual. Rather than simply reacting to problems and conflicts as they arise (which so often leads to hindsight and regret), you can take action proactively to enhance your family stability and, in the process, give your child the maximum opportunity to develop a healthy, productive life.

TWO

Step One: Developing Your Child's Self-Esteem

In spite of all the material advantages afforded children of affluence, they are at risk for many of the same kinds of emotional and psychological problems as children from financially impoverished backgrounds. The "golden ghetto" and the ghetto are strangely related in many ways.

First, in both groups, there is often a high incidence of parental deprivation. It may result from parental preoccupation with business, extended travel, relegating parenting tasks to servants, and over involvement with community and social activities. It can also be the result of single-parent families, or the need of a parent to work multiple jobs in order to buy the basic necessities. Whatever the cause, both affluent and impoverished children often find themselves isolated from their parents. The consequences for children of both worlds can be loneliness, frustration, and even depression.

Children from these two economic poles also share a high risk for developing a sense of hopelessness about their lives. The reasons may be opposite and yet the effect is the same. Impoverished children may have trouble imagining that their lives will get any better (or in some urban neighborhoods that they will live long enough to find out). Many affluent children also feel hopelessness motivated by the fear that they will never be able to duplicate the success of their parents or grandparents, and continue to live such a privileged existence.

Above all, however, both groups of children are prone to suffering from a deficiency in what is perhaps the single most important factor in emotional health and success in life for all human beings: self-esteem.

For impoverished children, because they often live under the stress and tension of basic survival in a hostile environment, and having limited opportunity to develop professional competency skills, they can have serious questions about their self-worth. The child of upwardly mobile and affluent parents, however, can also be plagued with these self-doubts, although the causative factors are different. These children often find it hard to believe they are "okay" because they constantly feel under pressure to perform at a level comparable to the achievement of their very successful parents. How, they wonder, can I ever measure up? Since the adults in their world are often controlling, overprotective, and indulgent, these children have limited opportunities to develop independence and a sense of competency, both necessary factors in high self-esteem.

In short, high self-esteem is not guaranteed by social class or related to disposable income. It is not a commodity that can be purchased—though it is more important than any that can be purchased. It cannot be given nor can it be inherited. It is, in fact, earned. A deficiency in self-esteem is often the reason children fail in school, act out in a delinquent manner, become involved in substance abuse, have difficulty focusing on a career, or attempt suicide.

If parents establish a strong foundation of self-esteem in their child's early years, it will remain throughout his lifetime. On the other hand, if such a foundation is *not* created, it becomes increasingly difficult to achieve this ultimate sense of personal contentment and self-respect as the child becomes older.

Self-esteem has become such a popular psychological buzzword that few would deny its importance. In fact, most adults would readily admit a desire to increase their own self-esteem as well as that of their children. But while the concept is generally understood intellectually, the parenting actions necessary to create self-esteem are seldom as clear.

Building high self-esteem in your child is therefore the general umbrella toward which all your parenting skills need to be directed. In order to make this your priority, you need a clear and comprehensive view of what self-esteem really is and how you, as parents, help to create it.

The Key to Ultimate Happiness

Self-esteem is a general sense of well-being vital to all humans. It incorporates a very basic, almost primal, feeling that no matter what is occurring in an individual's environment, he or she is inherently worthwhile and possesses the skills to live a happy and successful life. Dorothy Corkille Bigs, author of the highly acclaimed book, *Your Child's Self-Esteem*, expresses it in this manner.

> Self-esteem is how a person feels about himself. It is his overall judgment of himself—how much he likes his particular person. In fact, self esteem is the mainspring that slates every child for the relationship that exists between the child and those who play a significant role in his life.

Self-esteem expert Nathaniel Branden adds: "Self-esteem is the sum of self-confidence and self-respect. It reflects your implicit judgment of your ability to cope with the challenges of your life and of your right to be happy."

Parents play a pivotal role in the development of a child's self-esteem. The process begins immediately—as soon as a child is born. Infants receive initial information about themselves and their world from the primary caregivers in their family. Are they smiling or frowning? Do they appear tense or relaxed? Is the voice sharp-tongued or soothing? Do they seem fearful or confident?

Infants cannot separate themselves from their caregivers. If the person holding the infant is uncaring, cold, preoccupied, angry, or anxious, the infant internalizes those emotions and believes himself to be responsible for them. If, on the other hand, the mother and father or other caregivers are attentive, relaxed, and cheerful, that infant feels good about himself.

As children get older, more complex interactions have an impact. For example, a toddler given freedom to explore the world will develop a sense of confidence and of ownership of his or her space. If, on the other hand, the parents and other caregivers impose numerous restrictions—the proverbial overdose of "no's"—the child may begin to doubt herself, to fear the unknown, and to feel unworthy.

Noted psychoanalyst and child development expert Erik Erikson cites five developmental stages from which children develop healthy feelings about themselves.

The first is *basic trust*. A child must have a sense of trust in the environment and the important adults in her life. This means she must be able to predict, with some degree of regularity, what will happen in a given situation and be able to gain a handle on "how things work." This is why the child with multiple, ever-changing caregivers may well become fearful of trusting, since a trusted adult may suddenly disappear from her world.

The second important area of emotional development concerns *autonomy*. In order for children to gain a positive self-image, they need to feel a sense of independence. However, powerful, driven parents often take over their children's lives in the same manner they control their employees. Not wanting too many chiefs in the house, they do not actively encourage a child to become strong and independent.

Issues of privacy are also critical in this stage. Children whose parents do not allow them a reasonable degree of privacy—physical and, most importantly, emotional—have difficulty in feeling well-grounded as separate and significant human beings.

The third stage Erikson notes is the experience of *initiative*. A child must be instilled with a level of energy that permits him to approach challenges with undiscouraged effort. Parents who are overly critical and demanding will put the child at risk in this regard.

Through initiative comes the next important task: *industry*, which refers to the ability to learn and be self-motivated. A child must be able to achieve goals and feel at least some degree of accomplishment. The feeling of success is extremely important to a child's sense of personal satisfaction.

The last of Erikson's developmental stages in childhood is that of *identity*: the child's need to have a sense of who he is and be reasonably comfortable with this awareness. It means having a true self rather than feeling and behaving as the child believes others want and expect him to.

My own research and clinical experience has led me to believe that Erikson's five components of healthy self-esteem can be distilled into two very important—and also very accessible—parenting concepts. The first is unconditional love, the feeling within a child that "I am a special, unique, lovable person." The second is the belief that "I am competent."

The following sections will give you a basic understanding of these critical concepts and how you can create an environment to foster these feelings in your child, and thus contribute to ensuring the development of high self-esteem.

Expressing Your Love

Loving your child unconditionally implies that your love is not dependent on any specific conditions or achievements. It doesn't mean that you don't get angry, annoyed, frustrated, disappointed, or critical of his behavior, but it does mean that even at those times when you have and express such feelings regarding the behavior, you show respect and reassure him of his value as a human being. If you, like many successful people, tend to be more judgmental and less unconditional in your attitudes and relationships, giving your child this message of unconditional love may be a problem.

In order to make a change, the easiest way for you to understand unconditional love is to consider it from your child's point of view. Your child must believe that you can accept every aspect of his person. He must feel comfortable expressing all his thoughts and feelings, even those that you might view as negative or hostile. If your child is made to believe that he shouldn't feel that way, or that some feelings are "bad," he will think that he is, in some respects, also bad. After all, he knows the reality of his feelings, and no matter what you say, they exist within him.

Unconditional love also means that your child feels he is treated with dignity and respect. He is not merely an extension of mother and father, but a unique and special individual who plays a vital role within the family system. He believes his contributions are considered as valuable as any other family member.

It is also important to remember that your child must experience unconditional love in his interactions with all the important adults in his life, including caregivers. Every person in your child's life needs to communicate to him continually the idea "you are valued just because of who you are; you do not have to perform or do anything special to be accepted by those who love you; you don't have to be pretty or clever or socially skilled or the best student; you are OK, period!"

At this point you might be thinking this can't be a problem for me because I really do love my child. But in understanding the process by which we develop self-esteem, it is important to note that the emphasis is on the feeling *your child* has of being loved, not on your experience of loving your child. In other words, you may love your child passionately, but unless that child recognizes and feels unconditional love, high self-esteem is not likely to result.

In all your interactions with your child, your focus must always be on the child's feelings. Keep this in mind as you ask yourself not just What am I doing? But also, How will my child perceive what I am doing? If I were my child experiencing this interaction, what would I think?

In my clinical experience with affluent families, I have seen countless instances of a gap between the parents' expressed love and the child's perceived love. Some examples follow.

Case 1. The parents have a deep love for their children, but because of poor choices or bad luck, they hired caregivers who spend a large amount of time with the children but have not been very loving, or have come and gone with regularity. The parents, unaware of the impact on the children, have failed to reassure them that the cause of the instability is not due to the children's bad behavior. Thus the children perceive that they are not lovable, although this is obviously not the parents' intent.

Case 2. The parents have achieved great success and now want "only the best for their child." Unfortunately, in so doing, the parents set up behavior and achievement expectations that immobilize the child and make him feel unloved when he does not reach their goals.

Case 3. The parents with good intentions try to shield their child from life's disappointments and failures, but in so doing, think that only they know what is best. As a result, the child feels discounted since the parents rarely consider her opinion in making decisions, or give her an opportunity to learn from setbacks and failure.

Case 4. The parents, due to pressures in their own lives, have limited family time. As a result, their moments with the children are tense and stressful. Unfortunately, the children are unaware that they are not the cause of the stress, and feel in some way that they must be bad.

Case 5. The parents are celebrities, larger-than-life images idolized by an adoring public. Often in these cases, the parents fail to realize that their children may have internalized a feeling of being unworthy of such special parents, and they don't reassure them of how important they really are.

This can happen not just to parents who are nationally known. Civic leaders, important professionals, recognized executives, prominent members of the community, local heroes, even parents who are popular teachers, may also have a child who needs to know that he or she does in fact deserve such special parents. Since you are the adult, it is up to you to discover if your child feels your love is unconditional. While there are no absolutes in knowing when and how a child perceives love, you don't have to be a mind reader. Use your words; talk to your child about your love.

One way to do this is simply to ask your child from time to time this question: How do you know that I love you? Ask it directly—

in those specific words. Whether you are dealing with toddlers or teenagers, you may be very surprised to learn that what you consider signs of your own expressed love are not what your child considers love at all.

Successfully married couples learn, over time, how to express love in ways that a spouse can understand. It might be a simple smile or wink, or a meaningful word that, even when used only occasionally, reminds both husband and wife that they love one another. And so it should be with parents and children; but it is not. Children are more sensitive in this regard. They need continual reminders about your love, and they need to experience it in direct ways.

One father recently told me how he discovered through this kind of open exchange of feelings that his son, Eric, felt loved when he was struggling with a task and his mother and father did *not* come running right away. "Eric said," the father told me, "that when we let him work things out himself and [do] not try to do everything for him, that it let him know we trusted his ability. That made him feel really loved. He felt we were there for him if he *needed* us but that if we let him not *need* us all the time he felt more loved." The father used this insight about his son to better their relationship. Of course, for some other child, the opposite might be true. She may perceive love only if the parents come running to her assistance at the very first sign of a problem.

Conversely, also ask your child if and when he feels unloved. Again, ask him directly. "Are there times when you feel I don't love you?" You may be stunned to discover how your child interprets your words and actions, including many you may have never considered.

For both questions, listen intently to what your child says. Then, use the information to modify to the best of your ability your behavior wherever you can. You may find that a few small changes will make a world of difference to your child's perception of your love. Through these kinds of honest and sincere discussions about love, you can avoid miscommunication, and thereby close the gap between your intended expression and your child's interpretation.

Finally, one of the most forgotten ways to communicate unconditional love is to remind your child of your feelings whenever you think he might be in doubt. If, for example, you have just completed a difficult discussion or heated argument, always try to end it by assuring your child that you love him and that any negative emotions you have expressed are the result of your sincere love. This simple reminder can go a long way toward enhancing your child's perception of your love, even at your worst moment in his eyes.

Helping Your Child Feel Competent

Love alone is not sufficient to create high self-esteem. I am sure you know yourself of examples of affluent children who were loved, cherished, pampered and indulged by their sincere and affectionate parents, but who were unable to function with any degree of maturity and responsibility in the adult world because they lacked the foundation of a positive self image. Such children never develop a career of their own, float from one relationship to another or become involved with other problem children who likewise fail in their endeavors.

Although these children were not unloved, they lacked the feeling of competency. To be successful in life, children need to receive from surrounding adults the feeling that they are both loved and competent. Competence means a child could make the following belief statements:

- I can physically take care of myself.
- I can handle most problems at home and at school by myself.
- My ideas, opinions, and decisions count.
- I can think and function for myself.
- I can deal with pressure and stress.
- Other people recognize that I can take care of myself and my responsibilities.

- I am not afraid to take a risk or fail.
- If I make a mistake, I learn from it so I won't make the same mistake again.

In spite of their advantages, affluent children are often at risk in the area of competency. Living with strong, capable, and concerned (sometimes to the point of intrusive) parents who frequently tell them exactly what to do and how to do it, and being attended to by doting hired help, these children can easily become handicapped in their development of independence and self-discipline.

Place yourself in this hypothetical position. Imagine that you are learning to play golf. It is a challenging game, requiring practice and training. You proceed to the first tee with your new set of clubs and your instructor. You take your first swing and miss the ball completely. Then, on the second swing, the ball barely rolls off the tee. At this point your instructor says, "Don't worry about it; I'll hit that for you." He proceeds to step up to the ball and drive it toward the green. "Nice shot," he tells you with a wink, then drives you to where the ball landed. What kind of message does this give you? It is going to make you feel capable of mastering the game? Will you be excited to get to the second hole? Not likely.

If, on the other hand, your instructor responds to your inability to drive the ball by reminding you how long it takes to master that skill you would be reassured. If your trainer pointed out how good you already are at tennis and indicated that your athletic ability proves you have the natural talent to be an excellent golfer, you would feel confident. You would keep trying until you began to achieve some degree of success.

Needless to say, the situation is exactly the same for your child. If you perform tasks, make decisions, and fail to give your child reassurance he can succeed independently, the feelings of competency will obviously not result. As with unconditional love, you set the environment for instilling in your child his own perception of competency.

We will explore the techniques of developing competency throughout this book, especially in Chapter 5. However, what you can do immediately, if you are not already so doing, is to begin expressing confidence and support for everything your child attempts. Show your child your concern and interest in his endeavors, but not to the point of suggesting that without you, he or she would fail. Additionally, give your child the opportunity to try new challenges, without interceding or helping prematurely if you believe he might fail.

When parents focus on a child's positive attributes and express a genuine respect for the child's efforts, they will empower that child to cope effectively with challenges and to develop a sense of competency in her own innate skills.

Watching What You Say and Do

One factor that often interferes with a parent's attempt to foster unconditional love and competency is implied negativism. Often without even being aware of the implications, parents will utter statements that have no constructive value in a situation, and will thereby undermine a child's sense of worth and competency.

What follows is a list of typical comments I frequently overhear between parents and children. Since positive self-esteem develops when a child receives information from the world that says he is lovable and competent, would any of these statements give this message? Would these statements make a child feel competent or loved? Do you ever say things such as:

- You have a way of always doing the wrong thing at the wrong time.
- You owe it all to me. If I left things up to you, it would be a disaster.
- I don't know how you would manage without me around.
- What did I do to deserve you?
- I can't wait until summer when you will be away at camp and I can have some peace and quiet.
- I can always count on you to mess things up.
- Get away! Leave me alone!

- You're driving me to drink and your father to a heart attack!
- Don't be such an idiot [or some other negative name].
- Don't you ever apply yourself?
- I'm embarrassed to admit I'm your mother [father]!
- I can never depend on you.
- Your sister [brother] never put us through this.
- You are so irresponsible and lazy.
- If it weren't for you, I could . . .

Realize that children do not only listen, they also watch. They pay attention to you and they know when you are not paying attention to them. The following is a typical example of how parental non-verbal behavior can quickly devalue a child.

Jason comes home from junior high school, bursting with the news of his day. "Mom, guess what happened?"

"Just a minute." Mom is busy talking to a friend on the telephone—for the next hour. The next time Jason tries to tell her, she is busy preparing dinner and listens half-heartedly. Jason senses this.

When Dad gets home Jason tries to get his attention about what happened today at school, but Dad is immediately consumed by the television news, the mail, and a phone call. "Can you tell me about it in five minutes, Jason?" the father offers, clearly preoccupied. This time, Jason drops the subject completely. He decides that all the exciting things of his day really aren't very important after all. Other examples of parental behavior that undermine a child's self-esteem include the following:

- intruding too quickly to complete tasks that your child is having difficulty with
- helping your child with his homework while complaining and appearing agitated throughout the process
- insisting that a task your child wants to undertake is much too hard for him and that he should wait until he is older or until someone can help

- continually criticizing your children's choice of friends while trying to force friendships you consider desirable
- threatening to send your child to live with your ex-spouse, grandparents, or to a boarding school, military academy, or juvenile hall
- comparing siblings or reminding your child of your superior competency at that age

At this point, don't be alarmed if you recognize yourself as a parent who may sometimes make these negative statements or actions— minor doses will not destroy a child. With your new awareness, however, you now need to avoid additional instances of implied negativity. As your child notices your new positive tone and encouragement, you will have taken a big step toward effective parenting to enhance self-esteem.

Self-Esteem Influences Three Critical Areas

Positive self-esteem plays a critical role in a child's overall psychological development. Three areas, however, are particularly affected by a child's self-esteem: social skills, emotional growth, and learning. Recognizing when a child is lacking self-esteem in these three areas is as important a parenting capacity as recognizing when a child is physically ill.

The following stories should strike a resonant chord for parents whose children may be experiencing problems in any of these areas. We will examine the two ends of the spectrum, a child with high self-esteem and one with low self-esteem. In all probability, your child will not fit perfectly into either mold, but will fall somewhere in between.

However, if you do identify your child at the low self-esteem end of the spectrum, your concern is appropriate. In most cases, by following the suggestions in this chapter and throughout the remainder of this book, you will be able to turn the situation around with time, effort, and a sincere dedication to changing your parenting techniques.

Self-Esteem and Social Skills

Brandon is full of self-confidence and personal pride. At school, his outgoing, positive, assertive manner draws others toward him. Because he is not threatened by the achievements of others, he is the child who will be quick to compliment their success, and he will receive the same type of support in return. Any good-natured teasing on the part of his peers does not bother him because he is secure about his own position. He is comfortable letting others have the opportunity to stand out and be noticed.

At home, Brandon is popular among his neighboring children. If he invites a friend to play at his house after school, he is not hurt if the child declines. Brandon simply invites another friend and does not dwell on the refusal.

Taylor's world is quite different. Taylor is a tense, anxious, fearful child who spends much of his time near the protected shelter of his parents or teachers. At school, he does not venture out onto the playground during recess, telling his teacher that others do not play with him because he is not good at sports. Of course, he has never given himself a chance to try, since even the possibility of a rejection is too upsetting to think about.

At home, Taylor spends much of his time alone. He finds it difficult, if not impossible to invite other children to play with him. If Taylor invites someone to his house, and the child declines, Taylor would immediately think, "It must be me. I am not a worthwhile person and others know it." He therefore does not develop his own friendships, and waits quietly for others to notice and invite him.

Moral. The child with high self-esteem feels comfortable with other people, and is able to take the risks of meeting new people. He is not preoccupied with what others think of him or fearful of offending someone. Because he likes himself, he assumes that others will like him. And he is often right—people are generally attracted to someone with self-confidence.

The child with low self-esteem, however, does not believe he is a worthwhile person and always blames himself for not having friends. His social skills perpetuate a vicious cycle:

I can't believe anyone likes me → I'll just stay away from other children → since everyone avoids me, it must be that no one likes me → and so on.

Self-Esteem and Emotional Maturity

Brandon wakes up in the morning, eager for a new day. He does not become upset with teasing from his siblings, and, in fact, is very good at giving it back in a light-handed manner. When his parents ask him to clean his room or perform a chore, he does not become frustrated or burst into tears. If his mother criticizes something he has done, he can listen to the information without becoming defensive, and then can apply it to the task at hand. Brandon recognizes that criticism of a particular behavior does not mean he is a worthless person. He knows he is not expected to be perfect, and that he has many things to learn.

Taylor, on the other hand, is subject to big, emotional mood swings. He may wake up one morning feeling unhappy and anxious, another morning feeling pleased and cheerful. He is frequently aware of something bothering him—a slight headache, upset stomach, or pain in his legs. He dreads having to face that unfriendly group of children in his school. If someone starts to tease him, he hopes he won't start to cry as he has done in the past. However, because his emotional responses are so obvious, Taylor is the easy scapegoat in the school yard.

In the classroom, Taylor is very guarded and defensive. When his teacher tries to discuss an incorrect answer on one of his papers, he argues and refuses to listen. He sometimes feels his teacher purposely tries to embarrass him.

Moral. All children experience emotional turmoil, but those with strong self-esteem tend to deal realistically with their emotions. When frustrated, they look for solutions rather than allowing themselves to become worked up into a rage. When disappointed, the high self-esteem child may become angry and depressed, but not for long. Because he is not ashamed of his feelings, he is free to experience them, rather than try to push them down. He knows that such uncomfortable emotions go away with time. Because children with high self-esteem feel capable and confident, they do not expect perfection from themselves, knowing that they are OK in spite of temporary setbacks.

Children with low self-esteem have the opposite experience. When dealing with life's frustrations, disappointments and failures, they are often tortured by feelings of anger and guilt. They then blame themselves for feeling this way, thereby exacerbating the original feeling. In many cases, their emotional pain leads to physical symptoms, further compounding the original negative feeling.

Children with low self-esteem often overact to situations, bursting into tears at the slightest criticism. They want to feel better about themselves but do not know how.

Self-Esteem and Learning

A new lesson unit is being introduced today and the teacher instructs the class to pay close attention so that they will understand how to do the follow-up work.

Brandon feels excited with anticipation as he readies himself for a new challenge. He recalls the difficulty he had on the last assignment, but feels very proud that he was able to complete it by himself. He remembers, too, that the teacher even complimented him on the report he turned in. He knows this new assignment will provide him with just another opportunity to test his academic prowess.

Taylor, on the other hand, is already beginning to feel a stomachache. "That last assignment was too confusing," he recalls, "I just couldn't figure out anything by myself. Thank goodness Dad was able to get me that tutor. Without her help, I wouldn't have known where to begin." Taylor tries to listen to the teacher's presentation, but he feels so anxious, it is hard for him to concentrate. "Oh well," he assures himself, "I will just go up to her after class and she will help me. At least she will write down what I need to give to the tutor so she can do this project for me."

He glances around the classroom and notices the other students are beginning to work on the assignment, but since he was unable to concentrate on the teacher's instructions, he doesn't know what is expected. Finally, he asks to be excused to see the nurse and feels greatly relieved when he can escape.

Moral. For children with high self-esteem, learning is fun and even inspiring. They not only have the desire to do well in school, they have the personal belief that everything is possible. They know they are capable of succeeding in their own way—even if they lack the raw intelligence of some of their fellow students. This confidence enables them to tolerate the challenge of learning difficult material, and to concentrate and remain focused until mastery occurs. Children with high self-esteem are not afraid to try different or creative approaches to problems because they do not fear being wrong.

The unfortunate child with low self-esteem tends to approach the challenge of new learning with discomfort and anxiety. The minute the work becomes hard, panic sets in and his automatic response is to assume he can't get it and to quickly give up. He becomes dependent upon parents, friends, or tutors to help him with the work, thus denying himself the opportunity to experience a challenge or the true feelings of success. Children with self-esteem problems have more frequent illnesses, miss more classes, and thus risk falling behind and further compounding their feelings about their academic inability.

Negative feelings and behaviors about learning can also perpetuate a vicious cycle:

I can't do it → and so I don't do it → so I fail → this proves that I am inadequate, that I am incompetent → therefore I can't do it → and so on.

Don't Delay, Begin Today

These examples should dramatically illustrate the importance of establishing a solid foundation of high self-esteem, and the consequences of not doing so. Since every aspect of your child's life will be greatly affected by his or her self-image, recognizing when there is a problem must become a priority for any concerned parent.

High self-esteem is not a feeling that spontaneously occurs. It is the result of thoughtful, encouraging, supportive interactions between a child and his family, primarily the parents. When positive self-esteem develops in a child, and is reinforced at every opportunity, its impact is profound and lasting. It is clearly one of the most valuable gifts any parent can give a child. With this basic knowledge and understanding of the methods of enhancing self-esteem, you can already begin to use more effective methods of parenting. Learning the action plans is what the rest of this book is about.

Roadblocks to the Development of Positive Self-Esteem

Self-esteem is very much like motherhood and apple pie. There appears to be universal agreement as to its importance for the child and the family as a whole. With such wide acceptance, why don't all children of paradise reach adulthood brimming with positive self-esteem? Why don't all affluent parents automatically express unconditional love and encourage competency in their children?

Family Chaos

Family chaos comes in all flavors and is sometimes more apparent than others. Certainly marital problems, mental illness, and substance abuse or other addictions, be it alcoholism or compulsive gambling on the part of one or both parents, create serious family problems. But so can constant travel, intense competition, perfectionist parents, and unrealistic expectations—all common characteristics of affluent families.

Children are very enmeshed in the events in their lives. If the family is chaotic, they will feel anxious and insecure, often blaming themselves for the problems they observe, and their self-esteem takes a nose dive. Affluent parents need to be especially aware of this, because their elegant homes and the money to buy any luxury or service do not immunize them from the effects of a chaotic or dysfunctional family system.

Sadly, I have conducted many parent conferences in which it quickly became apparent that problems between—or within—the parents were so severe that these had to take priority, and that without some resolution, these parents would have little hope of accomplishing any of the positive parenting steps their child might need. Affluent parents—for whom such problems may often be well concealed beneath a veneer of material excesses—must be forthright and deal honestly with the underlying instability in the family system if they hope to ensure high self-esteem in their children.

The Parents' Self-Esteem

One personal issue that parents should explore is whether their own self-esteem is high or low. Parents with low self-esteem can have tremendous difficulty being positive and actively encouraging the strengths of their children. Since they are often wearing "negative" glasses in viewing the world, such parents tend to be overly critical and obsessed with perfectionism. Without realizing what they are doing they can project their own pressures onto their growing child.

Low self-esteem can also lead the parents to feelings of insecurity about a child's love. It can make a parent overly possessive and fearful of a child becoming independent.

Jennifer, a mother I recently encountered, represents a typical example of destructive possessiveness. Having grown up in a wealthy but dysfunctional family, Jennifer married a stable, industrious man who provided her with the security she never had as a child. Erik, however, was very ambitious, often traveling for his business and leaving Jennifer at home with their two young children. On an unconscious level, Jennifer redirected her energies toward her children, making her role as Super Mom a means to give herself the feeling of self-worth lacking in her relationship with her often absent husband.

Jennifer involved herself in her children's activities with a vengeance, from becoming an active school volunteer to leading the local scout troop. However, as the children grew older and wanted to participate in activities in which she could not become involved (summer camp, excursions with school friends and their families, sleepover dates); Jennifer refused to let them go. By the time her oldest daughter, Carole, was ready to enter high school, the continual fights over Jennifer's need to control Carole's desire for freedom brought the daughter into my office in tears and rage, threatening to run away. It was only through family therapy that Jennifer learned to recognize how desperately she needed her children to mask her own feelings of low self-esteem. She was soon able to create a life of her own and channel her energies into independent activities that could give her lasting feelings of self-worth.

If you recognize low self-esteem issues within yourself, take the necessary steps to enhance your own positive feelings. Of course, this is easier said than done, but it is important to realize that by doing so you will not only enrich the quality of your life, but your children's as well. Remember, you are the major influence in the lives of your children and even though at times it may seem contradictory, they desperately want your approval. They look up to you as a role model, and your own positive attitude and behavior are perhaps the most important influences you can control.

THREE

Step Two: Making Each Moment Count

There are only twenty-four hours in the day and your busy schedule is taking up most of them. You glance at your appointment book crammed with meetings, and even though it is only 10:00 A.M., you are already feeling behind. The demands are great, the deadlines critical.

You check the itinerary of the impending business trip, hoping your return flight will arrive on time so that you can catch your daughter's performance in the school play. You can still recall the disappointment in her voice three months ago when a prolonged meeting in Atlanta caused you to miss her act in the school talent show.

Flipping through the past week's calendar, you notice that every evening was filled with events that were either of professional significance or were necessary for your own brief-but-essential moments of relaxation. When was the last time your family ate dinner together?

There is no question that time presents a critical problem for successful, affluent parents. Your lives are often so full that each day leaves you with limited time and energy to devote to effective parenting. Even when you are physically home with your children, you may often not really be there, remaining preoccupied with thoughts about an important decision at work or a philanthropic activity. Sometimes you must conduct business by telephone from home at night, or friends stop by to socialize.

For the affluent parent, the pull away from the family is understandable, at least in part. On one hand, your drive and commitment to career goals have created your financial success and you love what you do. On the other hand, you know that there is no question about your commitment and devotion to your family. You simply must divide your passion and attention between many equally attractive pursuits: career, hobbies, friends, social-service causes, and children. Although you might admit that your activities outside the home are much more interesting than arguing with a fussy three-year-old or dealing with the emotionality of a temperamental teenager, you rationalize that your children are well cared for because either your spouse is caring for them or you have hired a responsible caregiver to substitute for your presence.

In spite of the validity of the affluent parent's conflict, we cannot ignore that parents are the most important influence in the lives of children. When you are not available, regardless of the reasons, your child suffers to some degree. After all, the child reasons, if my own parents don't want to be with me I must be unlovable. How can I expect anyone else to love me? We can observe the result of this mistaken belief in children in many ways: anxiety, depression, anger, and low self-esteem.

For the parents, too, the personal price they pay for this conflict is guilt. Most are disturbingly aware that their devotion to their children may not be as total or complete as the idealized stories of families lead them to believe it should be. They know Norman Rockwell would not use their family as a model, but they nevertheless wonder if it could be otherwise.

To this, my answer is yes, it can be otherwise. With so much at stake in your child's development and happiness, your decisions about time are crucial. In this chapter, I hope to help you not only gain a perspective on the importance of your time at home, but also guide you toward the most effective kind of time management when matters beyond your control limit your time with your children.

What is Enough Time?

At some point in my work with parents, I will invariably be asked if there is a certain amount of time they should spend with their children. My response of "As much as you can" generally evokes a nervous laugh, as parents then realize how impossible it is to expect anyone to put a specific time allowance on their commitment and attention to their children.

I would love to make this dilemma easier for parents by giving a precise prescription for time, but there are too many variables involved. Even within the same family, one child might require more time than another. However, by educating you about the specific benefits your family time creates, you will be able to make a more informed decision about your personal arrangements.

There are three important developmental areas for a child in whom time is a critical factor: bonding, role modeling, and developing competence and intellectual growth. The more time you spend in each of these areas, assuming it is positive and healthy, the more you will significantly enhance the sound psychological growth of your child.

Establishing the Bonds That Tie

From the moment your baby is born, the parenting time you spend with him is of the utmost importance. Dan Stern, a prominent psychiatrist, has concluded from his research that children begin to learn from the very first day of life. By the end of the first week, not only has the infant stored numerous bits and pieces of information regarding the world and the environment, but he is also beginning to form some nonverbal categories: responsive mother, loving dad, kind world, hostile environment, and caring adult, to name a few.

Once these categories begin to form, all additional information is filtered through them. If the baby looks around and sees happy, smiling faces and the adult caregivers are appropriately responsive to his needs, the baby feels that the world is a safe place and adults can be trusted. If, however, the child is dealt with in a perfunctory manner, the infant develops an initial perception that the world is unresponsive or unemotional, and much future behavior may arise from this point of view.

Most infant studies now emphasize the importance of the early bonding experiences, the connectedness that develops between an infant and the adult caregiver. Needless to say, the ideal candidate for the primary objects of a child's bonding are nurturing, loving mothers and fathers. However, in many affluent homes, the infant's primary bonding may actually occur with the nanny or nurse, who is most intensely involved in the caring of the newborn child due to the absence of the parents.

Allowing a child to bond only with a hired professional can be very risky. The caregiver may quit or you may find it necessary to dismiss her. Obviously, the infant does not understand such circumstances. The only thing the child comprehends is that the individual whom he has trusted physically and emotionally has gone. The child is left frightened, anxious, and feeling abandoned. Infants and small children may respond to such abandonment, which may happen more than once, with a reluctance to trust future relationships.

For the young child, the disappearance of an important caregiver may have an additional dimension. Not only might the child have to wrestle with the pain of abandonment, she may believe that in some way she was the cause of the caregiver's departure.

To further compound the problem, a revolving door of caregivers creates an environment of inconsistent care. Each nurse or nanny has a different style of interaction. One may be lively and happy, another harsh and cold; one might practice strict discipline, another overindulgence. We cannot expect household help to give our children the same kind of consistent parental care or values that we would if we were available. Nor can we expect to have a lifetime commitment from them.

There is, in fact, evidence to support the belief that some of these individuals, who themselves may have grown up in poverty or in dysfunctional families, may have an underlying resentment and hostility toward their privileged charges. Their jealousy may be only on a subconscious level, but it can come out in a type of detachment, impatience, or punitive manner with your child.

I have personally dealt with situations where cases of child abuse, both physical as well as psychological, were occurring from the child's hired caregiver. It is therefore of critical importance for parents to be physically present to supervise the interaction between a child and a caregiver, particularly when a new individual is coming into your home. Whether or not you have concerns about this matter, it is important to talk to your child about the types of activities he or she do together with the caregiver, as well as the feelings he or she may have for the person. The unhappy or traumatized child will be more than willing to share this information, if the parents have expressed a clear interest in listening.

If it is necessary for you to be out of town for extended periods of time, arrange for a family member or close friend to keep in daily contact with your children so that the caregiver will not be able to have a potentially unhealthy amount of power and control.

This analysis is not to suggest that using a nanny is inherently negative or that all affluent mothers and fathers who rely upon hired help will necessarily see their child bond with someone other than themselves. However, you must recognize that a child cannot connect to an abstract notion of mother and father or to a smiling face in a photograph if you are away too frequently. It takes physical presence to establish this basic bonding. When your time is restricted, then your limited interaction must make an especially positive impact.

If your career or community obligations frequently require your absence from home during these formative years, reassess your priorities and the manner in which you handle these demands. Could that business meeting be arranged for lunch instead of dinner? Is this trip absolutely necessary, or might the desired result be accomplished through the use of our burgeoning technology (telephones, video conference calls, e-mails, and so on)? Is that volunteer board position crucial at this time, or could your time be more productively spent in family activities? Do you really have to attend the charity fund-raiser or would your mailed check serve the purpose?

I recognize that many of these decisions are difficult to make for the busy and engrossed parent, but for your child's sake, creating time for your family must be given an equal priority to your professional and personal commitments.

Someone to Look Up to

As children mature and strive to create a personal identity, they look for role models from whom to pattern their own behavior. Children are, to a large extent, imitators, and therefore role models are some of the most important teachers children have. They observe and copy nearly every aspect of their parents' behavior, and through this observation and imitation they learn a great deal about who they are, and how to be.

One of the most memorable lyrics of Stephen Sondheim's *Into The Woods* states: "Children will look to you, for which way to turn, to learn how to be. . . ." For better or worse—and I hope mostly for better—if we are there for our children they will model themselves after us—not just when they are children but for the rest of their lives.

If you are concerned with your children growing up with a value system compatible with yours, then it is important to ensure that you—and not surrogate parents—are your child's primary role models. The people you hire to work in your home do not necessarily share your values, ethics, or morals. Exposure to the attitudes and values that reflect another lifestyle can be a positive influence, but only if your child is well grounded in his own. The only way to ensure that you are the primary models for your children is ultimately to spend enough time with them to ensure their recognition of you as the teacher of values.

Time to Teach Competence
and Stimulate Intellectual Growth

In order for children to develop positive self-esteem, they need opportunities to feel competent, to be given challenges so that they can experience accomplishments and the resulting confidence that success breeds. They also need intellectual stimulation if they are to develop positive attitudes toward learning, as well as good study habits.

In each of these areas, parental involvement is the crucial factor in providing the right environment. If parents are not with children on a regular basis, they cannot consistently provide the stimulation or the feedback necessary for the child to grow in intellect or competence.

Often not realizing the importance of this, many affluent parents who leave their children exclusively in the care of hired employees have expectations that simply cannot be fulfilled. First, since an employee's primary responsibility is to provide service, he or she may not contribute to the child's need to have experiences in competence because they do things for the child, rather than requiring the child to assume personal responsibility. Second, although most caregivers are usually capable of caring for the child's basic physical needs, their own intellectual background may be limited, making it difficult for them to provide experiences that foster intellectual growth.

If parents recognize that a healthy environment means more than nutritious food, clean and comfortable clothing, and abundant toys, they will realize that they need to play a more significant role in their children's lives or, as will be discussed shortly, they will need to train servants to structure their children's activities so that they provide opportunities for learning and for self-sufficiency.

Quality Time—Beyond the Buzzword

Busy, active parents often focus upon the concept of quality time in an attempt to assuage their guilt at not having more actual time to participate in the lives of their children. They find it comforting to believe that the actual number of hours spent with a child is not so important and that the same benefits can be derived from making limited time "quality" time. They may feel that it is no longer necessary to spend several hours per day involved in the life and activities of their children, since fifteen minutes of quality time could do the same trick.

However, as a clinical psychologist, I find myself increasingly uncomfortable with this buzzword *quality time*, since all too often this concept is used merely as an excuse for not making children and family activities a number-one priority in a parent's life. It is therefore imperative that we try to establish some kind of operational definition of what quality time in the truest sense of the term must be.

Quality Time is Made up of Very Special Minutes

Quality time refers to any type of interaction between parent and child that results in the child feeling important and special. In order to create this, parents must demonstrate a genuine respect for the child, his interests, his attention span, and his pace of activity. You cannot have quality time if you are not present in mind and heart, as well as in body.

Like unconditional love, the emphasis in quality time is on the child's feelings and perceptions. Only when his or her needs are satisfied will the parental involvement be special. If a parent plans an activity that is high on the parental interest scale, but low on the child's, it does not count as quality time in the youngster's eyes.

The following examples of parents making their moments with children quality time suggest several methods by which you can implement this general principle.

Michael, an investment banker, and Susan, a successful modeling agent, have a five-year-old daughter, Elizabeth. During the week, they usually see their daughter for only a few hours in the evening. Michael, therefore, has made Saturday mornings a special time for him and his daughter.

They begin the morning by sharing breakfast together, sometimes at home, sometimes in a local restaurant. Then it's on to the park where Michael and Elizabeth climb, slide, see-saw, and have plain, unadulterated fun. Then they might take care of a few errands, or just walk down a street they've never explored before, window-shopping or talking about whatever Elizabeth wants to discuss. Without fail, they end up in the library where, together, they pick out books that Michael or Susan will spend time reading with Elizabeth while one or the other takes care of his or her personal errands.

What is significant in this ritual is that these Saturdays are something Elizabeth can look forward to, and depend on. When she is with her dad or mom during this time, she feels she is number one, and this positive feeling stays with her even when her parents are at work or busy at home.

Phyllis is a high-profile community volunteer whose calendar is filled with meetings covering a variety of social issues. But regardless of her schedule, she insists on always being home when her three children return from school. They share a snack together and review all of the details of their day. Phyllis leaves her telephone answering machine on during this time so that she is not interrupted. Her full attention is directed toward the children. She does not attempt to complete other tasks, like preparing dinner, addressing cards, and letters, or watching television, while listening to her children.

As a result, Phyllis's children feel highly valued. They have learned that what they say is important and worthy of discussion with their mother, that she sincerely cares about their interest. With such confidence, these children have been quick to develop independence and do not feel neglected when their mother's commitments require time away from them.

Larry, a very successful entrepreneur, directly expressed to me a concern about his lack of involvement with his growing children because of the attention required by his growing business. He didn't feel it was possible to arrange his life so that he could successfully satisfy both his familial and professional needs. When we evaluated his daily schedule, he realized that one of the problems was his inability to get home from the office before 8:00 or 8:30 in the evening. By that hour he had very little time left with his children before their bedtime. His free time simply did not coincide with theirs.

In analyzing this situation, Larry was able to develop an alternative plan. He would leave his office at 6:00 P.M., spend time with his children, including family dinner, and then return to the office to finish up whatever work remained. When he began to implement this schedule, Larry made some striking observations. Since his colleagues knew he would be gone by 6:00 P.M., they made certain that items requiring his attention were handled before that deadline. Additionally, Larry found that he could organize his working time more effectively so that he rarely had to return to the office and could complete any necessary items from his home office once his children were in bed. He learned how to work "smarter" not harder. Although his business productivity never diminished, his parenting effectiveness greatly increased.

Involving children in your own projects is another way to create time together. Martha, a high-profile community activist, helped her son and daughter create a junior division of a major charitable cause in which she was very actively involved. The son and daughter developed a number of projects in support of this worthwhile cause and, at the same time, were able to share many special moments with their mother.

There are many creative methods to arrange quality time within a busy schedule. Affluent, successful parents are by nature talented and oriented toward effective problem solving. By committing some of that talent and energy toward solving the dilemma of your limited time, you and your children will benefit immensely.

Unfortunately, for some people, creating quality time does not come naturally. They may need to force themselves, or be forced by external events, to reevaluate their priorities in terms of their relationships with their children.

David, a lawyer, lived with such a swirl of activity that he wasn't aware of the disintegration of his marriage until he found himself being served with papers for a divorce. David's relationship with his two sons was, until then, quite distant. He was hardly ever home—working late on weekdays and playing golf on weekends. Even when he was home, he was usually buried in extra paperwork or occupied with telephone conference calls. Now, suddenly divorced and no longer living with Michael and Brad, he was finally forced to choose between estrangement or the forming of a real relationship with his sons.

With specified visitation periods limiting their contact with each other, time with his sons became very important to David. He realized that he had to establish priorities in his life that would permit him to have a free calendar when the boys came to stay with him. He couldn't just have them for the weekend and let them lounge around while he played golf or worked. He had to become involved with them or they might choose not to visit. Today, David has managed to build a very positive relationship with his children. It is only unfortunate that it took the trauma of a divorce for him to create quality time with his boys.

The Application Of Quality Time

Beyond these general guidelines, several additional issues are important to consider as you begin to implement quality time in your family.

Intellectually Stimulating Time

Many affluent parents often view quality time as centering around a type of intellectual interaction between their child and them. Every moment spent together becomes a teaching moment, but the result unfortunately is a stressed feeling in both parent and child. Quality time does not mean pressuring your child to learn through such activities as drilling with flash cards, doing math problems, undertaking a forced reading program, or accompanying you to a cultural event of your choosing that may be of little interest to your child.

Quality intellectual time can be better implemented by simply talking with your children, telling stories, asking and answering questions, playing games, and making one another think. For the young child, don't just read the stores; invent stories together. Let your child create a new ending for a favorite tale. For older children, discuss what you read by asking questions, speculating alternate ideas, and find out what your child thinks without pressure to find a "right" answer.

There are many ways to develop a relationship with a growing child that will enrich you both. At dinner time, refer to current events, soliciting the ideas and opinions of each family member. Encourage your child to develop his imagination through such activities as creating performances for the family, working with puppets, or writing poems. When you watch television together, make it an opportunity to talk about significant issues that arise from the programs. Explore your community. Plan day trips to unusual, stimulating places where your child can have first-hand experiences with diverse activities such as museums, the theater, historical landmarks, special festivals, special parks and other experiences with nature and even interesting businesses. Begin collections: stamps, coins, butterflies, minerals, and so on.

The goal of intellectually stimulating time is to transform learning experiences into an enjoyable activity. Presenting your child with a perception of learning as exciting and stimulating is the foundation for lifelong habits and attitudes that will significantly contribute to your child's academic success. As long as you don't insist that there be a specific intellectual product from these experiences, but let them be a sharing of focused time, they will produce a happy and useful interaction.

Quality Time Can Be Just Hanging Out

Quality time does not have to involve any spectacular activity. You need not pack dozens of activities into a day so that your child becomes exhausted and irritable. Quality time can be simply time when parent and child are together in a relaxed frame of mind, merely enjoying each other's company. In the parlance of your kids, you need simply to *hang out* with them.

If you ask your children what they do when they hang out with friends, they will usually say, in their own way, that they are just being with one another. No one has to perform or be judged in any manner. When children just hang out with their friends, they talk about any subject of interest, express any type of opinion, or share their mutual appreciation for similar activities.

Ironically, we all had this skill of hanging out when we were children, but in the process of maturing and developing a more purposeful orientation in our lives, it became lost. Particularly for the high-achieving adult who feels that free time is a very limited commodity, hanging out may seem like wasted time. After all, you may reason, where is the end product? Without a specific instruction, direction, or goal, what is my child learning? But for your child, the positive feeling of spending time with you, while having your friendship and love, is the only goal needed. This is exactly why parents must recapture their ability to "hang out" with their children.

If morning is your best time, for example, take advantage of your natural biorhythm to hang out with your children. Make breakfast your family time for sharing, rather than hectic or silent, with newspapers drawn like walls around everyone's heads. Instead of having your children driven to school by a driver or carpool, perhaps you could do it yourself and thereby create quality time for fun and conversation with your children.

One company president, attending a seminar during which I was discussing the concept of hanging out, approached me with his sudden insight. He had wondered why his children always eagerly looked forward to going away to their family mountain retreat, even without their friends around. He now realized that this was the only place where he was truly relaxed and unstructured in his time with them. They weren't rushing to be on time for an event, and he wasn't instructing, advising, or directing. There were no schedules or deadlines. He would just be there with them, walking, talking, laughing, and playing games or sitting quietly in a boat, fishing. This is a perfect example of quality time between parent and child.

Let Your Child Understand Your Time Constraints

Often what was a quality-time activity ends on an unpleasant note because parents do not let a child understand a time limitation. Your child is engaged in an activity when you look at your watch and realize you have another commitment and that your allotment of quality time is over. Of course, your child is not ready to stop what she is doing; you haven't warned her that your time is almost up. She protests, you become irritated. Suddenly all the pleasantness is forgotten because of the negative ending.

When you have limited time, you need to establish this fact in advance. Tell your child, "I would love to go to the park with you, but I will have to be back in the house in one hour." When you are then at the park, give your child a ten-minute warning before you actually have to depart. This approach demonstrates respect by indicating that you do want to spend time together and don't wish to rush the activity, but that you have time constraints to work around. By doing this, you are also setting a good example about time management so that your child can begin to learn to budget and prioritize his or her own activities.

Maintain Quality Time When You Are Away from Home

For those parents who frequently travel, Alexander Graham Bell created a wonderful invention, the telephone. As obvious as it is, many parents fail to use this to stay verbally and emotionally involved in the daily lives of their children.

Children see travel as an adventure. Even if your business travel is far from exotic, your child's romantic image of your trip only serves to enhance the meaning of your call. The child thus can say to himself, "Even though Mom and Dad have so many interesting and exciting activities occurring, they haven't forgotten about me. They are interested in what I'm doing." This can be profoundly validating to your child!

In fact, try phoning home when your spouse is not available and letting your child know that you have called just to talk to him or her in a private conversation. You might also conclude your call with a message your child can relay to your spouse, adding to his or her sense or responsibility and independence.

Traveling parents can help a child feel included by explaining the nature of the trip and even sharing with the child some of the objectives you are trying to accomplish. Pick up little souvenirs (postcards, maps, refrigerator magnets) so that your child can further feel a part of your adventures. It need not be a major gift; a small item that helps your child know where you were and what you were doing can be very meaningful.

If you are away on a special or important occasion (birthdays, Halloween, Valentine's Day, religious holidays, first day of school, beginning of exam week, first Little League game), send a card to acknowledge the event. Keep a supply of cards on hand and calendar these into your appointment book if you know you will be away.

If it is at all possible, take your child on an occasional business trip, preferably during a school break. This gives your youngster a chance to participate more fully in your life and to develop a greater understanding of your frequent absences. It also provides a very valuable time for parent and child to be together, away from the usual daily home routine.

It is important to note that if you expect your child to value education as a priority experience in his or her life, it is generally not beneficial to withdraw the child from school for a prolonged period of time on a regular basis. The message this action inevitably communicates is that other activities are more important than school. However, if you decide that it is important for your child to accompany you on a trip, then you should make every effort to bring the school environment with you. This can be done by obtaining all assignments in advance from the teacher, and then setting aside some portion of each day for school work, or by requiring your child to keep a daily diary in which he or she gains the experience of writing and recording events as well as thoughts and feelings. Talk with the classroom teacher in advance, and if possible, have her arrange a special project assignment based on the location of your trip. Finally communicate to your child your feelings regarding the importance of school, and explain why you feel that this travel experience will supplement the school program.

A very special relationship can occur when a parent travels individually with a single child. The family system can often submerge the individualities of its members, with neither Mom nor Dad able to sustain a lengthy and meaningful conversation with one child without being interrupted by siblings. But if you routinely plan parent-child overnight excursions, each child has the chance to develop a truly personal connection.

Mark Your Calendar for Parenting Commitments

If you look in your appointment book and note that you have scheduled time with an important client or friend, it is not likely that you would schedule a conflicting activity for the same hour. Your children deserve the same kind of scheduling commitment. In the course of your busy week, write in those times you have promised to your child as if they are imperative appointments, equal to your business and social responsibilities.

Support the activities of your children. While the junior high school talent show, the drama-class workshop, or a high school soccer game may not be as stimulating as first-run theater or professional athletics, and your tendency is to think there is another event in a month anyway, you still owe it to your child to demonstrate your interest by being there. If your child is giving time and energy to a project, it has significance for him. Taking the time to support those efforts with your presence *and* your enthusiasm is quality involvement. A sensitive and concerned parent will not ignore activities of such obvious importance to his child.

It is such a painful disappointment to children, who are hoping their parents will come to a special school activity, to see other parents arriving, and finally to realize with resignation that theirs are missing. All too often parents promise to attend, and then forget or get a "better offer," believing that not showing up won't really make a difference to the child. The tears I have seen children shed in these situations would quickly change any parent's mind.

If you cannot attend an activity in which your child is involved, be sure to tell your child that you recognize the importance of the event and fully explain what your scheduling conflict is. But whenever possible, look honestly at your conflict, evaluate your own priorities, and determine which event is really the more important one.

When dealing with older children, make sure that whatever time you schedule with them is time they have available. Children of paradise, ever wanting to emulate their busy parents, often find ways to crowd their own schedules with friends and activities, so in instances when Mom or Dad suddenly sets aside some time for quality interaction, they may have already made plans. Parents often react to this with frustration and hurt feelings, or the expectation that the child will immediately cancel the other arrangements in order to participate in the family activity. This is a mistake. When you force your child to participate, you communicate the feeling that his arrangements are not important, and the child then translates your message as a put-down rather than as indicating how important you feel it is to be together. The result is usually a sullen and irritable child ruining a family activity for everyone.

Your child's social independence should be encouraged and praised. Honor his or her commitment as you would honor your own—and he or she will do the same. When scheduling quality time, negotiate with your child so that the time is mutually agreeable.

Are You a Hurried Parent?

Another of the most important time issues for affluent parents is not time itself, but the psychology of time. In his book, *The Hurried Child*, psychologist David Elkind makes an eloquent plea to all parents not to hurry their children during their critical developmental years.

> Children need time to grow, to learn, and to develop. To treat them differently from adults is not to discriminate against them but rather to recognize their special estate. . . . Recognizing special needs is not discriminatory; on the contrary, it is the only way that true equality can be attained. . . . All children have, vis-à-vis adults, special needs—intellectual, social and emotional. Children do not

learn, think or feel in the same way as adults. If we ignore the special needs of children, we are behaving just as if we denied Hispanic or Indian children bilingual programs, or denied the handicapped their ramps and guideposts. In truth, the recognition of a group's special needs and accommodation to those needs are the only true way to insure equality and true equal opportunities.

Children need encouragement, guidance and patience—not a push for acceleration. The ambition that is inherently within each child needs to be nurtured—not forced by outward pressures.

Affluent parents have a far greater risk of hurrying their child than most other parents. In the world of high-power, high-finance, and high-tech, the time-is-money philosophy runs rampant. Cellular phones allow traffic snarls to become business conferences; portable dictating machines make shaving time productive for one's profession as well as one's hygiene. Being immersed in the time-equals-money mores, affluent parents often have little awareness of the extent to which they inflict this kind of pressure upon their children. Ultimately, this issue boils down to a single question: How hurried are you? How would you answer the following questions?

- Do you blow the horn and change lanes frequently while driving?
- Do you feel strongly irritated when you are put on hold preceding or during a telephone conversation?
- Are you frequently running late for appointments?
- Are you often engaged in two activities at the same time?
- Do you hurry other people's speech by interrupting them or by completing their sentences for them?
- Do you have trouble staying focused on the speaker with whom you are conversing?
- Are you a rapid eater? Talker? Mover?
- Does "wasting" time bother you?
- Do you hate to lose any game or athletic contest?

- Do you question why others don't work as quickly and effectively as you do?
- Do you have little time to relax?
- Does family mealtime often become stressful?
- Do you frequently feel tense and irritable?
- Are you often reminding your kids to hurry up?
- Are you quick to anger?
- Do you pride yourself upon completing each task or assignment as quickly as possible?
- Do certain muscles (such as arms, neck, and back) often feel tense and taut?
- Do you have too many things to do and not enough hours in the day to do them?
- Do you rush your child to and from activities because you have a problem with your own schedule?
- Are you panicked without your palm pilot, your Blackberry or cell phone?

If you have answered yes even to only a few of these questions, then chances are you are a hurried individual, and it is probable that your own hurry-up syndrome will negatively affect your children. In a climate of hurry up, parents often do not consider their child's inner clock.

Children perceive time from a different perspective than adults. Their attention span is much shorter and thus they often become impatient. Five minutes of waiting can, for them, seem like an hour to us. Yet, when a child is engrossed in an activity he or she enjoys, thirty minutes can seem like five minutes. Therefore, to create positive experiences with our children, particularly the younger ones, we must make every effort to view an activity through their eyes.

As highly productive adults, it is probable that you are able to minimize your time expenditure on any given activity and thereby squeeze many events in a day. However, your child does not necessarily have your same speed and stamina. If a parent forces a child to operate at this level, the results are frequently disastrous. Instead, both you and your child will benefit if you plan your day, utilizing your knowledge of his or her interest areas, attention span, and physical stamina.

I have often seen an overtired, uninterested child being dragged through a museum while the exasperated parents prod him along. These parents were obviously well intentioned in their desire to expose their child to culture. But what might have been a thirty-minute positive experience easily became, two hours later, a nightmare.

Even a simple task such as eating dinner requires sensitivity to your child's time clock. Many adults may quickly finish a meal, being accustomed to eating on the run or anxious to do something else as soon as dinner is over. But instead of recognizing that a child may need to eat in a slower manner, they interpret a child's behavior as dawdling and chastise the child to hurry up.

I recently worked with an affluent couple, both professionals in high-pressured jobs, who had a four-year-old daughter. Every Saturday morning the two parents encountered the same resistance when they tried to get the toddler ready and out of the house to accompany them on the errands they could not complete during the week. Fights erupted, tears were shed, and, as the father put it, "Everyone lost."

I asked these parents if they had any idea why their daughter was so resistant. "No," the mother replied sheepishly. "We've even been too busy to think about it." In examining this conflict from their daughter's point of view, the parents began to realize that the activities in which they involved their daughter were in conflict with her inner clock. Through our discussion, it became clear that their daughter's inner clock needed to slow down on weekends. Since she'd been very young, Rebecca had been in daycare all week, requiring her to be dressed and out of the house by seven o'clock. She needed two days a week vacation from this fast pace, doing what *she* wanted to do in a relaxed manner. Understanding this enabled the couple to make important modifications in their weekend routine that would accommodate both their and their child's needs.

Acknowledging and respecting your child's inner clock will help you avoid being a hurried parent. But as you begin to allot sufficient time for family activities and create a relaxed atmosphere; remember also, if your children see you return to your usual hurry-up mode the moment the fun is over, they may still feel the pressure. Because you are your child's role model, what he observes in you reflects upon his self-image. When he sees a harried parent, he may likely start to believe that the entire world operates at a harried pace. When you are able to stop and smell the roses (at least occasionally), your entire family system will experience dramatic stress reduction.

Recharging Your Batteries

Time is not the only determinant to a quality interaction. Your energy, too, is a crucial factor. Many parents take their energy supply for granted, not doing what is necessary to assure that they have enough to meet the challenges of the entire day and still have some left over for the family when they come home at night.

Every morning you arise with a fresh supply of energy, but it is finite commodity. In the course of the day, the pressure and demands from your career or community obligations can emotionally drain you. If you do not consciously recharge, by midday you can find yourself running on empty, grinding the gears of your raw nerves.

Affluent parents who are operating in demanding situations must pay close attention to the methods they use to handle the negative stressors in their lives. Some, such as alcohol and other drugs, may seem to provide immediate relief, but create far greater long-term problems. There are many healthful remedies for managing stress. However, the first step must be the recognition of the problem. Consider the following questions:

- Do you feel stress increasing when your children return home from school or when you finally come home after a hectic day involved in other activities?

- Are your major requirements from your family peace and quiet?
- Do you want to hide away at the end of the day?
- Do you sometimes wonder if you can make it through the evening until your child's bedtime?
- Do you find yourself angry and yelling at the slightest provocation?

If you answered yes to any of these questions, you are overworking your "positive-energy index." In this frame of mind, the time you spend with your children is obviously not likely to be of high quality. The depletion of your positive energy can cause you to overreact to the slightest stresses or demands from family, and can lead to low levels of tolerance, respect, and nurturing. And those who will suffer most from your parental fatigue will be your children.

This common situation was clearly verbalized by a young executive during a recent consultation. He exclaimed, "Every night as I drive home, I tell myself that I am not going to lose it tonight. I'm going to stay calm and cool. I'm not going to let anything get to me. But the minute I open the door, I am pounced upon and within five minutes I'm yelling at everyone. I just need some quiet time when I can change clothes and get relaxed before I have to deal with my family."

One important change you can make is to allocate a transition time between work and home. In switching from the working world to the home world, you should allot yourself a period of winding-down time before returning home. With your mind well-separated from the problems of the day, you can open the door and be ready for positive interaction and quality time with your children. Perhaps you need to stop at a gym and participate in an exercise routine or engage in some other kind of activity that will help to drain off the negative stresses. Even walking around your block after you have parked your car may be all you need to create a transition time.

Wait a minute! you might be thinking. This chapter is about the problems of limited time for children and now the author suggests

I spend even less time with my family by stopping at a gym on the way home? Isn't this a contradiction?

The truth is that two hours of quality time is far healthier for children than four hours of negative interaction, the very kind you risk having with your children if you have run out of positive energy at the end of the day. When it is necessary to recharge, to build up your positive-energy index in order to nurture and encourage your children, then this becomes your priority.

The more effective, long-term solution to the problem of perpetual negative stress is to evaluate your current situation, determine what areas are causing you the greatest amount of stress and then do something about it! Obvious as this recourse may seem, many affluent parents never act on it. If ignored, stress and its complications can have serious physical and psychological ramifications.

If you have a serious ongoing problem with stress, you should explore one of the numerous stress-reduction programs available privately as well as through hospitals, community organizations, and at the workplace. Bookstores are filled with popular books, audio tapes, and video cassettes on this subject, introducing readers to a variety of methods including meditation, yoga, biofeedback, visualization and positive self-talk, diet, exercise, participatory sports, regularly scheduled vacation time, hobbies, and psychotherapy. It is important to explore at least one of these techniques. By educating yourself about the various options and listening to your own needs, you can find your own best way to create a more positive and energized state from which to operate within your family.

Hiring the Help

If careers or community commitments absolutely necessitate your frequent absence from the home, you may have little choice but to hire competent individuals to care for your children. But affluent parents must be careful not to underestimate the importance of the quality of that care. A warm, affectionate, nurturing caregiver can enhance the healthy development of your child, and the effects of an austere, aloof, punitive caregiver can be quite damaging. By becoming aware of some of the potential hazards of delegating the care of your children to others, you can make wiser, more informed choices about the kind of person you want to trust to be a surrogate parent to your children.

When surrogate parents are hired to work in your home, it is with the realization that they will be spending a significant amount of time with your child. During the interviewing process, most parents are primarily concerned with the issues of physical care and safety for the dependent child. Is the person competent, reliable, and responsible? Does he or she smoke, drink, or use any types of drugs? Would he or she know how to respond to a medical emergency? Will this person be responsible for protecting your child from unsafe situations? Is he or she in good health, with the physical capabilities and basic intelligence to handle the job?

These issues are essential questions, but they are far from adequately comprehensive. They tell us very little about the basic personality makeup of the person who will significantly influence the emotional and psychological health of your child.

As much as possible, you also need to find out about their attitude toward the entire child-rearing process, how they discipline and set limits and the skills and techniques they have previously acquired that can enhance the self-esteem and sense of competency of your child. While many caregivers are highly proficient at tending to the physical needs of your child, they are not necessarily as skilled at relating in the warm, nurturing, encouraging manner that fosters the development of self-discipline, curiosity, and learning.

You need a caregiver who can stimulate creativity, play with your child, answer the multitude of questions children ask as part of their intellectual advancement, and, in general, someone who has the desire to put forth an extra effort where necessary. It is easy and tempting for the capable but uncaring caregiver to leave the child alone, mesmerized in front of the television while she is occupied with other things.

Every hired caregiver brings along her own personal orientation based upon her background and the family system from which she came. It is important to find someone whose values differ as little as possible from your own. You must, therefore, emphasize in your initial interview with that person what your concerns and requirements are regarding her interaction with your child. Make the rules and boundaries clear to everyone. Be sure your caregivers are agents of *your* child-raising philosophy. In almost all cases, these individuals will appreciate the clarity and consistency of rules and boundaries as much as your child.

I therefore suggest spending as much time as possible when interviewing candidates. Begin your interview with open-ended questions that give the respondent a chance to reveal more of her basic orientation to this task rather than simply answering yes or no. For example, you might ask:

- How would you spend a day with my child if you could do anything you wished?
- What do you think are the most important activities for a child of this age?
- What type of chores should a child of this age have?
- What do you think are the three most important responsibilities of this position?
- What discipline methods do you use?
- When should a child be disciplined?
- How do you like to spend your free time?
- How would you handle the following situations?

    Tantrums
    Refusal to eat food
    Unwillingness to go to bed at nap time or at night
    A child's refusal to cooperate
    Running away on the street
    Hitting a sibling
    Delay or refusal to complete homework

Also find out your prospective caregiver's opinions on the following questions:

- At what age do you think a child should be dressing, bathing, feeding himself, taking care of all personal hygiene?
- Is a specific bedtime important? If so, why?
- Do you enjoy reading for yourself?
- What have you read lately?
- Do you enjoy reading to children?
- What is your favorite game to play with children?

Questions of this nature will give you a much better picture of the personality, character, and attitudes of the person who will play such a critical role in the life of your child. Also, once you've hired a caregiver, his or her answers from such an in-depth interview can make you aware of any weaknesses, so that you can provide the necessary instruction to ensure that the interaction with your child will be positive and serve to enhance the child's self-esteem.

Regardless of qualifications, it is crucial after you've hired someone that *you* spend time with the party involved to establish what this surrogate parent's role will be and the manner in which you expect your child to behave. Your child should see you give this caregiver permission and authority to set limits and enforce consequences if rules are not followed.

A frequent problem for families hiring caregivers is that the children do not respect the surrogate's authority. They find ways to intimidate them, or to defy the structure they were hired to provide. I have worked with families in which a young child will threaten, "If you don't clean my room for me I'll get you fired!" Without clear support from parents, most employees will not stand up to such threats and will give in to inappropriate demands. But you must not allow your children to wield indiscriminate power over the surrogates you have chosen to help raise the child. The only solution is to assure your child's caregiver that on matters of discipline that you have already established; you will support the agreed-upon consequences, and then be sure that your child knows it.

Consistency gives children the feeling of security. They need to feel confident that the rules and boundaries they are taught are not in constant flux. Children without consistent rules and boundaries often engage in negative behavior in order to test the waters, to search for the ends of the boundaries. What often underlies the most outrageous behavior on the part of a child is a cry not for more freedom but for less freedom and more limit setting. And behind this is often the need for more time with parents.

Rules and boundaries should be created by parents, but they must be maintained consistently by everyone who is in charge of supervising that child in the home. Rules should not be created in your absence without your consent.

Your child's caregiver has to take the place of very special people: you. By devoting the necessary effort to make a careful selection and by remaining involved in the supervision of your child's care, you are making sure that you are with your child in many ways even when you are not physically there.

Time and energy are two critical ingredients in the recipe of effective parenting, and you will see how they come into play in almost every issue in this book. The affluent family must therefore pay close attention to how these limited resources are allocated so that their children are not at the end of the receiving line.

Unique Problems of Time for the Child of a Celebrity

Parents who are local or national celebrities face an added dimension to the problem of limited family time. The high-pressured executive or well-heeled heir can clear the calendar in order to give a child undivided attention, but when high-profile celebrities try the same, they often do not enjoy equal control over the outcome. The moment they are out in public, they are often besieged by fans and admirers who do not consider that they might be intruding upon special family time. Whether at a restaurant or on vacation, celebrities find it nearly impossible to escape interruptions.

Some celebrities must cope with a conflicting dilemma. Even through private time is limited, in order to maintain their success; they must conscientiously remain in the public spotlight as much as possible. The late John Ritter, television and film star and the son of the famous singing cowboy, Tex Ritter, said about his father, "There were times when I was really jealous of the public. I wanted more time with him. He was away about half of my life doing radio or going to Nashville."

Many other children of celebrities have reported frustration over seeing the parent but not really seeing him, in the sense that they often saw their mom or dad more on television than in person. The child of one celebrity mother bitterly told me that her mother was so rarely home, she watched her mother's television show so as not to forget what her mom looked like. What made the situation even more painful was the fact that her mother was in a situation comedy that involved other children. This child became enraged as she watched her mother playing the role of a caring, involved parent on the television screen when she never could recall having those kinds of interactions with her at home.

If you are a parent in this category, the suggestions throughout this chapter should be especially valuable to you. Your children are your most important fans. Be sure your moments together are of the best quality time.

FOUR

Step Three: Raising
A Self-Motivated Child

I recently conducted a parenting program at a highly competitive private school. In the audience were two pregnant mothers who sat attentively, and then approached me after the presentation.

"We've been listening carefully to you," one said, "and we're very concerned. This is the first pregnancy for each of us. What can we do to make sure we do everything right? What kinds of books should we get? What are the strongest preschools in the area? My sister-in-law told me about Montessori but my neighbor says Alouettes is the most progressive. We want to be sure our children will really be competitive! What should we be doing in preparation?"

The desire of these women to maximize the potential of their children was admirable. They cared and they were willing to devote considerable time and energy to the success of their yet-to-be-born children. Yet, at the same time, I was extremely concerned. I couldn't help thinking that if this was the parents' attitude *before* their children were even born, by the time the kids were old enough to put sentences together, they would likely feel overwhelming and debilitating pressure.

These were two mothers-to-be already creating expectations that might not have any basis in reality. What they will expect from their children will be based primarily on what they fantasize their

81

children becoming, not necessarily on what their children are capable of or interested in becoming.

Are parents such as these two mothers unusual? Unfortunately, not at all, especially in families of the affluent who so frequently want nothing short of the very best *for* their children and *from* their children. While the parents' motives are rooted in love and concern for their child's well-being, their unrealistic expectations can nevertheless become a tremendous burden, putting the child in the position of having to please the parents first and himself second.

When a child operates solely to fulfill parental expectations—appropriate or not—he may never feel, consciously or subconsciously, pleased by his efforts or satisfied with his successes. As a result, such a youngster may spend much of his childhood feeling like a failure. Ironically, the lifelong pain children experience as the result of unrealistic parental expectations is usually far greater than the pain from which the parents are trying to protect the child. And the disabilities that can result may be exactly what the well-intentioned parent has tried to avoid.

Expectations: What's Unrealistic?

Whenever I discuss unrealistic expectations with parents, I inevitably get such questions as: What is wrong about setting one's sights as high as possible? If I don't expect the best, won't I get inferior output? Shouldn't concerned parents want their children to be the best they can be? Isn't it like a business? If I don't push my employees, I get nothing. We would never make our quotas. Why are my children different?

All are understandable questions. But what many parents fail to realize is that children can only be the best *they* can be. Arbitrarily deciding what your children can and cannot do makes you vulnerable to creating unrealistic expectations.

To put it more simply, an unrealistic expectation is any unilateral standard a parent imposes on a child without fully considering his or her unique abilities and interest. Needless to say, any expectations parents might have that predate the birth of a child are, by definition, unrealistic. The two mothers above fall into this category, as does the father who says his son will be the next Mickey Mantle and then has a daughter and never lets her forget his disappointment.

Within this broad definition, however, one can distinguish three different categories of unrealistic expectations: expectations of excellence, of maturity, and of commonality.

Expectations of excellence are frequently the ones to which affluent parents are most prone. Because they have the best house, the best car, the best career, why shouldn't they expect the best child?

If you expect your child to have a report card of straight "A's," to become class president, to shine as the star of the school play, to captain the football team, or if you have determined a specific career for your child, you are in danger of setting unrealistic expectations of excellence. The goals are based not on your child's interests and abilities, but on what you subjectively believe to represent success.

There are two serious consequences of expectations of excellence. The first is that they create unbearable pressure for the child, as the child is aware only of how outstanding his achievement must be in order to please the parents. The second is that expectations place an emphasis on the *product*, virtually ignoring the *process* of learning or achievement. Thus, they emphasize *external* rewards rather than internal motivation for excellence and self-satisfaction.

The second category, expectations of maturity, involves a preconceived notion of how quickly children should develop, be it physically, emotionally, or cognitively. Because of the more sophisticated lifestyle of the upwardly mobile family—such as exotic travel, fancy restaurants, social functions—affluent parents have a tendency to put their children in situations that require them to behave or to think beyond their chronological age. Expectations of maturity create problems for a child in two major respects. They create pressure by assuming that rapid development is the best development. In fact, children, who often start out slowly finish on top. These parental expectations hinge on a false assumption, namely that a child's rate of maturity is something the child can control, which he cannot.

Expectations of commonality are those that demand your children grow up to be exactly like someone else, be it a sibling, a friend's child, or you. As in the other two cases, unrealistic expectations of commonality portend numerous potential problems. The child may be afraid to express his own feelings and desires for fear of hurting the parents. The expectation denies the child's unique individuality, and presumes that your interests are the only valid ones. When rigidly imposed, the expectation very often leads to intense frustration, anger, and resentment.

Sometimes parents combine expectations into a potentially volatile mix, such as: If I could get straight "A's" and quarterback the football team while holding down an after-school job when I was only 15, why can't you? The problem here is that adults often have selective recall about their own childhood and adolescence. Comparing their memories to their children's lives not only creates unnecessary pressure, it is often not even honest!

You can avoid all of these manifestations of unrealistic expectations and still raise happy, achieving, capable children. By understanding the pitfalls of pressuring your children to succeed and modifying your behavior accordingly, you will help them to develop the only truly positive, healthy, and motivating expectations: the ones they establish for *themselves*.

In Search of Excellence

Whenever I speak to groups of privileged children about the advantages and disadvantages of their lifestyle, one of the most frequent complaints expressed is the pressure to achieve. They sense it from their peers, with whom they feel an intense competition. They feel it coming from their private schools, under demands from the parents who are paying for this high-priced education, to maintain high achievement scores and prepare the graduates to be accepted into the most prestigious and competitive high schools and universities.

But the achievement pressure privileged children get directly from parents is the most unrelenting and the most potentially damaging. When these parents push too hard, the message they send their children is: Nothing you do is good enough. This is in clear contradiction to the basic principles of fostering positive self-esteem, "I am worthwhile and I am competent," the main ingredients for healthy, achieving children.

Although affluent parents seldom mean to inflict such a painful message upon their children, there are a number of reasons why they are prone to setting up unrealistic expectations of excellence.

First, many successful parents are so accustomed to applying pressure on themselves that it becomes a habit, a way of living. They expect nothing less than superior performance from themselves and their employees, and a natural extension of this is to expect the same achievement from their children. Their own drive for excellence may also be tied up in what they believe are the prerequisites for success as prescribed by our American Dream: a visionary attitude, ambition, a willingness to set for oneself the highest goals, and a driven persistence to make them a reality. They want their children to adopt this philosophy as well.

While this determination may work well as a personal guideline for these adults, it is not an attitude conducive to effective parenting. When this type of individual creates too much stress in his or her business life, employees can quit or physically remove themselves from the uncomfortable situations. But children do not have this option, unless in desperation, they run away from home.

It is one thing for a parent to pressure him or herself. That internal stress can be a positive motivating force. However, when you impose your standards of excellence on your child, they become negative forces that often decrease rather than heighten motivation. Even if this pressure appears to have a temporarily positive effect, its long-term consequences are usually disastrous.

Erin is a tragic case of an affluent family's push for excellence. The oldest child of a hard-driven businessman father and a community-activist mother, she was constantly pushed by her parents to achieve, and she quickly learned that she could only get her parents' approval by gaining outstanding recognition at school and within the community. To do this, Erin involved herself in a multitude of activities—editor of the school newspaper, student-government leader, organizer of the food drive for the homeless, member of the varsity tennis team, and so on—while at the same time maintaining top grades throughout her high school years.

Her mother and father beamed with each honor and award their daughter earned, especially at her acceptance into a prestigious university. As a reward for her outstanding achievement, she was given a new car as a high-school graduation gift.

Erin's parents did not realize, however, the enormous strain under which she operated in order to keep all those balls juggling successfully in the air. Nor did they recognize the fact that Erin needed this continuous acknowledgement from others, not only to make them notice her, but to make her feel good about herself. By her teen years, perhaps even earlier, Erin had become a success junkie. The school honors and other activities held no real or intrinsic satisfaction for her. She was focused on pushing herself to the next level of success only to maintain parental approval.

Sadly, three weeks before her high-school graduation, Erin ended up in the psychiatric ward of a local hospital as a result of a suicide attempt. In her therapy, she expressed fear of disappointing her parents, but more profoundly, she felt a sense of emptiness at the thought of not being able to maintain her superhuman level of personal achievement.

Erin may be an extreme case, but I have seen many affluent children fail to live up to their potential because of the pressure. Invariably, they do not suffer from a lack of motivation; they suffer from the wrong kind of motivation: external expectation, rather than internal drive. Their drive results from the parents' expectations, not their own desire to achieve internal satisfaction. In one way or another, these children often simply burn out, or worse. The acclaimed film *The Dead Poets Society*, in fact, depicts the sad result of suicide when a father tries to force his son to follow his directives.

Another reason for creating the push for excellence among affluent parents is an inability to see their children in an objective way. Living at the top of the social spectrum, they believe that anything is possible, and that by pushing hard enough, their child can become a super achiever.

I frequently encountered this syndrome during my tenure as the Beverly Hills School District psychologist. The following scenario from a parent meeting is illustrative.

A teacher expresses concern about Adam, an eight-year-old who is performing poorly in class. The teacher reports that Adam has all the accompanying problems of not being able to keep up academically with his classmates. Often he appears passive and withdrawn, and when I meet him, Adam freely admits to me that he's unhappy and doesn't like to go to school.

The school assessment team conducts a thorough evaluation, including intelligence testing, a social/emotional evaluation, and an appraisal of language development, motor skills and academic achievement levels. The results of this battery of tests reveal a child of high average intellectual potential, highly anxious, with poor self-esteem and lack of confidence in his ability to succeed in class. Additionally, I learn his older sister is an excellent student.

I then schedule a conference with Adam's parents. Our meeting is very early in the morning because his father, a doctor, has an appointment at eight o'clock and Mom is in the midst of a large project and has to catch a nine o'clock flight to Chicago. I meet an attractive couple, immaculately groomed, clearly world beaters ready to conquer again that morning. Once we have dispensed with the formalities, Mom and Dad take the offensive.

"We know Adam is bright," Dad says.

"He's gifted," Mom punctuates. "He just doesn't try hard enough!"

While it might seem unusual for parents to be determining giftedness, it is understandable. Parents, in general, can have some degree of difficulty in seeing their children objectively, but affluent parents often have more trouble in this area. These high-powered and often highly intelligent individuals may spend limited time with their own child and even less time with other children. As a result, they have a narrow frame of reference for evaluating their own child's development, and substitute instead a fantasy about their child's intellectual prowess.

In the course of a conference, I always try, in as positive a manner as possible, to give the parents a more realistic appraisal of their child's ability, noting areas of strength and interest.

But these parents resist the facts of this situation and are not interested in helping me to uncover what family dynamics may be at the root of their son's learning difficulty. Their minds are fixed. "We've hired the best tutors money can buy!" the mother offers.

"Adam just won't apply himself. He won't settle down. All he wants to do is play," the father adds.

"Why do you suppose that is?" I ask.

Mother and father shrug. "I'm not sure, but I know I wasn't always the greatest student in the world myself," the father says. "I was a slow starter, you might say, but once my innate ability kicked in I was an ace. I know the same is going to happen to Adam, but in the meantime I've got to make sure he keeps his goals high and doesn't fall behind."

These parents would rather believe that they have an exceptional child who is not trying rather than a more average child who is having a real learning difficulty that they could help.

"We've been too easy on him," the mother says. "I think we just haven't put enough pressure on him."

But Adam's problem, generally, is not in his intellectual ability. It is that learning has become an emotional issue for him. Because he cannot live up to his parents' unrealistic expectations, he has come to feel that there is no point in trying. He is already a failure. He clearly knows he is a disappointment to his family. His parents have admonished him to try harder, but, in fact, he is trying as hard as he can. Now he is afraid that nothing he does will ever satisfy them. As a result, any school activity becomes a source of anxiety and stress for him. Without psychological intervention, it is unlikely that Adam will ever be able to achieve even average potential.

Unrealistic expectations are not an exclusive problem for children of average intelligence whose parents feel they have greater potential. Even truly bright or gifted children, given too much pressure from parents to achieve, can develop the feeling that nothing is good enough. The consequence of this, however, is that a child in this situation simply gives up, and the push for excellence backfires. The parents have effectively removed the sense of pride and self-worth the child might have developed in his own accomplishments, whatever they might have been.

Lastly, some affluent parents exert pressure simply because they assume that children are, by nature, lazy and will not strive for excellence if they are not prodded every step of the way. Sometimes the parents aren't even aware of how they are communicating this pressure. But through their continual "constructive" criticism— such phrases as "Apply yourself" or "Pay attention" or "You can do better if you just . . ."—or through a constant focus on what could be improved rather than on paying attention to what was achieved, such parents implicitly accuse the child of laziness or lack of sufficient effort. How often I have heard a child complain, "I'm trying as hard as I can. What do they want from me? I guess I can't do anything right."

One father, a Fortune 500 CEO, told me: "There isn't much point in talking about what you've done right. If you just sit around patting yourself on the back, you don't move forward. You have to look at where you fell short or you'll never get anywhere."

Criticism and chastising may be motivational for the executive whose success has already been established, but children don't have the tangible reinforcements adults have—the graduate degrees, penthouse offices, or big bank accounts—to remind them of their achievements and maintain their self-esteem in the face of challenges. Parents are a child's cheering section, and without encouragement, and applause, children will lack the persistence to rise above the challenges.

You Succeed in What You Like

If setting high expectations, consciously or unconsciously, does not guarantee excellence from children—and, in fact, may produce the exact opposite effect—what can parents do to ensure that their children will reach their potential? What are realistic goals parents can have that will encourage children to stretch to achieve their best, yet not overwhelm?

The first part of the answer to creating truly realistic expectations begins with understanding a very basic truth: people, whether children or adults, are most successful in activities in which they are internally motivated, that is to say, activities in which they personally choose to be involved and enjoy. They rarely succeed for more than a short period—if at all—when someone is standing over them constantly pushing, demanding, or criticizing.

Young children naturally want to learn. They delight in the positive attention they receive for their accomplishments and will continue to achieve in areas that bring an encouraging response from parents. When entering school, most children remain eager to please. They want to be chosen as classroom helpers, to have their papers displayed on the bulletin board, to participate in the top reading group and to receive good grades on their report cards. They don't need a parent to give them motivation. That already exists. But if their efforts to achieve are continually met with criticism or demands for greater productivity, the stress will destroy their natural motivation.

When children operate to please themselves—to learn things and to master tasks of personal interest—we see the greatest degrees of success. True mastery and talent, in fact, come almost exclusively from internal, not external motivation. One striking example is the story of the famous composer and conductor, Leonard Bernstein, whose father tried to steer him away from pursuing a career in music. When asked why he did so, Mr. Bernstein, Sr., replied, "How was I supposed to know my son was going to grow up to be Leonard Bernstein?" Unable to dissuade his son from music, Mr. Bernstein, Sr., tempered his own expectations for himself that motivated him to achieve his considerable success. He did not need excessive parental pressure, and perhaps if he had had it, he would not have grown up to be Leonard Bernstein.

Parents can encourage an innate drive for excellence only if they respect the unique interests and passions of a child, and allow the child to be involved in setting his own goals. If an activity makes a child feel good, if it creates positive internal feelings, then the child will develop strong motivation to pursue it and to achieve to the best of his ability. This is the quintessential formula for motivation:

ACTIVITY + POSITIVE FEELING = MOTIVATION

Think for a moment about those activities in which you willingly and enthusiastically participate. Isn't the key factor of your drive the satisfied feeling you have during the activity or after it has been accomplished? Isn't that the source of your motivation?

Of course, there is an equally simple but profound formula for the lack of motivation, or avoidance:

ACTIVITY + NEGATIVE FEELING = AVOIDANCE

Now imagine an activity you dislike: writing a tedious memo, having lunch with an antagonistic client, organizing a chaotic desk or closet, and so on. Isn't it easy to think of a multitude of reasons to avoid the loathsome task? The same will be true for your children. If a task creates a negative feeling, if it has become an unsatisfying, frustrating, or boring experience, a child can be very creative in his rationale for avoidance, for why there are better things to do, or why he won't even try since he knows he will not be successful at it.

Negative feelings frequently occur when a task is not appropriately correlated to the abilities of the child. In school, for example, one reason children become frustrated is simply that they are not intellectually or physically ready for a certain challenge. When children are given work that is beyond their ability (since curriculums are planned for the ability level of the majority of students) they will become less and less motivated to try. For other students, the curriculum may be too easy. The work is not challenging enough and they become bored. Boredom is a common and strong motive for not engaging in an activity.

However, even when a child is capable of a task, he will experience negative feelings if no matter how much he might achieve, his parents never seem satisfied and they impose their perfectionist need upon their offspring. Consider for instance the following scenarios:

- A child has conscientiously worked on a book report and the parents comment, "With a little more effort this could really be outstanding."
- A young child decides to surprise Mom by making her bed, but she responds, "The cover is pretty messy. Let me show you how to do this better."
- A child has struggled diligently to complete a project and the parent suggests that she copy it over again so it will be perfectly neat for the teacher.

How are these children going to feel about themselves? How can they develop positive feelings about their efforts when the parents have made the task a negative experience? Although some parents may think their criticism is constructive, their desire for perfection is destructive and serves only to feed the avoidance formula.

Avoiding the Brass Ring Syndrome: Process Over Product

The question now becomes: How can I encourage my child's own internal motivation to achieve and do well with the tasks which confront my child?

Herein lies the second part of the answer to how parents can foster a healthy climate supporting their child's goals: they must change their emphasis from *product* to *process*. This encompasses making a shift in your priorities from the *results* of your child's efforts to the *effort itself*.

Although these two concepts, process and product, are very much intertwined, it is important for parents to recognize the critical difference of their focus. Processes occur on a continuous basis, while a product may take a considerable period of time to reach completion. Children are always involved in some type of process; however, not every child will always be able to obtain the sought-after final goal, the ultimate product.

A concrete example of this difference is the case of the remarkable young swimmer, Michael Phelps, whose achievements at the

2004 Summer Olympics made history. After winning eight medals in one Olympics, including four individual and two team gold medals, he accomplished what only one other Olympian in history—a Russian gymnast—had done before, and the debate will continue for years as to whether he has surpassed the legendary Mark Spitz as the greatest swimmer of all time. All this at the age of 19!

However, for young Phelps to reach the summit of his sport involved years of grueling process. He had to adopt a much disciplined routine that required considerable focus, concentration and sacrifice. He had daily practices, working even when his body was aching and fatigued. He had to fight back tears and exhibit good sportsmanship when others won. He came to the 2004 Olympics after finishing only fifth in his one event in the 2000 Olympics. But back he came. Much of his teenage years were spent in the pool, while his contemporaries were partying and playing. He was fortunate, indeed, that this sacrifice resulted in the achievement of a lifetime: the gold medal and a place in the history books.

But for every Michael Phelps, there are hundreds of other young athletes who are making the same sacrifice, going through the same laborious processes, and yet they do not receive the final product, the gold medal. These young athletes are just as deserving of being acknowledged and acclaimed for all their work and effort as the designated champion, Michael Phelps. If these unrecognized champions are to maintain high self-esteem, their families and coaches must continually and positively acknowledge the process involved in their competing.

Not paying sufficient attention to the process and daily accomplishments of children is a parenting challenge that can occur at any socio-economic level. However, I observe it with much greater intensity in people who are accustomed to achieving and getting something tangible for their efforts. Affluent parents see themselves as winners, not "also rans." They have been able to reach their positions by staying focused on a goal, and getting it, be it money, a title on the door, a position of control, articles written about them, and recognition and respect from their community.

However, if parents are focused only on these end products, how can their children feel valued and validated if they don't reach this level of acclaim? What happens to the child who loses the class election for president or the lead in the school play? What happens to the child who works as hard as he can and is able to receive only a "B"?

In order for your child to feel validated all the time, you must shift your focus and responsiveness to your child's process and not the product. Process can be rewarded every day. A specific product (the gold medal, an "A," or whatever) may be forever elusive.

When children do *not* feel that they are always expected to be the winners, they will relax and enjoy whatever they're doing for its own sake. More importantly, they will feel good simply about the process of their participation. Even if they aren't the best they can still have positive feelings about their efforts and will not feel they have been a terrible failure or disappointment in the eyes of their parents. When these children do achieve external success, the drive will have come from within, not from parental pressure.

Identifying Process in Your Child

High-achieving, affluent parents already possess an operational understanding of process over product. Think, for example, about how you approach a large and important project. Would you continually remind yourself of its enormousness, asking yourself over and over if it will ever be completed successfully? Most likely not. As achieving adults, we usually cope with challenges by dividing them into small, more manageable units. We set time tables, and delegate responsibility for specific tasks. Then we immerse ourselves in doing the work, focusing primarily on our daily accomplishments. Soon the long-range final goal does not seem so improbable.

In this same way, you should be looking to acknowledge the small, every day steps in your child's life. Your focus should be tied to effort, not achievement. When children feel successful about their competence in small tasks, they will have the confidence to push themselves willingly to the maximum. Success is a feeling everyone enjoys. It drives us toward greater effort and mastery.

Parents can recognize process in children of any age. In toddlers, they can observe such traits as concentration, independence, persistence, and responsibility. For example, if your three-year-old son is engaged in doing a puzzle and shows a great degree of concentration, ignoring the potential distractions around him, acknowledge that process of sustained concentration. "It's great that you never give up. That will really help you figure out the puzzle." Or if your four-year-old daughter stubbornly refuses your help tying her shoes because she wants to do it herself, don't become annoyed because you want to get it done quickly. Instead, compliment her responsibility and persistence in the face of frustration.

Encouraging process over product with small children also involves recognizing the essential role of play. Hard-driving parents often do not realize the importance of unstructured play as a part of learning and as a confidence builder. But considerable research has shown that it is instrumental in helping children develop intellectually and creatively. If you take your child to the park, for example, it is important simply to allow him to find his own challenge and enjoy it at his own pace. The process of his activity is more important than whether or not he makes it to the top of the jungle gym. Play should not be work.

Once your child is in school, emphasizing process will help inspire your child's internal ambition to succeed. Because children spend a considerable portion of their lives in school, much of their self-esteem and motivation stems from how they perceive themselves in this environment. If parents can help them feel successful in school, and enjoy the process of learning, they will help their children become successful in life.

In order to do this, parents should be aware of the diverse processes that create confidence in learning. Too often, they simply give their children the general admonition, "I want you to be a good student." But what exactly does this mean to the child? Unfortunately, the implication is usually Mom and Dad will acknowledge you if you bring us tangible evidence that you were a good student. Thus the child must wait for an excellent grade, a special note from the teacher, or an award in the class before he begins to feel that he is in fact a "good" student.

On the other hand, if parents recognize the smaller actions that contribute a genuine enjoyment of learning and encourage them along the way, children will naturally develop greater internal motivation and become the best students they are capable of being. The following are examples of some of the processes you can look for:

- concentration and attending to the task at hand
- the ability to listen and follow directions
- eagerness and enthusiasm to learn new information
- organizational skills
- confidence to ask questions
- new and creative ways to solve problems
- confidence to stay with a challenging task and not give up
- the ability to work independently
- good study habits
- conscientious follow-through on a task begun
- consideration for the teacher and other students
- ability to cooperate in a team project

You can observe and encourage each of these processes in many types of interactions and activities—if you are aware of them and responsive to your child. For example, if you see that your daughter's friends are calling her to get the homework assignment because she pays attention, let her know that you have noticed it. Or, if your son sits right down after, school and begins his homework, acknowledge how responsible his behavior is. You can also observe examples of these traits in non-school-related activities.

Even when your child enters high school and college, parents can still have a major impact by the manner in which they recognize process and praise success. I recently met a young man, Jered, whose parents had sent him to the finest boarding schools, and expected him to remain at the top of his class. He did well enough to gain admittance to the same prestigious Ivy League college from which both of his parents had graduated. But in the middle of his sophomore year, he recognized that, although he was academically good enough to be an average student among the brightest students in the country, no matter how hard he tried, he would never meet his parent's expectations for a top-of-the-class product. Struggling to maintain his parents' standards, he lost confidence in himself and wanted to drop out and get a job to remove the stress.

In working through the crises with his family, I was able to get Jered's parents to realize that they had to shift their emphasis from a product (top grades) to a process (Jered's enthusiasm for the subjects in which he had a personal interest). They would have to support goals that would make Jered feel worthwhile and avoid communicating expectations that would seem overwhelming.

Fortunately, these parents were successful. Soon, Jered stopped seeing his remaining years at college as an imposing burden and was able to view them as a tremendous opportunity to discover where his interest and talents lay, and then enthusiastically pursue them.

The Language of Encouragement

At this point you may be wondering exactly how to go about recognizing process in your child's daily life. Perhaps the most important technique is using the "language of encouragement" as frequently as possible. This type of interaction focuses on your child's strengths and the progress, however small, that he makes each day.

In order to have a better understanding of how to implement this new language, we need to make a clarification between the terms *encouragement* and *praise*. Don Dinkmeyer and Cary D. McKay, in their parenting program, "The Systematic Training for Effective Parenting," draw an important distinction between the two words. Although praise and encouragement appear to be the same thing—as they are, after all, both a kind of positive reinforcement—they differ profoundly in emphasis and effect.

Praise is a verbal reward given for an accomplishment. It is most often given for winning, for being the best, and is therefore tied very closely to product. In effect, the parent who praises is saying, "If you do something I consider good, you will have the reward of being recognized and valued by me." When we praise our children we are telling them how proud we are of their accomplishments and by so doing we emphasize to the child the level of performance we expect.

Encouragement, on the other hand is given for effort or for improvement, however slight. By focusing on the child's assets and strengths without any consideration for what the child might have achieved, you recognize process. Encouragement gives children internal motivation by telling them that the act of trying and doing one's best is its own reward.

If we praise a child who has not succeeded externally at a given task, it may often come out as a false compliment. But there is no such thing as false encouragement! The table below summarizes the distinctions between praise and encouragement.

Praise	Encouragement
Focus is on accomplishment of an end product: the *what*	Focus is on the process of an activity—the *how*
Related to a specifically designated standard	No predetermined standard of accomplishment
Limited in its application—not everyone will accomplish on a daily basis	Unlimited opportunities for application; applies to ongoing activities occurring on a daily basis
Fosters intense sense of competition	Does not create competitive model—there are no competitors
Winner-loser orientation—the most accomplished are praiseworthy	Every child can be a winner
Does not encourage cooperation for the good of all	Acknowledgment given to cooperation and interpersonal skills
Rewards the tangible success	Rewards intangibles: effort, attitude, determination, persistence

You can apply the language of encouragement by taking the following actions.

Comment Upon Effort and Improvement of Any Kind. Many affluent parents do not regularly recognize a child's efforts, or worse, communicate in ways that demean their child's accomplishments, assuming they are "a given." They reason: "Well, of course, he's learned how to use a computer, throw a football, and so on—he's my son!" But when parents neglect or minimize a child's effort, they take away the sense of accomplishment from the child.

The more you can verbally acknowledge improvement, no matter how small or seemingly natural, the more your child will want to find new and more pronounced ways to improve in all aspects of his or her person. You may need to search hard for improvement in your child, and sometimes it may be improvement of which the child himself is not yet aware. But letting your child know that you notice every small step will help strengthen his image as a success-prone individual.

Comments such as: "You were having so much trouble starting that paper, but now you've really got the hang of it." or "Your practice swimming really shows. Your form looks much smoother now." let your child know you realize that success is accomplished in small steps, not in one fell swoop.

Even when notable results do not come forth; continue to look for improvement no matter how slight. If, for example, your teenager has committed himself to getting a good report card, but when his grades come out, not all subjects meet your expectation, comment first upon the areas that have shown improvement. By telling your child that you recognize these, he will feel more motivated to try for more.

You can also use the language of encouragement in your child's social development. If your son tells you about a conflict with a friend or friends, remark about ways in which he has already grown in his relationships, and express confidence in his ability to resolve his current conflict.

Solicit Your Child's Ideas and Opinions. Successful people have complete confidence in their judgment; that is why they succeed.

Soliciting their child's opinion is something they are unaccustomed to doing. They are more accustomed to deciding, not asking. But effective parenting requires a change.

Supportive parents recognize and communicate respect for their child's ideas and opinions. In order to begin this process, find issues about which your child may have a valid opinion and then give it consideration. For example:

- Ask your child for ideas about an interesting weekend family activity.
- If you can't make a decision about a family project, ask your teenager to make it. An example might be deciding between two equally appealing color schemes for remodeling the kitchen.
- If your child has a reason for not doing something you think he or she should do, listen to that reason and, even if it is unacceptable to you, show that you will give it consideration
- Whenever possible, praise your child's thinking. "Good thinking!" is a phrase all children love to be told.
- Ask for an opinion about a current event

Thinking is a process. When a child feels that his thinking is a positive attribute, he will be not only encouraged to use his mind, to be creative, and to assert his intellectual autonomy, he will also gain a tremendous sense of competence, confidence, and self-esteem.

Appreciate special Qualities and Characteristics. While it is important for your children to know that you love them no matter what they do, letting them know specifically what it is about them that you especially appreciate and admire can greatly enhance the support your child feels coming from you.

Telling your child how very thoughtful it was to bring a friend a homework assignment, or how happy you are that your son entertained his little sister while you had to run an important errand, or recognizing your child's sense of humor and letting him or her know how much joy it brings you are all encouraging responses that validate special qualities.

Even a statement as simple as, "Thanks for helping with dinner, I can always count on you to give me a hand," lets children know that you are paying attention to them, that they can please you in small as well as big ways.

The trick for parents is to recognize the "special genius" in each of their own children, whether or not it is reflected in school grades or other external measurements, so that it can be celebrated and encouraged. New and exciting research into the nature of human intelligence has found that there are numerous domains of intelligence, many of which may not be challenged or rewarded in a traditional school setting. In fact, Harvard University researcher and psychologist Howard Gardner posits in his acclaimed book, *Frames of Mind*, that each person possesses at least seven different and distinct intelligences: linguistic, logical-mathematical, musical, spatial, bodily-kinesthetic, intuition, and interpersonal. Most of these are neglected by our traditional educational system. This explains why even high school dropouts have achieved dramatic success when they were free to follow their own natural instincts.

It is not infrequent that parents—successful in life without having necessarily been successful themselves in school—will put tremendous pressure on their children to be academic stars right from the start. Affluent parents need to recognize that school is not the only stepping stone toward success in adult life. I am not suggesting that any parent cheerfully accept a report card full of "D's" and "F's," but rather that, for some children—especially children who are often competing in school with many verbally or mathematically talented students—an early emphasis on high grades can be destructive. When a child of at least average intelligence brings home failing grades, a more in depth analysis is called for.

- Does the learning style of that particular prestigious school match the learning style of your student?
- Are there undiagnosed learning disabilities involved?

- Could emotional issues be interfering with attention, concentration and comprehension?
- Is substance abuse a factor?

I recently attended a large meeting where all the participants would be considered among the movers and shakers of the business world. The speaker at the podium, himself of considerable achievement, suddenly posed the question "How many of you out there were Phi Beta Kappa?"

Everyone looked around as only a few individuals raised their hands. And yet if he had asked those same people whether or not they wanted their children to win such academic honors, the majority would probably have admitted that they did.

Some children will not always follow the traditional path to success. Parents have to be flexible enough to support a child's personal intelligences if he is to achieve his fullest potential. Encouraging your child's strengths not only ensures that your expectations will be reasonable, it also enhances that child's self-confidence.

Effective parents need to have many of the attributes of a skilled detective. They must find the hidden talents, abilities, and inner strength of their children, so that these can be celebrated.

Speak Also When You are Pleased. Sometimes it seems that basic human nature is to complain about that which displeases us but to remain quiet when all is well. Of course, life does not always run smoothly and our children are not perfect. But while parents need to let children know what behaviors are unacceptable, scolding and other negative expressions should be the exception, not the norm.

Consider, for example, Alex and Lauren, who return home from a very exhausting day. Their two children greet them at the door, and then return to the den where they have been playing. After a half hour, however, the two youngsters erupt into a loud argument, and both parents rush into the den, angrily admonishing the disruption. For thirty minutes the children have played wonderfully without any supervision, but was any notice given to the positive behavior? What kind of message does this give these children about attracting their parents' attention?

When parents only notice a child's negative behavior, the child will often begin to misbehave as a means of getting parental attention. Thus, the attention you must give your children with regard to their negative behavior needs to be counter-balanced with positive encouragement whenever things are going well. Catch your child being good as many times a day as possible.

Criticize Constructively. One of the most important roles that parents can play is that of teacher. Children need guidance. When they make mistakes, parents can help them learn through new information and corrective action. Speaking the language of encouragement does not mean avoiding criticism, but it does mean doing so in a *constructive* rather than *destructive* manner. Follow these recommendations to ensure that your criticism is constructive:

1. Find something positive in the situation to which you can make reference, such as effort, good thinking, improvement, and so on before you comment on a problem or error. For example, "I have noticed you are trying to be more careful about doing your homework when you come home from school rather than waiting until late in the evening when you are more tired."

2. Avoid demeaning comments about your child's personality or attitude—that is, "You're always goofing up," "You're such a wise guy"—and stick to the specifics of the problem.

3. Express your feelings about the situation and include your belief that your child can correct the behavior. Example: "I am bothered by this comment from your French teacher regarding your missing assignments, but I feel confident you and I can figure out the solution."

4. Work together *with the child* to establish a concrete plan of action to improve this issue in the future. Example: "How do you plan to handle this problem? Let's work out a plan, and write it down."

5. When you notice even the slightest improvement in the situation, encourage this forward progress. Example: "I

noticed your French book on the kitchen table. I think it is a good idea on your part to do the homework first before other things can distract you."

Remember: *con*structive means building up, *de*structive means tearing down. Only the former will encourage your child to make improvement.

Believe in the Success of This Approach

Highly successful, achievement-oriented parents have the greatest difficulty fully accepting the concept of process over product and feeling comfortable using the language of encouragement. Many of these parents, I have discovered, are concerned about "toughening up" their children, preparing them for stiff competition in high school, college, and beyond. They honestly believe that the best way to achieve this is through external pressure. Some parents even feel that if they do not maintain high expectations, their children will become complacent, and never reach the potential they, the parents, wish for them.

Admittedly, it may be difficult for you to find the fine line between expecting too much of your children and not expecting anything at all. Like Goldilocks in the story of *The Three Bears*, you may need to try several beds before you find the one that is "just right." More importantly though, if you remember that the goal of your efforts in establishing realistic expectations is to help your child find his or her own "just right," rather than <u>yours</u>, you will not find yourself in this quagmire.

The following dialogue I recently had with one concerned father movingly exemplifies the fears many parents have, and how you can challenge those fears. After a workshop on the issue of process and product, this father approached me, and said: "If I have to keep saying something good about every little insignificant thing my son Michael does, I am going to be raising a wimp. He will always be whining for some attention, even though his efforts are not outstanding. I can assure you that my folks were not coddling me all the time, and look at what I've achieved. Come to think of it, I don't remember my Dad ever really giving me any compliments."

I asked this father, "How would you describe your relationship with your parents?"

"Well, I suppose that a psychologist wouldn't think it was so great. We were never very close, and he was a pretty tough sort of guy. In my house, you sure did what you were told to do, or else. But then, my father had to work pretty hard to support the family, and that was really his whole life, working and sleeping, sleeping and working."

"Is that the type of relationship you want with your son?" I queried.

"Of course not, I remember always wishing that I could have been closer to my own dad when I was growing up. But on the other hand, I became tough myself and have been very successful."

As I reflected on the conversation, I shared this with the father: "When I hear you describe your father, it sounds as if you are talking about a strict disciplinarian, but I don't hear you saying that he was always criticizing your achievement and pushing you to try harder and harder."

"Well, maybe that is true," he responded. "To tell you the truth, he wasn't around that much to really know what I was doing as far as school goes. He just didn't want any trouble from the school, and expected us to get passing grades."

"So if your dad wasn't the one who was stressing the super performance, what do you think motivated you?" I asked.

"I guess I just wanted to have a better life than what we had. I went to school with some pretty wealthy kids, and I remember looking at their clothes and fancy cars, and I decided that one day I would be able to afford that, too."

Like many affluent parents, it was clear that this father's motivation came from inside. I therefore reminded him: "you drove yourself to achieve, not the tough attitude of your father."

In the end, this father realized that his motivation for success was prompted by two things: economic necessity and his own internal drive. Although his son, Michael, may not have the economic hunger his father had, he deserved the same opportunity to develop internal motivation.

This is why encouragement is so important. If a child is always pressured and worried about not meeting a parent's high expectations, she will not have the confidence to be competitive. This is the type of child who becomes the wimp the parents fear they will raise. Genuine toughness comes from self-confidence. It comes from recognizing your strengths and knowing that others appreciate them. The child who has been encouraged to develop his own motivation is more likely to achieve in life, because he will believe in himself regardless of whatever external results occur.

When a child feels a positive about what she does, she will push for greater and greater challenges, and she will also have the bonus of a close and supportive friendship with parents.

Eight Going on Eighteen: The Push for Maturity

Affluent, successful parents often place their children in adult social situations and expect them to behave in a sophisticated manner at an early age. We take them with us into the first-class cabin on airplanes and into posh hotels when we travel. We request that they sit like little angels at expensive restaurants; we dress them in designer clothing to attend a party and then become upset when they spill chocolate mousse on it. In essence, we have a tendency to forget they are children and need to behave as such.

According to such prominent developmental psychologists as Jean Piaget, Eric Erikson, and Arnold Gisell, children grow, learn, think, judge, reason, and make decisions in well-delineated stages. These stages are common to all children regardless of their ethnic or cultural environment, or their parents' worldly accomplishments. Each child passes through these stages at a different time and at a unique pace, and the speed of development is not related to intellectual potential.

While all parents tend to focus on the traditional milestones of infancy, whether their child is walking by age one, for example, or talking by two, they are often totally unaware of the much more subtle developmental processes and growth rates underlying other areas. Furthermore, the disparity in reaching these milestones among different children can be quite dramatic.

For example, consider these four simple instructions: "Get a sweater; brush your teeth; take your clothes out of the den; and meet me in front of the house." While one child may be able to follow them effortlessly, another child of the same age may not yet have developed the ability to remember and process more than two sequential instructions. Without a clear understanding of a child's developmental status, a parent may erroneously believe his child is not listening, paying attention, or trying hard enough, and consequently respond in a punishing manner when the child fails to follow the instructions.

The mere act of sitting still, to illustrate another example, is an activity requiring a conscientious effort for a child under ten. This has been demonstrated scientifically by Martha Denckla, professor of neurology and pediatrics at Johns Hopkins University. According to Denckla, the frontal lobe of the brain has the capacity to control a child's natural curiosity and energy, but this capacity remains undeveloped until approximately age ten. Denckla demonstrated that a younger child, placed in a situation that requires sustained restriction of physical activity, will almost assuredly fail.

A well-publicized example of this could be seen during the wedding of Britain's Prince Andrew and Sarah Ferguson. Considerable media attention focused upon the behavior of young Prince William, then four. He was seen playing with his hat, squirming about in his seat, seemingly inattentive to the formalities. But was this behavior that deserved a reprimand? Prince William was, in fact, behaving like a typical four-year-old. To expect him continually to pay attention would have been completely unreasonable and unhealthy, even for one born into royalty.

Affluent parents may push their children toward early maturation with the best of intentions. Utilizing their material advantages, they fill virtually every minute of their child's waking life with activities designed to promote rapid development. Rather than accepting the fact that developmental cycles will progress naturally, these parents create busily scheduled lives that can leave the child in a state of mental and physical exhaustion and make learning a chore.

In general, parents must be aware of the dangerous habit of over-programming children simply because they want him or her to begin an activity at as early an age as possible. David Elkind, in his book, *The Hurried Child*, describes the negative ramifications of rushing our children through childhood without really permitting them unstructured time when they can play and pursue their own interest. When very young children require an appointment book—or a PDA—to guide their scurrying from piano lessons to dance lessons to tennis lessons to educational-enrichment programs to programmed play activities, they will not become more mature, merely overloaded and stressed out.

In order to assure that you do not let your expectations of maturity become unrealistic, you must constantly be aware of whether the demands you make on your children are truly appropriate to your child's stage of development. When you see that your child is frustrated, you should ask yourself if the child's frustration is an indication that the task may be inappropriate for his or her maturity. Even though it may have been appropriate for a sibling at the same age, you must remember that each child is unique.

When a child expresses displeasure about an activity he or she is supposed to be enjoying—such as any extracurricular activity—an effective parent listens. Children, in their own way, will voice objections. They may plead fatigue, a stomachache, or other minor physical complaints. They may complain about the behavior of another child in the program or an attitude on the part of the instructor. They may become regressively dependent, whining, or fearful if you are not within their sight at all times. All of these behaviors can be a signal to you that your child is not developmentally ready for this activity yet, and that your unrealistic expectation is causing emotional trauma.

It is important to remember that a slow start is not necessarily symptomatic of limitations in any ultimate achievement. Making a slow-starter feel inferior, however, *can* be detrimental to future achievement, and therefore it is important to be sensitive to your child's developmental stage and avoid making demands that are not appropriate for his current level of maturity.

Unrealistic Expectations Based on Comparisons

Affluent parents may also create unrealistic expectations for their children based upon the achievements of siblings or of the children of friends or relatives. They seem to feel that comparisons will help to stimulate the achievement drive of their children.

I once taught a workshop in an affluent Midwestern suburb in which a young mother approached me afterwards, very concerned because her four-year-old daughter didn't want to go to the special preschool ballet class at a popular children's dance center.

"Why force her?" I asked.

"Everyone goes there!" the mother replied.

"Everyone?" At this point I gently reminded her that 99.90 percent of the four-year-olds in this country have never even heard of preschool ballet, let alone participated in it.

"But all my friends take their children there," she again offered. Sadly, she had fallen into the classic trap that comes with parenting in affluence: "If everyone else's child is doing it, mine should be, too."

Major problems are caused by creating expectations for children on the basis of comparisons. Because such expectations are often developmentally unrealistic, they can create a sense of inadequacy in your child. No child should feel he is being negatively compared to someone else and that he may be behind in some manner. Comparative expectations can sometimes be based upon incomplete information, in which case you wind up comparing your friend's child at her best to your own child at her worst.

Comparisons within the family are particularly damaging. A successful sibling will be a daily reminder to the less accomplished child of his inadequacies. I have seen more than a few capable and competent children and teenagers who feel completely inadequate because of the shadow of an older, younger, or even twin sibling's accomplishments. Although children themselves may make comparisons, the actions of parents can greatly increase or decrease the negative impact of this shadow.

It is critical for you, as parents, to be particularly alert to the importance of celebrating the differences among all your children. Recognize the strengths and talents in each of them and focus upon the positive without comparing.

One of the things I often ask parents to do is to write down five special qualities about each child in their family. These can be accomplishments, achievements, talents, or personality traits such as even-tempered, dependable, helpful, thoughtful, or humorous.

Take a moment to do this now. If you have trouble with this exercise, you are probably not truly celebrating the uniqueness of each of your children and may be inappropriately making identical demands upon each family member.

It is not uncommon among busy, affluent parents, whose time with children may be limited, to note that they can easily talk about the "star" of the family, but the more subtle talents of the other children in the family give them pause. If you cannot identify the special needs and talents of each of your children, however, how can they be recognized and encouraged?

Like Father, Like Son

Most parents see their children, at least some of the time, as miniature versions of themselves: fathers with their sons, mothers with their daughters. Our children often look like us, and they are our biological creations. But many affluent parents have a particular tendency to attempt to make their children just like them. For some, this is based on a desire to relive their own childhood experiences through their offspring. For others, the unconscious reasoning may be more akin to thinking "If being like me has worked so well for me, it will work for my child as well. If I have been rewarded for my traits and interests, so will my child be." In either case, the result is that such parents encourage and pressure their children to be exactly like them, from enjoying the same sports, hobbies and foods, to insisting that they enter the same careers.

The truth is, most children do want to imitate their parents, but they want to be like them in their own unique way. When parents expect their children to share the same views, to have the same interests and passions, to appreciate the same clothes, they are creating unrealistic expectations.

A few years ago, I knew a father who was an outstanding golfer. Tom made his living as a successful surgeon, but when he was younger, he could have opted for a career as a professional golfer. Unfortunately, his son possessed neither Tom's natural talent nor obsessive interest in the game. Tom, however, remained stubbornly blind to this fact, and for several years had worked regularly with his young boy so that he would be able to play on the high school golf team. When that time came, the boy did qualify for the team but then suddenly quit playing altogether.

Tom was devastated. Only after numerous family counseling sessions could this young man verbalize how angry and stressed he felt with his father's continual instructions, angry outbursts, and demands for increased perfection. This father's unrealistic expectations had destroyed any positive motivation his son might have to participate in an activity that could have resulted in pleasurable quality time together.

Unfortunately, variations of this story occur frequently among affluent parents and their children. Merely substitute golf for any other sport, or singing, dancing, art, music, and the like, and you will have the story of a million unhappy parents and millions of angry children.

Children need encouragement to initiate hobbies and passions, but they resent having their minds made up for them. When parents are too aggressive in trying to control these interests, they convey this message: "You are inadequate and incapable of finding your own way." Their imposing position fails to respect the child's own interests and abilities and will only foster resistance and rebellion.

Another reason for unrealistic expectations of comparison may lie in the unfulfilled ambitions of the parents, which they are now trying to satisfy through their child. Even the most successful individuals may have regrets about not accomplishing something or not achieving a certain goal in their life. In order to relive this experience, the parents force the child into activities or areas in which he has neither the interest nor the talent.

Parents must be careful not to live vicariously through their children in these activities. Are you enrolling your child in violin lessons because it makes him happy or because it makes you happy? Are you trying to relive your life through your children? These are questions every parent should ask himself regularly.

Parents must also avoid valuing only those personality characteristics in their children that they feel will lead to that child's achievement of material success. I have had numerous accomplished fathers worried because their sons lack their aggressive and competitive nature. They seem somewhat threatened if they perceive their boys developing a reserved, thoughtful, or sensitive personality. When I query them on this position, they remind me that it's a rat race out there and their children need to be able to "make it."

But effective parents do not force their children to be aggressive and competitive beyond their nature. You must learn to make your children feel valued whatever their personality and character. The resulting confidence they will have will guarantee that they indeed "make it."

The psychologically healthy way to inspire children is again through encouragement and invitation. If a child appreciates one of your interests, that is wonderful. If not, don't insist; try another area of mutual interest. If you do find common ground with your child, do not insist that he or she perform or appreciate the activity exactly as you do. Let your child develop his or her own love for the activity. Let your child feel that the activity or interest is as much his as it is yours.

If you do not find common ground, let your child develop his or her own loves. Perhaps you can learn to be interested in these as well as your own. After all, that is what you are hoping your child will do.

Think about your reason for wanting your children to be like you in the first place. If it is that they might enjoy the things that you have come to love, remember this: demanding that your children simply be parental clones does not promote this enjoyment.

Perfection is Elusive

When raising children in a privileged environment, parents must remember that as perfect as they may desire their children to be, they are just human beings. They need to be challenged, but not overwhelmed. They should certainly know that you expect them to do their best, but also that failure can be an important learning experience.

You can model this philosophy by letting your child know that *you* are not perfect. If children perceive their parents as incapable of anything less than perfection, the role model will be overwhelming. Admitting you are wrong or that you make mistakes can be a tremendously illuminating experience for your children. It permits them to learn that it's acceptable to be wrong, and that you don't expect yourself or anyone else to be right all the time. You become more humanized and the model you present to them appears achievable.

It may seem trivial to admit when you are wrong to a child, but it serves an awesomely important function. Maintaining an image of being right all of the time (or at least an almost God-like percentage of the time) may be important in the world of business or in various professions, but at home and imposed upon your children, it cannot help but to create a negative perspective from which your child and your relationship with your child may never recover.

When reflecting upon your expectations, your child's individuality is the ultimate barometer. If you can develop the ability to look analytically at each of your children and to encourage them in their own talents and interests, you will create an environment in which even the most privileged child will feel confident and internally motivated to thrive and produce, to work hard because effort has its own intrinsic reward.

Just as daily water and nutrients feed the developing flower so that it may produce its spectacular blossom, so, too, can our children blossom in an atmosphere that is both structured and flexible, that promotes self-motivation and is rich with daily doses of encouragement.

FIVE

Step Four: Developing
The Competent Child

Danielle and Matthew were a highly successful couple with a large manufacturing business. They had waited many years between their marriage and the birth of their first child because they wanted to be sure they had acquired a reasonable level of financial stability and the personal maturity to give their child every advantage they could offer.

Materially speaking, the best was exactly what their son Max got. From the day he returned home from the hospital, he settled into a lavishly furnished nursery, which later became a bedroom resembling a toy store. He was attended constantly by a nanny, and then other servants as the parents hired more staff. It did not take this bright child long to discover how to manipulate his caregivers to do pretty much whatever he wanted them to: cleaning his room, making him special meals, letting him watch television and stay up beyond his bedtime.

Almost from his first day at school, Max complained that the work was too hard. He was continually assisted in his homework, first by Danielle, and later by a battery of tutors, some of whom he coerced into doing the work for him. Max also had social problems in school. His classmates did not like him, finding him selfish and self-centered. He was excluded first from playground games, later from parties—until he was largely isolated from his peers.

As homework in his competitive school grew increasingly diffi-cult, Max began to develop a multitude of illnesses, which kept him out of class a considerable amount of time. When he was at school, he was a familiar face in the nurse's office. His illnesses stopped at around the age of thirteen, approximately the same time he began to overcome his isolation and find a circle of friends. Danielle and Matthew were now relieved to see their son in better physical health and answering telephone calls from friends, although his grades were still miserable. But what relief they had was short-lived.

By the time he was sixteen, Max had begun to associate with the other troubled students at his school. His behavior at home changed dramatically and his physical appearance became unkempt and disheveled. However, his ever-protective parents excused these changes by rationalizing that all teenagers go through difficult times.

Soon Danielle and Matthew began to miss valuables from their home. An investigation revealed the frightening truth: Max had developed a drug addiction and he and his friends had been steal-ing from their own homes in order to raise money to support their drug dependencies.

Still, Danielle and Matthew remained "good" parents. They did not want to subject their son to the trauma of being placed in a drug rehabilitation program, and the idea was embarrassing to them. They attempted to deal with the problem instead by taking Max to a variety of different psychiatrists. With little progress made two years later, they finally agreed to place him in the more intensive program.

Max did not continue his education beyond high school, and his father clearly realized that he would not be able to contribute in any meaningful manner to the operation of the family business. In fact, on the occasions that he did attempt to work for his father, Max's employment became a demoralizing influence on the hard-working and capable executives. Max is presently drifting from one activity to another, living on a monthly allowance from his parents.

Danielle and Matthew are heartbroken and disappointed par-ents. They tried to do everything for this loved and wanted child, but Max never seemed able to realize the potential that he pos-sessed. What went wrong? How did they fail him so badly? How could they have prevented this unfortunate outcome? How could they have such a "bad" kid coming from such a "good" home?

This story, with minor variations, repeats with distressing frequency in the families of the successful and affluent. I have met many heartbroken parents, their hopes and dreams shattered. Sometimes, as if to defend their position somehow, they will tell me about another child, who, from their perspective, was truly neglected while growing up, yet now is a highly accomplished young adult. They cite that the other parents were never physically present or concerned with that child's choices, while they were always there, helping their own child with everything, making sure that he or she had the best. And now they wonder how this could have happened, and what mistakes were made.

Unfortunately, it is seldom the child who is the root cause of the problem. It is the well-intentioned parents who, like Danielle and Matthew, have failed to give their child an important chance, the opportunity to develop competency skills.

The Importance of Developing Competency

Throughout this book, I have been referring to uses of competency as a necessary factor in creating high self-esteem. Competency is a learned ability children acquire when they are permitted to handle a variety of independent tasks, even if they do not succeed in all of them. When too much is done for a child, there is no opportunity to acquire this skill.

The issue of competence first emerges in the crib as the infant begins his independent exploration of the world. There, a baby begins to move his hands and legs, fascinated with his own motions. He reaches for objects and, as soon as contact can be made, he utilizes his senses of touch, sight, and taste to learn about each new stimulus in his life. As mobility increases, the child will expand his horizons, crawling to different objects, attempting crude manual manipulations in his learning process.

At this important developmental point, the structure of the child's world is crucial. These are actually the child's first experiences with feeling competent. As he learns by trial and error how to reach, to grab and grasp, to hold, to let go, and to pick up objects, he experiences a sense of control over his environment. Knowing that he can initiate an event is a powerful feeling. He thinks, "I'll touch that toy," and then he does it, and does it on his own.

Children who feel competent enjoy the thrill of their own accomplishments. They don't' feel dependent upon the all-knowing adults in their lives. They seek the challenges of new and difficult situations with eagerness and enthusiasm. "Let me try it myself!" is their constant refrain. And how proud they feel to be able to do things independently and make choices for themselves, to stand back and realistically see their unique skills and talents in action.

But just as competence can begin in the crib, it can also be stifled there. The degree of adult intervention is very critical in this time of intellectual and emotional development. Children need to be encouraged in their self-exploration with appropriate toys and objects. If these do not abound, children will, in their natural curiosity, reach out for inappropriate objects and their world will become a place of continual parental reproval, intervention, and control. If this becomes the dominant parent-child interaction, even an infant can begin to feel that she is not competent, that she should not initiate an action.

When a child feels that his spontaneous instincts are bad, he can ultimately become extremely passive, always waiting for the omnipotent adult to tell him what to do next. Especially with ever-attending servants, a child will wait for someone else to do everything for him.

While this kind of behavior may seem to the parents to be laziness, in most instances it is not. Children in these circumstances honestly do not trust their own initiative, their own inclinations. They feel dependent upon others to make decisions and take action for them.

Of course, no parent can always provide complete freedom for children—be they infants, toddlers, or older—to explore and experiment. Children are genuinely helpless in many areas and must depend upon adults to provide many essential needs as well as to assure them of a generally safe environment. Toddlers cannot be allowed free reign to learn everything through experience. One would not want an eighteen-month-old, for example, to learn about boiling water by overturning the pot from the stove.

The key, however, is for parents to create a balance, an environment where safety can be maintained, but independence encouraged. Parents must establish this not only in terms of physical exploration, but also in intellectual freedom and cognitive curiosity. That is, the truly competent child must feel it is worthwhile to use his or her own mind to develop ideas and solve problems and that these ideas and solutions are valued.

Affluent children, despite all of their advantages, face a number of potential obstacles to fully developing this feeling of competence. What follows are the four most common obstacles for these privileged children.

Lack of a Competency Bank Account

In an average middle-class family, children have many opportunities to become competent, a majority of which do not occur by parental design but through necessity. With fathers as well as mothers often working full time and little if any hired help, the children are forced to learn to feed and dress themselves, put away toys and otherwise keep their rooms clean, as well as assume responsibility for personal hygiene.

As these children grow, they are often given increasing responsibilities within the family system, such as helping with meal preparation, house cleaning, pet care, grocery shopping, gardening, lawn mowing, the taking out of garbage, baby sitting younger siblings, and so on. Without extravagant—or, in some cases, *any*—weekly allowances and in need of pocket money, older children will often enhance their sense of competency by obtaining paying jobs, such as baby-sitting, bagging groceries in the local market, or washing cars. These activities provide real life experiences in self-reliance and the opportunity to demonstrate responsibility as the children mature toward total independence.

Jobs of necessity can never be underestimated as a powerful means of developing competency. Many highly successful individuals began working at a young age with the proverbial newspaper routes, after-school retail-clerk jobs, or weekend car-washing and lawn-mowing enterprises. While usually the result of financial necessity, these jobs pay considerably more than the monetary rewards in the long run. The working child develops greater self-assurance by assuming responsibility and then accomplishing the task without the help of parents or substitute caregivers.

As a result, many children from lower and middle income families develop confidence that they can assume responsibility for themselves, their family, and the community without the ever-present assistance of a parent. Their decisions and judgments are given consideration and respect. With each new work experience, they use the opportunity of personal achievement to add to their personal "competency account." And it is this internal account from which they will then draw when presented with life's more arduous challenges in adulthood.

By contrast, most affluent children have little opportunity to make deposits into this "competency account." Household chores and other potential opportunities to develop competency through the initiation and completion of tasks are handled by others. Even the most basic tasks, such as cleaning their own rooms, are done for them. This kind of "help" deprives a child of the chance to do for himself and, perhaps more important, to feel he can accomplish what he sets out to.

It is not uncommon for toddlers in wealthy homes to be fed, bathed, groomed and dressed by parents or caregivers long after the child has reached an age when she would be quite capable of adequately performing these tasks for herself. Some of these children may not even select what they will wear each day, or in which play activities they will engage until they are long past the age when they are capable of making these routine choices. In such cases, these children miss out on the opportunity to develop the competency that comes with exercising self-determination.

When affluent children begin school, their parents may use money not only to provide the best education, but to ensure success, to hire tutors to help with homework. In and of itself, this concern is well-intentioned. It is a way for affluent parents to express their support for their children. But this positive message may not be the one the child receives. Instead, the child may interpret this kind of help as an indication that, if left alone, he would not be able to succeed. He can only function intellectually if there is an adult assisting.

Take, for example, a common pattern I have seen in school work. Justin writes up his current event for social studies class. His mother reads it. Although Justin's work was adequate, Mom sees a few awkward sentences, a redundancy or two, missing punctuation, and a clearer manner of expressing Justin's ideas, so she rewrites the paper, then hands it back. Justin turns in the revised paper and gets an "A." Unfortunately, this is his mother's grade, not his, and Justin knows it.

While helping your child with his homework is not always destructive, doing it *for him* in order to ensure success does not build confidence. Although you may feel you are creating a safety net for your children, the net can ultimately become a web of self-doubt.

Look, But Don't Touch

The beautiful homes in which affluent children are so privileged to live are often, ironically, an obstacle to the development of competency. In such elegantly decorated homes, there are often entire rooms off limits to the children or, worse, without specific limits but many "No! Don't touch that!" restrictions. I have even seen new homes in affluent neighborhoods in which the child's room looks like a page right out of *In Style*—aesthetically magnificent but completely nonfunctional from a child's point of view.

These surroundings cannot co-exist well with the creative crafts and play space children need. Activities such as painting, gluing, finger painting, chalk drawing, and many other learning experiences are not only fun but provide an opportunity for the child to learn. Sitting quietly in a neat, orderly room and looking attractive does not, to a child, feel like much of an accomplishment.

Children begin to develop competency and independence by exploring, manipulating, and playing within their environment. Inquisitive children, of course, do not understand the value of antique furniture or fragile sculpture, but they will come to understand, after enough scolding or punishment, that they should curb their natural curiosity. Being told, "Don't touch that," or, "If you break that dish . . ." or, "Don't make a mess," in so many situations undermines their cognitive development and their ability to feel in control and responsible. The result in these cases is a passive and dependent child, waiting to take direction from others since her efforts at personal initiative are so often criticized or restricted.

Parents Who Protect

Many wealthy parents lead lives that place them in strong supervisorial roles. Whether in their professional careers or in their involvement with volunteer activities in which they take charge of a major project, these individuals are accustomed to making rapid decisions about significant matters and directing the work of others.

Eliminating, or significantly diminishing, this "take charge" orientation when parenting is not always easy. But parents who assume the responsibility for making all the important decisions without input from their children are actively encouraging dependency rather than helping them develop competency. In my work as a school psychologist in Beverly Hills, I have met many such parents.

Tobey and Jana were both corporate lawyers, personally very charming and caring human beings—but very controlling. I first encountered them because their son, Jordan, a heretofore well-behaved boy, began to exhibit disruptive behavior in his class.

"It's his friend, Ryan," Tobey said. "He has a bad influence on Jordan."

"When they get together they lose control," added Jana.

"We want Jordan moved to another class."

I explained to them that I wasn't sure a transfer was the best solution to the problem, as it was important for Jordan to develop the ability to behave himself whether or not his best friend was in the classroom. The world will always be full of "Ryans" and Jordan needed to learn to decrease his dependency on children who might exert a negative influence on him.

"But why let him continue to get in trouble." Jana asked, "If *we* can solve the problem ourselves so easily?"

"We don't want him to think he's a bad kid just because of these isolated situations!" Tobey added.

Although I could fully understand their concerns, I continued by explaining that children cannot always feel that someone else knows what is best for them and will solve their problems. Jordan might then start to depend solely upon their decisions and not believe he is capable of his own initiative.

In this specific situation, we reached a compromise: Jordan would be involved in solving this problem and a class transfer would only be considered if he was unsuccessful in correcting his actions. This way, choices and responsibility were Jordan's. If he could develop a plan to control his behavior around his best friend so that they could remain in the same class, then he could stay. As it turned out, he did, and in this way increased his sense of personal control and of responsibility for his own behavior.

Facing Failure

High-achieving, success-oriented parents often have great difficulty allowing their child to founder, or to experience failure in any way. In some cases, they experience the failure of their child as a personal stigma, a mark against them as if they somehow had failed. Other parents quickly and clearly see how to avoid failure, and so they automatically take over in order to spare their child any pain or disappointment. Still other parents have simply forgotten their own past failures now that they have finally arrived. They may not remember the important lessons they learned themselves from failure, or do not wish to relive their pain. Whatever the motivation, the end result is that such parents are rescuers, artificially maintaining their children on the ship of success.

However, children learn valuable coping skills when they are forced to deal with failures. They learn the importance of making careful, well-thought-out choices. They gain an understanding of the consequences of their choices, as well as how to learn from poor choices in order to start over again and create a new success from an old failure. It is easier for a child to learn these lessons early in life if he is permitted to practice with small failures. But if a parent is always rushing in to intercede and assist the child—to spare him from disappointments—how will this same child become prepared to cope intelligently when faced with the more challenging problems of life?

There is a vast body of literature by successful people who cite an early failure as a turning point in their lives. These individuals believe that the disappointments they were forced to handle at a younger age were directly related to their ability to succeed later in life. Lee Iacocca, for example, tells in his autobiography about his father preparing him for a life of success by teaching him that in the world in general, and the business world in particular, problems and failures are inevitable and that progress is a road that goes up and down. Those who succeed are not discouraged when they experience failure or setback, but are capable of learning how to create great success from them.

You are reading this book because you are conscientiously striving to be good parents, and, therefore you undoubtedly believe "What good parents would let their child suffer when they could do something about it?" The problem is that the most effective kind of parents are not *good* parents, they are *responsible* parents.

Good Versus Responsible Parenting

Most affluent parents have the best of intentions in their child-rearing decisions, but not all achieve their positive goals. One of the key factors lies in understanding the difference between being a good parent and a responsible one. The major differences can be summarized as follows:

Good Parents	Responsible Parents
Protects child	Encourages independent activity
Helps child with tasks that fall well within the child's ability level	Permits child to be responsible for every task the child can physically handle
Solves child's social and school problems by contacting the appropriate adult in charge	Encourages child to handle and solve his or her own problems whenever possible
Provides daily reminders for child's responsibilities ("Don't forget your books . . . jacket . . . homework . . . lunch . . .")	Recognizes that the consequences that occur from a child's forgetfulness will motivate greater personal responsibility in the future
Tells child exactly how to handle situations	Asks child for his or her opinion as to the most appropriate course of action
Feels that an adult's superior knowledge can save a child from frustration and failure	Lets child make his or her choices, recognizing that the consequences of a poor choice create a powerful learning experience
Feels guilty not giving in to child's demands; lets child take advantage of this	Can deny inappropriate requests; knows that child must learn respect for the needs of others
Tries to manipulate child through guilt ("Look at everything I've done for you!")	Guides child by helping him or her develop own self-regulatory behavior
Worries that others will pass judgment on them based on the behavior of their child; takes great pains to make sure child is conforming appropriately	Recognizes that each individual must be judged on his or her own merits

At the center of those differences is whether parents encourage their children to assume personal control, or whether they somehow encourage them to become physically, psychologically, and emotionally dependent upon others. Many affluent parents believe they can guide, direct or assist their children until some magical time when they suddenly become mature and responsible. In reality, the ability to become responsible for one's life must be learned through experiences occurring over a long period of time.

Whenever I hear parents exclaim, "When is Kelly ever going to grow up? She's sixteen years old and I think it's about time!" I immediately suspect that I am in the presence of a "good" parent— a parent who, without meaning to, has taken away many of Kelly's opportunities to grow up and now expects the transformational equivalent of divine intervention.

Part of the problem occurs because these affluent parents often forget all the experimentation and stumbling, the trial and error they were permitted to experience. The extent to which they were given the chance to fail and try again contributed to the rapidity with which they matured. David Elkind, noted this phenomenon in his essay, "Superkids and Super Problems":

> Many of today's parents have carved out their own successful careers and feel very much in charge of their lives. They see no reason why they should not take charge of child rearing in the same manner and with the same success. A successful child is the ultimate proof of their success. The result is that many parents are far too intrusive and over involved. By deciding what and when children should learn, they rob these children of the opportunity to take responsibility for their mistakes and credit for their achievements. Such practices run the risk of producing children who are dependent and lacking in self esteem. Today's parents want super kids, but what they are often getting are super problems.

You do not, however, have to create super problems. By becoming responsible parents, by recognizing the importance of providing frequent and continual opportunities for your children to operate in a self-sufficient manner, you can help them develop into capable, responsible, and accomplished young adults.

Making the Shift to Responsible Parenting

Responsibility and competency are long-term developmental processes, not overnight transformations. Making the shift from being a good to a responsible parent, however, can happen quickly. But this change requires first and foremost an awareness of the areas in which parents must relinquish control. There are four key areas upon which to focus with regard to enhancing your child's competency: self-help skills, social skills, school responsibilities, and problem solving.

Self-Help Skills at Every Age

Dependency can be a frightening experience for anyone. Think of how you feel when your car breaks down or your basement floods and suddenly you are helpless without a mechanic or a plumber. That's what it often feels like to be a child. Although Mother and Father may offer their help and additional hired help may be plentiful, every child still has the same innate desire as an adult to be able to take care of his own basic needs.

Responsible parenting recognizes this principle. As soon as your child has the appropriate manual dexterity, he should be encouraged to take an increasing initiative in personal tasks, from feeding himself to putting on his own clothes to brushing his own teeth and eventually to taking complete care of his personal hygiene.

Older children should be encouraged to assume greater personal responsibility. I have known several instances of teenagers who could not operate a washing machine or even make a hot meal for themselves. No matter how wealthy you are your child will benefit from knowing his or her way around your kitchen and being capable of preparing a meal for himself, rather than always relying on the culinary skills of the hired help.

Encouraging independence around issues of self-help can be difficult and frustrating to parents. Obviously, you waste less time and encounter less aggravation when you tie your five-year-old's shoes rather than allow him to fumble around and perhaps tie them incorrectly. In many situations, however, if you simply allow extra time, you can prevent your child's attempts at self-sufficiency from turning into a conflict with you. Although it may require extra effort, making your child's independence around the house a priority will prove a valuable investment.

Social Skills

In order for children to develop a feeling of confidence in relating to people outside the family, they need to be given controlled opportunities to assert themselves with others, even at an early age. For example, parents should allow children the freedom to choose their own friends—or at least to believe that they are doing so.

Obviously, until a child is four or five, mothers and fathers frequently find the playmates through the children of their own friends or neighbors. But it is one thing to tell a child, "Here is your new friend," and another to introduce the two children and allow *them* to decide if and when they will become friends. This simple choice gives the child a profound message about his or her own capacity to form relationships with others.

Another important aspect of social competency for children is learning how to participate successfully in group activities. Wealthy children often have limited experiences in this area. If you drive down the street on a warm, sunny day in an average middle-class neighborhood, you will see various groups of children informally playing together in the road or in front of the house. However, if you were to drive down a street in an exclusive neighborhood on that same day, you might not see a single child! Affluent children too often remain well-protected inside their homes or in walled back-yards. They may be with one special friend under the supervision of a parent or housekeeper, or engaged in a solitary video game. What they are not exposed to are the unstructured, group play experiences.

Unfortunately, security issues intensify the over-protective, natural instincts of "good" parents. For this reason, many privileged children are markedly deficient in what might be called "street smarts." Parents can somewhat remedy this by encouraging their children to participate in city-wide athletic leagues, youth social-service organizations, scouting programs, or a summer-camp program.

Children also need to be allowed to experience social conflicts without being immediately rescued. Upon seeing a visiting friend not getting along with their own child, overprotective parents will immediately intervene to solve the difficulty. They may attempt to bribe the children into behaving by, for example, inviting them to watch the latest popular DVD, going out to a favorite restaurant or even to an amusement park. In other cases, the parents will make a decision to terminate the visit rather than allowing the two children a chance to workout their differences.

Immediate intervention communicates to your child that only adults know what is best and will always be waiting in the wings to solve social conflicts. The child is thus denied the opportunity to acquire leadership, independent judgment, and negotiating skills. It will be no surprise to find this child becoming the compliant follower in his social group, easily influenced by more aggressive peers to participate in questionable activities even though the child himself may know it is not the right thing to do.

If you want your children to experience self-determination—to be leaders and not followers—the process of teaching independence should begin early and be reinforced continuously. Your child will not pay attention to or respect the voice within him unless you do.

School and School-Work Skills

School is one of the important initial challenges our children face. Confronted on a daily basis with social decisions and academic pressure to perform, the child with a strong sense of personal competency rises to these situations and with each success is stimulated toward additional successes. The highly dependent child, on the other hand, lacks the confidence that he can succeed independently. Conditioned to rely on parents and others, he will experience tremendous stress over the daily demands of school and homework. I have worked with several children who have told me candidly that they really don't have to listen attentively or complete class assignments because their tutors will come after school and "help" them.

Making sure your child does not become this type of overly dependent child means encouraging him not only to do his best, but also to do it independently. Do not do homework for your child! You have already completed these classes many years ago and it is not necessary for you to repeat the third or sixth or ninth grade now.

When you become overly involved in the homework process, you are communicating to your child your belief in his inadequacy. If this persists, your child will come to believe I can't do anything unless Mom or Dad or my tutor is there to help.

Too many accomplished parents become quickly involved in helping with homework as soon as they hear their child express a feeling of being overwhelmed. But children are continually faced with seemingly enormous challenges that can create fears about their ability to succeed in the future. I have had children in my office express such exaggerated fears as: "How will I ever know all the words there are?"; "I'll never be as smart as a grown-up!", "There are so many books to read; I'll never read them all."

However, when a parent's response to a child who is feeling overwhelmed is to "rescue" that child from the challenge in front of him, he may provide temporary relief, but the ultimate consequence is reinforcement of the child's self-doubt: the feeling that I can never do it on my own. Children in these situations need to be reassured that even adults don't know all the words or read all the books there are in the world.

Parents can help by teaching children good study habits such as keeping a daily assignment sheet, allocating a specific time for school work on a daily basis, keeping all materials and supplies in an organized manner, taking notes in the classroom, as well as supplying their home with a variety of supplemental learning materials (books, records, educational DVD's, computer learning games, and so on).

If your child asks you to decide what topic he should choose for a report, ask your child to name his favorite three subjects, and then encourage him to make his own selections for the options he established himself.

Learning is a challenging task. A child has to be able to tolerate a certain period of discomfort when new material is presented and he or she has not yet mastered the content. If the child is encouraged to believe that he will be able to succeed, this belief will create the motivation to stick with the task with determined concentration. The reward for this approach—the mastery of the task and the successful completion of the assignment—increases self-confidence and the sense of competency for the next challenge.

This philosophy equally pertains to the use of private tutors. Since many affluent children attend highly competitive schools with extremely demanding curricula, parents should pay careful attention to how a tutor works with their child. If a tutor does not follow responsible tutoring techniques which involve teaching their charges <u>how</u> to learn independently, he can undermine your child's independence and initiative. A tutor who supplies all the homework answers *for* your child simply for the sake of getting a good grade will create and reinforce a feeling of inadequacy. If the tutor does the work for your child, the child may boast to his friends about the easy ride he's getting, but inside he'll question his personal competency.

Ideally, a tutor teaches the child how to learn independently, largely by asking questions that encourage thinking. For example, when a child exclaims, "I don't understand any of these math problems!", the skillful tutor will not immediately launch into a detailed instruction of how to complete each problem.

A more helpful approach would be to ask the child to explain everything he *does* know about the problem, then follow-up with leading questions to help the child participate in the learning process. By articulating his current knowledge and answering questions, the child will begin to gain confidence in his own ability, which can ultimately lead to mastery of the assignment. This feeling also helps the child internalize a personal responsibility for the learning process and a sense of competency about meeting the challenge of the next assignment.

A responsible tutor should never do the homework. Instead, he or she should teach the child how to take an overwhelming challenge and break it down into its component steps, which will lead the child to independent effort and self-management.

Problem-Solving Skills

When a child presents a personal problem to which you, as parents, can clearly see the solution, how easy it is to supply the answer quickly. But easy solutions are seldom instructive. The only way to build competency skills in personal problem-solving is to let your child do it alone. There are, of course, many times when your child will ask for assistance, and you will want to offer some kind of guidance. But being supportive and helping your child actually solve the problem are two different things. The following series of steps can serve as a means to being responsible parents when guiding your child toward problem solving.

Step I. Clarify the specific nature of the problem by listening calmly and carefully to what your child is saying. Refrain from interjecting your comments or reactions while the child is talking. Encourage your child to share as much as possible by responding to the feelings he might be expressing. Summarize your understanding of the situation. Example: Mother to fifteen-year-old son: "I understand that you are very unhappy about being assigned to Mrs. Davis's classroom because you have heard that she gives too much homework and is a tough grader."

Step II. Ask your child for his suggestions for handling this situation. Do not supply your immediate opinion or express your own experience. Let your child do the talking first! Encourage your child to think of as many solutions as he can. Example: "How would you like to handle this problem?"

Step III. When your child offers solutions, explore what would be the probable outcome of each idea. Examples: If your child replies that he will just sit in the back of Mrs. Davis's room and not participate, encourage him to think about what the outcome of that action would be. "What do you think would happen if you did that?" Avoid interjecting a sarcastic or critical comment ("That would really be a stupid solution," "Your teacher would really have it in for you then").

Step IV. Encourage your child to pick a positive course of action. Example: If your child selects as the best solution sitting in the front and taking careful notes, compliment him on a wise selection.

Step V. After your child has selected an option, set up a time to follow up to see how well the solution is working. Example: "Why don't you try it for two weeks and then we'll talk about how you are feeling about the class?"

Although it is usually difficult at first to follow these problem-solving steps, parents must exercise control not to jump right in to give their advice and direction. During this entire procedure, your emphasis should be on helping the child to discover his own solutions so that when he or she is confronted with new problems, the child will have developed confidence and competency to handle a situation independently.

You might be wondering what a parent should do if the solutions offered by the child are not appropriate to the situation and the child does not realize it. The issue here is to be very careful how you criticize. Telling your child her idea is stupid or even not a good idea will not promote competence in decision-making and problem-solving. If the child does not see the inherent problem in her own reasoning, it probably isn't because she doesn't want to; she just has to develop further her reasoning ability. You can point out the faulty reasoning without being critical by posing it instead in the form of a question.

Using the example of the child in Mrs. Davis's class, assume he responds that the best solution is to sit in the back of her class and not participate. The parent then could ask, "Do you think that if you did that Mrs. Davis would want to give you a passing grade?" By forming a question rather than making a strong declaration, you are continually encouraging the child to become an active participant in the decision-making process.

This technique is not limited to use with older children. If a child can talk, he can be encouraged to use reason to solve problems.

I once presented a lecture on problem-solving to a group of parents whose children were in the next room engaged in a storytelling session. One mother in the audience raised her hand at my suggestion of using questions to encourage problem-solving in children.

"When can you start this? She asked. "At what age?"

When I told her that it can begin quite early, the mother gave me a quizzical look, and then shook her head. "My daughter's four years old. How would she have any idea how to solve her own problems?"

"What kind of problem is she having?" I asked.

"At day care, an aggressive boy keeps hitting Melissa when she is playing in the yard. I really don't expect my four-year-old to understand his aggression or know what to do about it."

At this point the children were finished with their activity and came into the room to join their parents. I asked Melissa if she would like to be my helper in solving a problem and she willingly came up in front of the class.

I began by telling her that I had been told she was having some difficulty with another student at her day care and asked her would she like to tell me about it.

After some initial shyness, the child warmed up to me and began talking about Evan: "He keeps following me around . . . while I'm in the school yard and I want to play with Sarah and Brook; he hits me . . . he pushes me, too."

I restated her problem to be sure that I understood exactly. Then I proceeded to Step II by asking her what she would like to do about this. She shrugged a couple of times. I smiled back, making sure I did not communicate impatience with her thinking process.

No matter how long it took her to think up a potential solution, I would wait; her thoughts deserved as much time as they needed.

When she finally spoke, she offered: "I could hit him back." But even before I could pursue this, she herself thought of the consequences of that action: "But then he would just hit me again."

I complimented her on her wisdom, then gently asked if she had any other ideas. Responding to my comment on her wisdom, Melissa suddenly seemed flushed with confidence. Then she quickly began to offer some more possibilities. "I could run away but he can run as fast as I can. I could not play in the yard when he's there." The wheels in her mind were definitely turning now; her eyes were bright, her voice animated. I glanced at her mother who was smiling with astonishment. Melissa continued: "I could tell the teacher about it, or I could use my words to try to get him to stop." Five options from a child whose mother was sure she could not possibly handle such a problem.

At Step V, Melissa decided that her best solution was to tell Evan that she wanted him to leave her alone. "How will you say that?" I queried? After a brief pause, she aggressively shouted out, "Evan leave me alone!" I felt quite confident that this action alone would handle Evan the bully, but to reinforce her ability to recognize other options I replied, "That sounds like an excellent plan. If that doesn't work what else could you do?" She immediately suggested that she tell her teacher.

Moving to Step V, I asked when she might try this. Without hesitation, she decided: "tomorrow morning."

The following week, her mother called me to report that Melissa had indeed been successful in dealing with her problem. This young child had just experienced a powerful exercise in establishing her competency and her mother learned an equally valuable lesson. Never underestimate the ability of a child to begin developing competency skills.

In fact, before you begin to assist your child of any age in any task, pause for a moment to ask yourself: Could my child handle even a part of this task independently? If the answer is yes, let the child do whatever he can! The reward for giving your child these kinds of learning experiences will be the development of a self-confident attitude and the eventual realization of the child's fullest potential.

Better Late Than Never

I conducted a conference with the parents of a twenty-one-year-old young man who was failing for the second time at college. The concern of these parents went beyond the immediate failure to their son's seemingly irresponsible character.

In exploring the family system, I discovered that both parents had always been extremely involved in every aspect of their son's life. "We've always had a very close family," was their appropriate rationale. They did, however, reveal additional information that ultimately pointed to the basis for their problem.

Keri, the mother, recalled how she and her husband had carefully researched and selected all of Michael's extracurricular activities. She said that if he objected to any of them, he was told that, in order to "build his character," he should remain with the activity until he'd achieved an acceptable level of proficiency (which was decided by his parents). Michael's mother and father also admitted to being critical about Michael's choices of friends.

With regard to their son's education, they indicated that they had made sure to get him into the most prestigious private school, and then made a commitment to do whatever was necessary to enable him not to fail for his sake—and for their own pride. They had hired numerous tutors who did his work for him and they justified it with the rationale that everyone else did it.

When Michael did fail a class exam, they made excuses for him, blaming teachers and school administrators, never allowing Michael the painful and valuable experience of directly facing his failure. When, on one occasion, Michael was picked up by the police with a very small amount of marijuana, his parents interceded with attorneys to ensure that Michael would not have any blemishes on his record.

Now that their son had just passed his twenty-second birthday, they were stuck with the realization that they had on their hands a poorly motivated, dependent young adult with no clear goals and direction. They began to panic but were, at first, unwilling to utilize the most potentially useful option they had: giving Michael the opportunity to function independently from the family.

When this was indeed suggested to them, the mother immediately voiced concern that Michael would continue to make "unacceptable" choices (his choices would embarrass her). She questioned how she could be a "good" parent if she compromised her values. But finally, she and her husband did recognize that they needed to permit their son to begin assuming his own responsibilities.

They decided to let Michael leave school, terminated all financial support, and permitted him to experience whatever failures he might encounter. It was clearly difficult for them to accept the fact that Michael would be *forced* to handle any problems, even if he wouldn't succeed at first.

He set out to get a job without his parents' help. His parents did not buy him a new suit or instruct him how to dress for interviews. They let Michael figure it out for himself.

Michael did not find a job right away, and when he did find one, as a courier for a real-estate company, he didn't keep it very long before being fired for tardiness, careless mistakes, and general lack of effort. But this time his mother and father did not rescue him from his failure.

Eventually, Michael found another position, this time as a retail sales clerk, and didn't make the same mistakes. He remained long enough to earn a raise and a bonus for his hard work and only left the job because he decided, with real interest this time, to return to college. He did not become an exceptional student—his grades were average—but he did graduate and, perhaps more importantly, learned some invaluable skills by being permitted to develop personal competency. He is currently employed and financially independent from his family.

The Time to Start Is Now

Affluent parents are often well-versed in many contemporary theories of child rearing. They may hover anxiously over their children; demonstrating concern if one deviates in any manner from the latest developmental theory. They actively guide, direct, and assist in all areas of activity in order to make sure their children follow the right track.

At this point, you now realize these characteristics to be that of a good rather than a responsible parent. You may even be feeling distressed if you identified with the former. I certainly do not want you to feel that you have failed by having been too good and not sufficiently responsible in dealing with your children. Remember, there is no such thing as a perfect parent. Failure in this area is not cause for shame or distress. It is, and should always be viewed as, merely a detour in the road, a sign that it is time to try, with an ever-open mind, another direction.

As newly responsible parents, you now need to begin to recognize where you may have erred, and where your efforts have achieved disappointing results. Then, use that information to become more successful parents. It is truly never too late.

SIX

Step Five: Learning How to Listen to Children

The youngsters were eager and enthusiastic throughout the Saturday rap session I was conducting. They seemed genuinely interested in discussing ways by which they could improve their relationship with their parents and other family members. These children represented students from a variety of schools in the affluent suburbs of the Los Angeles area, and had been picked to participate in this meeting because of the leadership and scholastic skills they had demonstrated throughout the year. I could hot help noticing what a physically attractive group this was. Each child appeared fit and healthy, well groomed and stylishly dressed.

Throughout the early part of the morning, our discussion had tended to be breezy and somewhat superficial. However, the conversation became notably more intense when the topic of communication was raised. "How comfortable do you feel discussing personal issues and concerns with your parents?" was the question I posed to open this segment of our talk.

"I would like to be able to talk with them," one youngster stated somewhat wistfully, "but they just don't understand and always end up getting mad."

"If I have a problem," another volunteered, "I feel bad enough already. I don't want to add to that having my parents getting all upset and emotional. I just go to my friends."

The honesty of the first two comments seemed to encourage the rest of the group to share their feelings. Here are some of their comments:

"I can't talk to my mom because she always overreacts and wants to get involved when it would embarrass me. I can talk better to my Dad, but they are always together so, in the end, we don't communicate."

"They just want to tell me their opinions and they never listen to what I have to say."

"My folks travel so much I have to make an appointment to talk to them."

"My Dad can't talk; he just shouts orders like I hear him do on the phone all the time. I'm just like an employee."

"When my parents are finished with their *lecture*, they refuse to listen to my point of view. They just say, 'We don't want to waste any more time on that issue.'"

"My folks come home and expect me to drop whatever I am doing because they want to talk."

"The minute I start to discuss something, my Dad starts to look at his watch, like he wants me to hurry up and finish what I have to say so he can do something more interesting."

"I've heard the stories about what a hard time they had growing up until I'm sick of it. Then is then, but now is now."

"If I try to disagree with my parents, they are always telling me how lucky I am to have all the advantages I do. But that has nothing to do with how I feel about something."

"If I have a problem, it always seems to be my fault and I end up being called lazy, stupid, idiot or some other things."

"My mom flies off the handle at the slightest problem. With Dad, you have to know what is happening at the company. If it's bad there, he's bad at home."

And so it went, each child adding his comments. What was of concern to me, as a mental-health professional was that the majority of these young people truly appeared open, honest, and quite verbal about their discontent. On one hand, it was clear they had important issues to discuss with their parents, and eagerly sought their guidance and direction. On the other hand however, their comments also clearly indicated that they were seldom able to communicate successfully with their parents, and this caused them great pain. When one young man shared that he did feel uncomfortable talking to either his father or his mother, the others gaped in awe, letting him know how lucky he was.

Unfortunately, my clinical and personal experience with these types of young people indicates that poor communication is a pervasive problem in the majority of these families. In addition to comments like those above that I continually hear from children, many parents in my seminars also express concern about the quality of their own communication with their children. Perhaps you can identify with some of the statements I hear from these parents.

"My kids don't pay attention to anything I say. Whatever I tell them seems to go in one ear and out the other."

"My daughter argues with me any time I make a suggestion. I don't know why she doesn't appreciate my help."

"Whenever I want to talk to my son, he is always busy with his own activity. He doesn't seem to make time for me."

"I find out more from my kids' friends than I do from them. I'm always the last person to hear about something new in their lives."

"It's amazing. I can sit down to dinner with my children, and by the time we are finished, everyone has argued with somebody at the table and nothing seems to be easily said."

With both sides, children and parents, feeling so negative about communication, it is not surprising that many of the family problems I hear about go unresolved for great periods of time, even though they could be resolved quite easily.

Needless to say, parents and children must be able to communicate. Good communication is the glue that unifies the healthy family system. It is the process by which strong and lasting bonds between family members develop. It leads to effective problem-solving, and the sharing of emotions both when times are joyful and when they are sad.

In a healthy family system, the communication channels between each and every member are always open. The parents do not drown their children in endless sermons and reprimands, but are able to listen and talk to them about any subject of concern. Each individual has the opportunity to express ideas and feelings to anyone without fear of sarcasm, ridicule, or punishment.

Good family communication teaches a valuable lesson to children, especially those who are the least verbal: everyone, regardless of age and articulateness, has something to contribute. This environment enhances the self-esteem of everyone in the family and allows all members to achieve competency in self-expression. Parents who raise children in this environment prepare them well for later life.

In an unhealthy family system, however, the channels of communication are often blocked or even nonfunctional. In the most destructive situations, there is no communication and the family members are virtually isolated from one another, or parental communication is used almost exclusively as a means of negative expression, leaving the children feeling worthless or enraged.

The purpose of these next two chapters is to increase your awareness of your communication habits and to explore specific techniques for developing a more effective approach. In this chapter, we will look at the receiving side, the listening process of communication. In the next chapter, I will address the giving of information, the manner in which parents talk to their children. While these two processes are in reality hardly separable, it is nevertheless useful to look at each component individually.

Listening Takes More Than Ears

Listening serves two very important purposes. The first is to receive information. Getting the facts right is a vital part of successful living, both in business and in your personal life. The second purpose is to let others, especially those you care most about, know that you value what they have to say. When you take the time and effort to really listen, you are saying, in effect, that the individual has special importance to you.

Few would argue that listening is an important part of effective parenting, but many parents assume erroneously that a pair of ears and a good mind guarantees the ability to listen. Affluent people, in particular, often overlook the listening skills they have utilized to become successful in their professional capacities when dealing with personal interactions. They may carefully absorb every detail of a complex financial transaction, apply their legal expertise in the courtroom, or control a board meeting with great acumen, but when it comes time to listen to their children at home, their behavior dramatically changes.

Unfortunately, many affluent parents do not fully acknowledge either of the two critical purposes of effective listening in their family. When they listen to their children, they may interrupt, speculate on answers, disregard data, and steer conversations in preconceived directions—all of which hinder their understanding of what their children are trying to communicate. Even worse, many parents with whom I have worked seem oblivious to the subtle and not-so-subtle emotional messages they convey when they fail to pay attention or listen closely to conversations at home. Rather than making their children feel special, their youngsters too often feel neglected, controlled, and unheard.

Parents are, in a sense, always on stage and our children are always watching. They are especially astute interpreters of both words and body language. They can tell when Mom or Dad is in a bad mood, detecting such clues as tenseness, rigidity of movement, or irritated glances. Parental indifference is quickly revealed by lack of eye contact and lack of forward body movement, or attempts to engage in another activity (for example, reading papers, watching television) while allegedly listening to the child. We express ourselves in powerful ways even when no words are spoken. The way we look at one another, the manner in which we hold our bodies, our gestures—all convey messages about what we are thinking.

Children are not content only to be seen but need to be heard. Their ideas and opinions need to be acknowledged and appreciated if you, as parents, truly want to enhance their self-esteem and sense of competency.

Effective listening does not just happen. It requires time, energy, interest, respect, and the ability to relinquish control. In each of these areas, you as parents must take the leadership role. Your attitudes in approaching these issues can be positive or negative. But without a conscious decision on your part to improve communication in your family, your children will not develop an equally healthy attitude.

Do You Make Time to Listen?

Those parents who lead lives of glamour, excitement, and challenge may not only feel mentally tugged away from their children, but are often physically pulled away from the home for extended periods of time as well. Therefore, when they find that they do have a moment of free time, they immediately expect to have their child's full attention.

The trouble with this approach, however, is that parents cannot expect communication with their children *on demand*. When you allocate only a few minutes in a hectic schedule for listening, the results can be very frustrating and disappointing. While you may complain that your children never tell you anything, my experience generally proves that it is more often the parents who are not available when the children have something of importance to say, rather than the other way around.

Children need to be heard while their excitement or turmoil is still fresh. They need to feel genuine interest and concern on the part of the listener. Not surprisingly, if your time is limited, your children will sense it through any number of clues you may give off, ranging from an obvious and direct verbal prompting to hurry up ("Get to the point, Amy, I'm already late for my appointment.") to more subtle, non-verbal actions such as fidgeting, glancing at a watch or engaging in another activity while the child is talking.

While children do not always have something critical to say, unless you make time to listen, you will never know!

What is Your Energy Level?

Of course, even if you do find ways to be available to your children when they need to talk, and afford them the time they long for, there is still the question of energy. When you have been operating at a high activity level full of pressure and stress, you will return home with limited listening energy.

I once had a teenager in my office, the son of a well-known sports celebrity, tell me that his father had a habit of sitting down on the living room sofa in the evening, and routinely asking, "So, son, how's life?" The boy would then begin describing his day, only to find his father closing his eyes and snoring before he could get out two sentences.

Effective listening takes work, it cannot be a passive activity performed when you are fatigued or drained. It requires your focus, concentration, and attention. To be an effective listener, parents must not only guard against the intrusion of distracting thoughts but must also maintain a high level of mental energy. If you remain drained from the events of your day, it is crucial that you recharge your positive energy level before interacting with your children.

Are You Really Interested

For many privileged adults, listening is a problem simply because their professional and social lives are so stimulating that by comparison the details of their children's daily lives and feelings can seem dull. For those parents who spend their days involved in multi-million dollar transactions, high-level decision making, or community development projects, it can be difficult to come home and get truly excited about a child's triumph in the class spelling bee. I have had parents in my classes who spend their day in conversations with celebrities, CEOs, and other prominent leaders admit that they simply find it difficult to spend an hour reviewing the social dilemmas of their 15-year-old child.

I once had a well-known pop singer and her husband in a parenting seminar. During the two hours of the workshop she was paged three times. Even when she was in her seat, I could see that it was quite difficult for her to become truly interested in the issues of effective parenting. After I concluded the workshop, she attempted to apologize for her distractions. "You must think I don't pay much attention to my daughter," she said, sheepishly.

"But really that's not true. "It's just that my career is so demanding. I feel like I'm on call all the time. But I try to include her in as many of my activities as possible."

Although I did acknowledge how positive it was to include her daughter in her activities as often as possible, I reminded her that, as exciting as she felt her life might be to her daughter, it was equally important that she make her daughter's life exciting to her. If her daughter was only a silent observer of her mother's frenetic activities, effective communication would not take place.

In order for children to develop positive self-esteem, it is essential that they feel loved and valued by their parents. And one important way this occurs is for children to know that what they have to say is worthy of Mom and Dad's attention. There is no more powerful way of communicating the worth of your child than by demonstrating your best listening behavior.

When parents make the effort to pay attention to their child's most trivial thoughts, feelings, and experiences, they will discover an entire new world. One client, a famous divorce lawyer, who participated in a workshop with me and then went home and applied what he had learned, later told me that he now feels most privileged during the moments his teenage son confides in him. He says that he misses this special intimacy whenever he has to travel on business. Listening became as valuable for him as I know it was for his son.

Do You Respect Your Child?

Effective listening also requires an attitude that can be difficult for many affluent parents: open-mindedness. When you are not willing to listen to your child's ideas, opinions, and feelings, you will not convey the message that you respect what your child has to offer. As a result, your child will not be inspired to speak openly with you.

Consider this simple analogy. How do you feel when you are in a social situation, talking to someone whose eyes are all over the room? Don't you feel personally affronted? Do you terminate the conversation as quickly as possible? Lack of interest in what you are saying is usually interpreted as lack of interest and respect in *you*, and most highly successful people recoil from such situations. Your children will feel the same way if you do not demonstrate interest in them.

Parents need to earn their child's respect just as they do the respect of colleagues and personal friends. While the cliché says that respect is something children should feel and show for their parents, it is truly a collaborative effort. Unless there is a respect from both parties in *any* interaction the relationship will not be emotionally healthy. Your family needs the same type of respect you show colleagues and associates, even when the content of the conversation may not be of absorbing interest to you.

There are two common obstacles affluent parents have to this two-way street of respect. First, because of their knowledge and abilities, many successful parents generalize their expertise to include numerous other domains and thus believe they are experts at everything, including their child's life. Although their conversations appear to include two people, such parents are really involved in monologues with themselves. While this problem can happen between parents and a child of any age, it is particularly a frequent issue of conflict with teenagers who are undergoing an important transformation to independence, and thus need to feel their ideas have value.

Secondly, being so focused on their own issues at work and at home, many affluent parents unknowingly adopt the attitude that the only important things are the things they know, and so they consider the information their children share to be trivial. When this attitude manifests itself in conversations, children will not learn to trust their own instincts to take pride in their own interests.

Children inevitably know less than parents do; they can be quite intimidated by demeaning parental behavior. Children need to feel that they are not just empty containers into which a mother and father pour wisdom. They construct their own knowledge about themselves from what they experience and they can only be validated if someone listens to what they have to say.

Can You Relinquish Control?

You are attending an important conference and the highly esteemed keynote speaker is presenting his ideas and opinions to the hushed assembly. At that particular moment, who is perceived to have the control in the room? The speaker, of course. Why? Because he/she has the microphone, or more specifically the "words".

During the day, many affluent parents may spend considerable time making decisions and instructing others. When they listen in the course of a business meeting, social engagement, or philanthropic event, it is usually to specific answers to their questions, or to information of immediate concern. Their focus inevitably is on what *they* need to know in order to do a job or accomplish a goal. In these circumstances, doing the talking, or at least controlling the agenda of the discussion, becomes equated with mastery and power, while listening implies, in some sense, subservience and a lack of control. Little of this may be conscious, but in meetings it is generally the boss who does most of the talking.

In meeting with your children, this is clearly a poor start for effective conversation. For some parents, sharing "control" may be simple, now that you are aware of the issue. Others of you, however, may need to work hard to make a dramatic transition from your natural orientation in your outside environment to your behavior in the family. While it is said that a man's home is his castle, remember that your children are not just pages in your kingdom.

What Are Your Listening Shortfalls?

Few parents at any socioeconomic level are without weakness in the area of listening. An honest evaluation of the level of one's skills in any area is the beginning of learning to improve them.

The following statements will provide you with the opportunity to take that honest look at yourself. How many of these statements describe you more or less?

1. I am usually involved in thinking about many things at the same time.

2. I don't have time to waste on idle conversation.
3. I often feel that people don't get to the point quickly enough.
4. It is hard for me to pay attention to information about an activity in which I am not directly involved.
5. I generally respond as soon as I think of a contributory idea.
6. If I have to wait for another person to stop talking, I frequently forget my own thoughts.
7. I am capable of listening while I am doing other things (scanning the newspaper, watching television, preparing dinner).
8. There are a limited number of subjects that really interest me.
9. When I get upset or angry during conversations, I don't get over it very quickly.
10. When people tell me about problems or concern, I immediately try to think of solutions.

If you identify with any of these statements, it is important that you recognize that they are indicative of personality traits you will want to correct: impatience, intolerance for the personal interests of others, emotional volatility, self-centeredness, and the need always to be the primary problem solver. All of these attitudes will seriously disrupt effective listening and deserve your prompt attention.

Steps to Creating an Effective Listening Environment

All parents can immediately implement the following six behaviors to create a positive climate for genuine listening. Regardless of the age of your children—in fact, these guidelines work for adults too—you will see a notable improvement in your communication when you add them to your repertoire of interpersonal skills. Practice these regularly and they will soon become a natural and valuable part of your communication habits.

1. *Maintain Physical Contact.* When your child is talking about something important, terminate any other activity. Look directly into his or her eyes, leaning your upper-body slightly forward so that your child does not have to look up to receive your eye contact. A slight body tilt conveys a message that what your child is saying is so important you want to be sure to hear every word.

Do not allow your eyes to wander up, down, or away form your child in any direction. If you are standing, either sit down or lower your body so that you will be at eye level with your child. Feeling a parent towering above is quite intimidating to a child.

2. *Be a Responsive Listener.* Save stoicism for the board room and allow your face to show some animation. Let your child feel that his words have impact and meaning for you by demonstrating a facial response.

React to what is being said in a supportive way. For example, when you agree with something your child says, shake your head in affirmation or express supportive words such as, "I understand," "I know what you mean," "I feel exactly the same way." Ask questions to encourage further elaboration of facts. Maintain eye contact and encourage your child to "tell me more."

From time to time, rephrase the information you are hearing so that you are sure you are listening accurately. Your child will feel very pleased when you demonstrate this special interest, and you will both know that you are on the same wave length.

3. *Be a Patient Listener.* Being a good listener means giving your child the opportunity to develop competency in expressing himself. Both young children and teenagers often require more time to express their thoughts than adults, but they shouldn't be made to feel self-conscious or nervous about it by a parent who completes sentences or reminds them to hurry up and get to the point.

Resist the temptation to interrupt or cut them off. You can't listen and talk at the same time. Finishing your child's sentence sends the message that you already know—or think you know—what he or she will say next. Mind reading does not constitute effective listening.

Being patient may also mean, unfortunately, being willing to hear what you don't want to hear. Although it may be easier to stay away from bad news by jumping to conclusions or cutting your child off, it is in dealing with these more difficult issues that effective parenting rises to the challenge.

4. *Be a Child.* If the subject matter of your child's discussion is not of great interest to you, try to focus in your mind on why this subject is important to your child.

Although the significance of an issue is relative to the individual, the feeling that your concerns are of interest to others is important to *everyone*. There is a reason why your child feels the need to tell you something. Focus on trying to understand why this event has meaning for your child; try to put yourself in his perspective and then imagine the weight of the issue. Visualize yourself at the age of your child and remember what concerns you had. Recall also the frustration or disappointment you may have felt when adults made it clear that they found what you were saying unimportant. Then get in touch with the excitement you felt when adults seemed to take an interest.

By disciplining yourself in this manner, you will find yourself paying much closer attention to what is being said. Furthermore, you will acquire a greater understanding of your child and a sensitivity to his special needs

5. *Be a Complete Listener.* Listening encompasses more than your ears. It involves your eyes and your perceptive abilities. Many researchers have documented the fact that body language is often more revealing than what the individual is saying. For example, the research of Dr. Ray L. Birdwhistel of the University of Pennsylvania has established the fact that 70 percent of the messages we communicate to one another are conveyed by body language, 23 percent by tone or inflection, and only the remaining 7 percent by the words themselves (so much for the omnipotence of a superb vocabulary!).

Always be alert to the communication in your child's body language. There are often incongruences between what a child says and what his or her body language reveals. In such cases, the body rarely lies.

Teenagers, for example, often demonstrate their feelings in body language such as a tensed jaw or angry eyes; although they will say that nothing is wrong. Do not disregard your child's turmoil simply because he or she does not verbally express it. If you think you can read fear, anger, or any other emotions on your child's face or in his body language, pay attention to the signals and use them to open up the verbal channels of communication about the issue.

6. *Don't Be Over Reactive.* Every adult has emotional hot buttons, words or behaviors that when expressed by others infuriate him and make him stop listening. For some of us, it is the use of profanity; for others, any angry, derogatory comment suffices.

Whatever the actual content, you need to find ways to control the initial blast of rage you may feel when your children push your hot buttons. Rather than reacting exclusively to your child's choice of words, you need to listen for the underlying meaning. Your child may be crying out for attention or for guidance and direction, but you will miss this message if your emotionality disrupts your ability to read between the lines. This is not to say that a parent must tolerate the use of profanity or other pejoratives. But if you focus solely on the verbal infraction, you may ignore an important warning.

One example of a very common hot button is a child's exclamation of "I hate you" directed toward the mother or father. Your tendency, of course, might be to retort, "Don't you dare speak to me in that manner!" and perhaps you would add some harsh punishment. In both cases, however, you will neglect addressing the real problem underlying this child's outburst.

When children use the expression *hate*, it is not in the same context as adult usage. This dreaded word usually emerges from a child because the parents have in some way thwarted the child's wishes. If you allow yourself to respond only to the inflammatory word *hate*, you will only make the child feel guilty about a real feeling, and you will miss the opportunity to teach your child a more acceptable way of dealing with anger. In situations like these, parents must not overreact, but learn to explore with their children why they are angry and what might be done to mange it.

Reacting to words rather than to their underlying meaning creates another problem. Your child will quickly discover how to get a response from you, allowing him to use your ire as a manipulative tool. For instance, if you want to discuss your child's poor grades in school and he doesn't want to, he may know that all he has to do is use a few choice words to distract you from the actual problem at hand. If you find yourself in that kind of situation, it is essential to keep control over your instinctive reactions so that you can regain the focus of the original discussion.

Implementing these six modifications in your listening behavior can immediately increase your effectiveness as a parent. It is not necessary that all six be started at the same time. In fact, you might be overwhelmed by constantly thinking of which new behavior you should be applying. But one by one, you should conscientiously practice each step, and very quickly, you won't need to think so hard about what you are doing. These techniques will produce such positive feedback, you will never abandon them. Combined with your new attitudes toward time, energy, interest, respect, and control, you will easily make significant progress in improving communication in your family.

Reflective Listening

When parents tell me that they feel they are frequently the last ones to know what is happening in the lives of their children, I discover that the problem often lies in their inability to establish a close bond of safety and trust between themselves and their offspring.

Beyond the six steps above, perhaps the most valuable and powerful technique to correct this situation is "reflective listening." Reflective listening focuses initially on the feelings of the speaker, not the external events that have occurred. When the speaker believes that his feelings are being recognized and validated regardless of what they are, a very strong interpersonal bond develops. In this way, you as a parent can encourage your child to feel comfortable sharing any information and problem-solving needs with you in a safe, nurturing, caring climate.

The following case will illustrate how reflective listening differs from other common listening behaviors.

Your fourteen-year-old son, Steven, angrily enters the house, slamming the door behind him. "Jones is a witch," he declares, referring to his science teacher. "I've been busy working on the stage crew this week, so how could I finish my project? How was I supposed to know she wanted to send them to the state contest today? She just freaked out and was really yelling at me in class in front of everyone."

A *director* type of parent might state, "What you should do is take the material, finish it up at home tonight and hand it in the morning."

An *arm-chair psychologist* parent might suggest, "Your problem is that you don't budget your time well. You try to be all things to all people and you end up getting pulled in too many directions, so you lose your focus."

A *smoother* parent might say, "Don't worry, Steven, your teacher was probably irritated because it was the end of a long day. You just relax and take it easy."

A *worrywart* parent might blurt out, "I sure hope this won't affect your class grade. You know this could affect your GPA for college."

A *know-it-all* parent would tell you how he handled a similar situation: "What I would do is talk to my teacher and see if there was another way I could get my project into the competition."

In each of these examples, although the parent might feel he was responding to the plight of his child in a helpful manner, it is unlikely that Steven will feel much better following any of these comments. None of these responses truly indicated that the listener was sensitive to how Steven might be feeling. In each case, the attention was focused on the external facts of the situation and what to do about it.

However, in order to connect with the speaker and encourage him to talk freely and openly, the listener must get beneath the obvious, external facts. The effective listener therefore needs to have the ability to hear the emotions being expressed, and then to reflect them back verbally to the speaker.

Think for a moment about how you respond when someone is sensitive enough to sense what your innermost feelings might be. Don't you feel very positive and drawn to such a person? Isn't it in the same way you are experiencing it?

The parent who listens reflectively therefore begins with an acknowledgement of the child's feelings. Whether expressed in words or actions, the idea is for you to go beyond the facts to determine the child's emotional state as best you can.

In the case of Steven, what were his feelings? Worry, anger, frustration, embarrassment? Any one is a possibility. Given the facts that the castigation occurred in front of a group of fellow students, embarrassment is probably a strong contender.

Thus a reflective response such as "It sounds like that was an embarrassing situation for you" will immediately make your son feel understood and he probably will want to carry on additional discussion about what he might do. Even if his feeling was not embarrassment, but rather, anger, as long as your response indicates you were trying to understand feelings in a supportive and tentative manner (for example, "it sounds like" or "it seems as if" instead of a strong declarative "I'm sure you were embarrassed!"), Steven will make the appropriate correction himself. "Well, I wasn't exactly embarrassed but I sure was angry." Feelings are the essence of our being. Therefore, when someone can connect at the deeper level of feelings, an unbreakable bond is forged. If your child feels you are trustworthy with feelings, then everything else is safe to confide.

The advantage of reflective listening is that by acknowledging feelings, you will encourage your children to share additional information so that if problem-solving is necessary, all the facts will be on the table. Even if a solution is not possible, your child's problems will seem less traumatic when they can be shared with someone who truly cares. When you attempt to reflect upon your child's feelings, you are making your child feel that someone really understands, or is at least trying to understand. This then stimulates the additional dialogue that may be necessary to develop appropriate solutions to problems.

Becoming a reflective listener is not easy for parents. It requires the ability and desire to step out of your own sensibilities and assume your child's point of view, without immediately giving advice or devising solutions. Many affluent parents are conditioned to dealing with their child's adversity with action: directing, advising, criticizing, or demanding. They are skilled in being precise and directive, then defending their point of view with their rhetorical abilities. But these are the types of responses that estrange parent and child.

The beauty of reflective listening is that there is no right or wrong—only the sense that you care enough to understand. When a parent acknowledges his child's feelings, this youngster will experience powerful understanding and support.

I can still recall the day that the effectiveness of this type of listening was initially etched in my own mind. While working at a junior high school, I encountered a fifteen-year-old who was involved in a fight in the cafeteria and was subsequently sent to talk to me, the school psychologist.

Into my office marched a wiry, defiant teenager. He warily draped himself into a chair, as if waiting for the inquisition to begin. His body language made it clear he had no beans to spill. How easy it would have been to commence with the standard "W" questions: "Why were you fighting? Who started the fight? What were you doing in the cafeteria when you should have been in class?"

I chose, however, to focus on his feelings instead. My first reflective comment was, "I understand you were surrounded by a large crowd in the cafeteria. I can imagine that fight was quite a frightening experience for you."

This reaction seemed to surprise him. He abruptly sat up in his chair. Then, responding to what he must have perceived as sympathetic understanding, he leaned forward to exclaim: "You better believe it! That punk was twice my size and he had his homies there with him." The young man then continued to express not only his fears about the fight but also the anger and insecurity that had led to the brawl. The talk poured forth almost non-stop while I carefully maintained my role as an interested and encouraging listener. Having verbalized all the issues, this young man was then in a position to look non-defensively at some ways to problem-solve that would not involve fighting, and came up with some excellent alternatives to handle future difficulties. Reflective listening had broken through his angry defensiveness.

Although reflective listening may not always create such dramatic results, it will ensure this much: your child will feel confident that his parent is really trying to understand his deepest feelings in a caring, nonjudgmental way.

I recommend practicing reflective listening whenever possible so that eventually it becomes a completely natural way of responding to your children in a variety of situations. It helps to begin practicing this technique when you are communicating with your child during non-crisis situations. It is easier to look beneath the surface then. By noticing feelings during the calmer times, you will be more prepared to be both an insightful as well as a compassionate listener at times when you might otherwise not want to hear about it.

If you are initially uncomfortable with verbally acknowledging feelings, at least silently identify them to yourself. Practice this exercise throughout the day during both your interactions with children and adults by silently answering the question "How is this person feeling about this situation?" It also helps to begin developing a more expansive "feelings" vocabulary. The following list of feeling words should help get you started.

angry	embarrassed	rejected
anxious	excluded	revengeful
annoyed	frightened	put-down
aggravated	fearful	pressured
crushed	hopeless	sad
defeated	inadequate	unfairly treated
depressed	intimidated	unhappy
discouraged	insulted	unsettled
disappointed	miserable	worried
devastated	overwhelmed	worthless
enraged		

When you develop the ability to respond routinely in a reflective way, you will never be the last person your child talks to about his most pressing issues.

Listening in Good Times and Bad

When your child returns home from an exciting event or has just received a special award, listening is a pleasure. In these instances, it is easy to respond positively to your child's enthusiasm, excitement, and joy. I have never heard of a child concerned about showing parents a report card with all "A's", nor of any unpleasant feelings or conflict resulting from this kind of interaction.

But life is not full of straight "A" report cards, promotions, and rewards. When negative events happen, negative feelings will accompany them, and it is at this point especially that parents need to make sure their children don't try to hide or suppress them.

Since successful parents set high achievement standards, many children I've worked with express fear of criticism and negativity from their parents. This in turn causes them to fear any type of failure so much that they withdraw. Often when a child begins to have a problem, the solution could have been easily remedied if he felt comfortable in sharing his concerns with his parents. But when a child feels he will not receive a supportive response, nothing is done until the situation reaches a crises proportion.

Kristina was having difficulty with her science class, failing the first test. However, she was afraid to discuss this with her parents and became so upset about the situation, she was frequently in the nurse's office complaining of a headache or stomach pains during science period. Then when she did receive a failing grade in the class, the feared family uproar occurred. However, if Kristina had been able to problem-solve with her parents at the beginning of the semester, the final failure could have been avoided.

In order to encourage open communication, parents must listen and accept whatever a child is feeling or experiencing: the good, the bad, and the ugly. All children—no matter how privileged—will have negative experiences and feelings. What is most important is that they learn to cope with these moments. Having parents willing to hear and talk about their pain is a major factor in determining a child's ability to develop a lifelong mechanism for managing difficult times.

Many highly successful parents have grown up in homes where frank discussions of feelings were not the accepted practice. This is particularly true for men, who were often encouraged to maintain a stiff upper lip, or simply to grin and bear it. As a result of such an upbringing, these parents may lack experience with acknowledging their own feelings. They are uncomfortable with words such as afraid, agitated, depressed, or anxious and would prefer not to hear them from their children. Their natural instinct is to deny rather than to probe when a child expresses something of emotional content. They may worry What am I going to do about fixing a negative feeling if I find out about it?

For other parents, their child's frustration and feelings of pain may also remind them of difficult events in their own lives. Since they have now come a long way from their own childhood, they may find it simply easier to forget or deny their own memories, and thus they cut themselves off from acknowledging and expressing empathy for their child's current problems and feelings.

The answer to such concerns is that parents are not required to fix their child's emotions. Just listening to and acknowledging your child's struggles are, in and of themselves, very therapeutic. Parents do not have to supply all the answers. In fact, as we have seen, if your children are to develop responsibility and a sense of competency, they need to learn to accept their emotions and to problem-solve on their own. Through exercising the six listening behaviors and reflective listening, however, your goal is to create a healthy family environment in which you, as parents, teach your children that you are always there for them.

Private Sharing Time

Lastly, one other highly effective way to begin establishing a strong connection with your children is through private sharing time. No matter how busy your schedule, every parent should be able to arrange at least 10 minutes each day to sit down alone with a child and listen to whatever the child wishes to discuss.

A natural time to do this with younger children may be at bedtime. For older children, other times in the day may be more practical (snack time or walking-the-dog time). Whatever time you and your child select must not be interrupted by other children, telephone calls, or anything short of a genuine emergency. By holding all calls, you are telling your child, "I value and respect you so much that I want to give you my undivided attention."

The amount of time itself is not the most important point. Even if you can only make yourself available in this manner for short periods each night, that brief contact can be extremely important for building a positive relationship with your child as well as enhancing the child's feelings of self-esteem.

Children need to know they have a safe place and time during which they can discuss anything. Private sharing time is never a time for negative emotional exchanges, or unsolicited advice and directions. If, for example, your child informs you during this private sharing time that you might be receiving a call from the school about a fight he had with another child, do not use this time to voice disapproval or dwell on the causes. It is time for compassionate listening, when you should allow the child to express anything without the fear of an emotional explosion. Thus, in responding to the above situation, you might simply say "I appreciate your honesty in sharing that with me. We will talk about the details of the situation tomorrow."

Private sharing time serves as an important communication base with your child, especially when he or she becomes an adolescent. If you have established this type of quality time together, your child will be accustomed to communicating with you in a safe, open and honest manner. When the nagging questions of adolescence have to be explored, you will have created a natural forum for doing so, and you will not seem like the intrusive personal investigator who suddenly becomes involved in the child's life at a time when the child is attempting to create a more independent position within the family.

Private sharing time is, above all else, a time to celebrate the parent-child relationship and the feeling of connectedness. Whether the connection is made by telephone during a business trip or in the car on the way to school in the morning, if a child feels secure and connected to his parents, that child will more than likely feel secure and capable wherever he is and whatever he is doing. No problem is insurmountable; no heartache unbearable, for the child who knows that Mom or Dad will listen.

SEVEN

Step Six: Learning
How to Talk to Children

Effective communication is truly a two-part process consisting of both receiving and giving information. While the previous chapter focused on the first important process, listening responsively and reflectively to what your child has to say, this chapter will examine the other side: talking with your child.

Being able to speak to your children is as important as listening to them. There are many times when you as parents must direct discussions with your children, for example when focusing the agenda, giving advice, providing feedback or criticism, or sharing your dreams and concerns. To handle these situations successfully, you must learn how to facilitate honest, open, two-way conversations. Not surprisingly, many of the same issues that interfere with listening—time and energy, interest, respect and control—also reduce the effectiveness of what affluent parents wish to say when speaking with their children.

In my parenting workshops, I have identified seven major road-blocks that affluent parents often encounter in speaking with their children. These barriers prevent you from developing consistently open channels of communication and an environment that encourages your children to listen when you talk. Becoming aware of these road-blocks and then taking conscious steps to avoid them will significantly enhance your ability to relate to your children, whether they are toddlers or teens.

Roadblock One: The Uninterested Parent

Just as effective listening means being genuinely interested in what the speaker is saying, effective speaking demands that parents have an active and personal response when they are talking with their children.

Unfortunately, busy and hectic lives often preclude time for parents to talk to their children in any manner but routine conversations. Living on automatic pilot during the week and sometimes on weekends, many parents find themselves treating home as if it were an extension of the office. They get up in the morning and immediately focus on what needs to be accomplished that day, directing children as they would employees and home matters like job tasks.

As a result, parents may frequently respond to their children's comments with short or curt responses such as "uh-huh" and "that's nice." The problem with this routine is that parents can give their children the message that they have nothing of value to share with them.

Children are aware of the often considerable difference between your interests and theirs. A parental display of no interest transmits to the child a lack of parental sensitivity to their issues. When children detect even a hint of this, they are not likely to see parents as trustworthy individuals with whom they can communicate.

In order to increase your skills as a communicator with your children, you must be truly prepared to discuss child-oriented issues, even though they may not hold the natural interest of your other activities. As it is said, the best defense is a good offense. Whenever you have an opportunity, initiate and encourage conversations with your children. Ask your child what happened in school that day, or what he did with his friends on Saturday, and be prepared to discuss the response you get. Be knowledgeable of your children's heroes, their current fads, who their friends are, and their tastes in music and books. Become involved in the private life of your children by showing you are ready to talk about whatever events are important to them. Shift your orientation from *I* to *you*.

If you expect your children to participate in whatever you have to share, and respect what you have to say, you must first develop an awareness, sensitivity, and involvement in the subjects that capture their imagination and attention. Regardless of your evaluation of the importance of the issue, the fact that your child is talking about something clearly indicates that the topic interests him.

Remember also that you and your children have differing perspectives on life. For example, you know now that not being invited to that special party when you were in junior high or not making a certain athletic team has not had a negative effect upon your life success, but to your sensitive child or teenage, these may be major and traumatic events. Many parents may ignore, or downplay an issue, believing that if they give something their attention, their child may further obsess about the topic. But failure to acknowledge your children's experience does not persuade them that they should ignore it. Rather, it may convince them to ignore you and to look for communication elsewhere.

Particularly with young children, if you can develop the ability to converse with them about any issue of interest to either you or the child, you will have gone a long way in preparing for the more difficult conversations of adolescence.

Roadblock Two: Negative Expectations and Self-Fulfilling Prophecies

Another common obstacle to successful communication occurs when parents bring negative expectations into conversations with their children. Although this is seldom done knowingly, because affluent parents are often judgmental and critical in their outlook on life, it can be difficult to isolate their children from this same perspective. Consider this analogy as an illustration of how negative expectations can color your view of a situation.

You are invited to attend a lecture given by a well-known authority. The speaker arrives at the podium and opens his speech with an inside joke about the chairman of the program. Since virtually everyone in the audience understands the humor, laughter is heard throughout the room and everyone is ready to listen to the speaker form a positive, upbeat frame of mind.

Now alter the situation slightly. Before the speech, a number of your colleagues have been gossiping about how the speaker, although brilliant, can be very cutting and sarcastic. Moments later, this same speaker arrives. With a warm smile he makes the same casual remark about the chairman. This time, however, the audience response is completely different. No one laughs or nods in agreement. Someone leans over and whispers to you, "this guy hasn't been here one minute and he's already criticizing." Without even realizing it, the speaker has alienated the audience due to its preconceived notions about his intent.

Following are some examples of how parents can bring a negative expectation of a child's behavior into a situation, and how it has an impact on their communication:

1. Your nine-year-old has a reputation within your family for being a troublemaker. He has conscientiously been trying to change this behavior, but since you anticipate poor behavior from him, you blame him for situations in which he was not involved.

2. You've caught your twelve-year-old daughter lying on a few occasions. Now, even when she is telling the truth about a problem at school, you assume that she is being deceptive, and accuse her of this when you discuss the situation that night.

3. Your sixteen-year-old son exhibited poor judgment by neglecting to tell you about a parking ticket he got. Now, rather than acknowledging any fresh example of sound decision-making, you constantly look for opportunities to remind him about his past irresponsibility.

In each of these circumstances, the negative expectations interfere with the parent's ability to speak honestly and fairly with the child. Not being objective in evaluating the situation, they will misinterpret basic facts, saying things that are inappropriate and causing anger and frustration. More importantly, negative expectations can become self-fulfilling, and instigate and reinforce the very behavior that caused the original distress.

A child's belief system is a powerfully motivating force, and is highly impressionable. Tell a child "you can't do anything right," and he will soon start to do things wrong. Advise your daughter that she's a slob, and her room will soon reflect your judgment.

Children raised in affluent environments often struggle with competency issues. As a result, parents must learn to be sensitive to the portrait their words paint. Instead of sharp criticism, give your children positive self-images by verbally acknowledging their strengths and expressing your belief in their ability to handle situations successfully. Note the following examples of how a parent can easily turn a response around from a negative to a positive reaction.

1. Your child has promised to improve his grades this semester, but his report card is not as good as you had expected. *Negative image*: "You said that you were going to work harder this quarter! What have you been doing in that algebra class, dreaming your life away?" *Positive image*: "You have really improved in English and History. You seem to be on the right track in most of your courses. How do you think you might improve in algebra?"

2. Your teenager goes to a party that becomes wild and the parents of the host send everyone home. *Negative image*: "Now you see why I can never trust your judgment. You're totally irresponsible. I don't see how I can let you go to any more parties." *Positive image*: "I am sure that you have learned something here about what can happen when you follow the crowd and don't use the good judgment I know you're capable of."

3. Your child angrily storms off the tennis court after losing the match during an important school tournament. *Neg-*

ative Image: You are always letting your bad temper get in the way of your game. *Positive Image*: It is frustrating to lose a match but your backhand play looked stronger as a result of your recent practice sessions.

Remember, your words to your children are like mirror reflections, telling them how the world perceives them: Make sure that regardless of the negative details, the overall picture your children see of themselves is positive.

Roadblock Three: Unclear and Vague Messages

Confident and successful parents seldom have trouble giving advice to their children. Unfortunately, they frequently do so without considering the level of understanding a child possesses. Young children in particular need information supplied in very specific, concrete ways. Consider the following example.

Ten-year-old Courtney is a painfully shy child who has had difficulty making friends in her new school. Each morning her mother reminds her to be nice to the other children and try to make some friends. Mother believes that she is being helpful and giving appropriate advice.

Unfortunately, Courtney does not understand operationally how to put the parental guidance into practical use. She desperately wants to have a friend, but she may not know what being friendly means in practical terms. Does it mean smiling at all the other students or does she have to go up to them and start a conversation? If the latter is the case, exactly how should she go about doing that and when? What can she talk to them about? Courtney is so overwhelmed with all the possibilities that she remains immobilized and continues to be an outsider.

In this case, the mother needs to communicate more specifically what being friendly might be. She might begin by asking Courtney what other children do in school when they are being a good friend. In this way, the mother and daughter can thus isolate some specific behaviors that Courtney can initiate in her quest for companionship: sharing a lunch-box treat, asking to join in a game during recess, inviting a child to play after school, or giving a fellow student a genuine compliment.

The important thing for Courtney is to be able to develop a specific action plan, three or four concrete behaviors she can begin to initiate in order to reach the more generalized goal of being nice to the students.

In the same way, communicating clear messages to any child means discovering what is comprehensible to that child. Vague terms such as *be nice, try harder,* or *cooperate* may seem positive, but they are not very useful or constructive. It is the equivalent of giving your child a nutritious meal without the utensils with which to eat it.

Children often need guidance from parents that is specifically oriented to actions they might take. Thus, when talking to your child, ask yourself:

- Am I clear and concrete in my request?
- Am I using the appropriate method of expression according to the time, place, and the age of my child?
- Will my child walk away from this conversation knowing what he or she might do in practical terms?

Although we will discuss the issue of discipline later in this book, if the advice you are seeking to give your child regards a behavioral problem, there is one method used in our schools that can be equally successful at home. This is to write a contract with your child clearly and concretely listing the behaviors to be implemented or corrected. Rather than simply telling your child that he must "get along with the other students *or else!*" By putting your guidance in writing, you can increase the chances of success. Examples of behaviors that might be listed on such a contract are:

- No hitting, kicking, pushing, shoving, or other hostile physical contact with another child is allowed.
- If another child makes you angry, you must report it as soon as possible to your teacher or to us.

- You must share toys with any child who asks to be included in a game you are playing.
- No name calling. Names such as stupid, fatso, or nerd are not permitted.

Additionally, it is useful to include in the contract the consequences that will occur if the conditions are broken. For example, "You will lose the privilege of watching television for the rest of the week." You can then sign the document along with your child, and let him or her know that you are putting it into effect immediately. This is only one method of attempting to correct a behavior, but it is important as an example of how to communicate with children in a specific and concrete way so that there is no confusion as to what the desired action should be.

Roadblock Four: Using Conversation Stoppers

The following story was related to me by Jenny, a fifteen-year-old high school student from a wealthy southern California suburb. Although she had never experimented with drugs, she became curious one day when, while passing the girls' rest room, she detected a strange odor. That afternoon, she asked her mother "Do you know what marijuana smells like?"

Now here was an opportunity for a parent and child to have a serious discussion about drugs in school. However, rather than opening a dialogue, Jenny's mother responded:

> "Marijuana! Are they smoking it in those bathrooms at school? Is someone trying to force you to take some? Is it that Nathanson girl? I knew she was a bad influence. I'm going to call her parents. How long has this been going on? I'll discuss it at the next Parent Association meeting and we are going to do something about this! How much of it have you breathed in?"

With a verbal onslaught like that, do you think Jenny will feel like telling her mother anything else that in any way might cause controversy?

This story illustrates one of the many kinds of conversation stoppers parents tend to have: the overreaction. Just as the boss with a quick temper is seldom informed about employee problems, parents who tend to close off conversations through a quick reaction of anger, hysterics or lectures will find that their children withdraw and become guarded and distant.

No one enjoys being on the firing line. Children learn very early to keep conversation with an "over reactive" parent limited to "housekeeping" items—that is, "Please pass the milk," "Where is the umbrella?" "I'll be spending the night at Jessie's," "I have to be at school for an early rehearsal tomorrow." Instead of opening up, they will conceal their inner-feelings and opinions. Sadly, the communication with their parents, the two individuals who should be playing the most important roles in their lives, becomes shallow and superficial.

Adversity is often a window of opportunity for parents and children to tighten their bonds. A parent should always look for ways to keep the conversation going through reflective listening. In this way, you are talking *with* your child—not just *to* him. Only when this occurs can your discussions last long enough to be of some benefit emotionally and functionally.

In Jenny's case, the mother might have begun with a reflective statement such as "You sound like you are very curious about the subject of marijuana." Then, as her daughter responds to this statement recognizing her feelings, the mother would have been able to follow up with a query such as: "Did something happen today that made you wonder about this?" She would thereby have opened a dialogue with the child in whom Jenny could describe what happened at school, and thereby give her mother insight into her questions and concerns. At that point, parent and child might have been able to follow up with an honest discussion of drugs that would help the child understand the dangers and effects.

Another situation: Nick announces at the dinner table that he is wasting his time at college and is thinking about dropping out. His father irritatedly responds: "Well, don't expect me to bail you out by giving you a cushy job in my company until you know what you want to do."

Nick's father demonstrates another powerful conversation stopper: the closed response. When you respond to your child in a manner that discourages a reply, communication shuts down. While the father's statement may express his honest concern, the presentation is just as alienating as Jenny's mother's. It discourages any further conversation or constructive problem solving and it certainly will not increase Nick's motivation to remain in school or generate enthusiasm for his studies. The remark cuts Nick off before his father can find out what is really bothering his son and precludes any chance of familial warmth and closeness. Nick will undoubtedly leave the table angry or hurt—and so will his father.

Since Nick's father had no idea what events have happened that have caused his discouragement, the most effective approach would have been a non-attacking, reflective response: "It sounds as if you are feeling discouraged with your program this year." In the same way that Jenny's mother would have been successful with this approach, Nick's father would have allowed his son to express his feelings on the subject, and then been able to pursue the conversation to a mutually satisfactory result.

Discounting a child's feelings is an equally common closed response, occurring when parents do not have the sensitivity to deal with an important issue for the child. Comments such as "Don't you think you are being overly dramatic to get so upset about an insignificant event" or "You are being so childish about this" are examples of discounting statements. So is the common response many parents have to a child's expression of concern: "That's silly. There's nothing to be afraid of (worried about, concerned over, and so on)." When a child is upset, parents must accept the reality of this feeling, no matter how things look through adult eyes. Statements that discount a child's feelings tell the child that the parent is not interested in truly knowing about his or her experience. The following statements illustrate additional common, destructive categories of closed responses that prevent further conversation:

- Criticism: "What an idiotic thing to do!"
- Interrogation: "Why were you there? What were you doing? Didn't you realize that you might get into trouble?"

- Frustration: "I'm not going to discuss that any further."
- Accusation: "What were you doing to *make* Becca so upset?"
- Insulting: "What's your problem? Why don't you ever use your judgment?"
- Threatening: "Shut up or you'll get a spanking."
- Patronizing: "You always have trouble figuring things out. Let me help you."
- Dictatorial: "I forbid you to continue seeing that girl."

If you find yourself using these types of expressions, the chances are your child will stop trying to tell you things that are important to you as a caring parent.

There are two important guidelines to help ensure that the messages you give your child will open rather than close a conversation. First, do not assume that you immediately and completely understand what your child wants or should do. Assume nothing, except that through further discussion you will learn and understand what your child is experiencing.

Second, avoid closed-ended questions that begin with the verbs Can you, do you, did you, and will you. It is too easy for your child to answer these interrogatives with a simple yes, no, or maybe, closing off further conversation. Instead, ask the questions a good reporter asks when trying to get a story: who, what, when, why, where, which, and how. These words necessitate fully articulated answers and can thus stimulate further conversation with your child.

For example, if you ask, "Do you have problems in school?" the answer is very likely to be a simple yes or no. You don't know much more information now than before you posed the question. On the other hand, asking "What is happening at school that seems to be upsetting you?" presents the opportunity for a more detailed explanation that can inspire further and deeper conversation.

Similarly, the question "Do you have any questions about your term paper project?" vs. "What parts of your term paper project are still not clear to you?" are worlds apart. The greater the opportunity children have for a positive, on-going dialogue with their parents, the stronger will be the lifelong communication channels.

Roadblock Five: The Angry Response

Imagine either of these two situations:

You have just returned home to find that someone has taken grape juice from the kitchen and spilled it on the new, white living room carpet.

You are tossing and turning in bed waiting for your daughter to return home. It is already one-and-a-half hours past her curfew time.

In either of these situations, many parents suddenly feel their blood pressure rising, and angry words start to pour rapidly from their mouths in an attack on their misbehaving youngster. The situation then becomes a major confrontation in which the parents perpetrate character assassination in order to vent their anger. They frequently demean some quality of their child, saying such things as:

"You are so irresponsible" (attacking responsibility)

"What type of an imbecile have I been raising?" (attacking intelligence)

"You are such a liar!" (attacking honesty)

"I will never be able to trust you." (attacking trustworthiness)

"How can you act like such a baby?" (attacking maturity)

"You are totally selfish and only interested in what you want to do." (attacking compassion)

However, when children feel themselves being attacked (particularly if they feel guilty about their behavior), their natural response is to protect themselves. In this guarded, defensive position, effective communication cannot take place. The minute that parents make a "you are" attack, the child will respond by defending the behavior verbally and psychologically. This may take the form of quickly blaming someone else for the transgression, or arguing the issue and thereby locking himself in a power struggle with the parents or by feeling rejected or even unloved—feelings that seriously interfere with the development of healthy self-esteem. Whatever the result, the child also does not respond to the problem needing a remedy, but instead will be focused on justifying his actions or else lying about the behavior that has created the eruption.

"You" statements are inflammatory because they appear to evaluate all the personal characteristics of the person, passing a negative judgment on his being. However, parents need to remember that what has caused their anger is not the child's basic character, but the specific action that occurred, that is, the grape juice on the rug, or the failure of a child to adhere to the curfew. You may have justifiable reasons for being angry, but a "you" attack will not achieve a constructive result, and can harm your child's self-esteem.

Instead of exploding in an attacking "you" message, parents can be more effective if they learn to give "I" messages.

I vs. You Messages

When delivering an "I" message, the speaker first takes responsibility for his own feelings, objectively describing the unacceptable behavior and indicating the reason for his anger. Just as you look for the underlying feelings when you use reflective listening, your goal in using "I" messages is to find your own underlying feeling when you are the speaker. An "I" message is constructed as follows: I feel _____ when _____ because _____.

The purpose of sending "I" messages is to communicate your feelings of displeasure in such a way as to influence the child to change the offending behavior. The three-part format above helps you to do this because you are speaking in a direct, precise, nonjudgmental manner. Your child will be more prepared to hear your concerns if he understands that there is a valid reason for your position.

Applying this formula to the two examples, a parent might say: I feel *angry* when *I return and find red stains on the white carpet* because *the rug may now be ruined.* Or: I feel *annoyed* when *I am unable to sleep* at night because *I am afraid an accident involving my daughter may have occurred.*

What makes an "I" message work? In the first place, when an individual states an opinion about another such as "You are so selfish", the listener will argue that interpretation and defend against the personal attack. However, if this same individual makes a statement about his own feelings, it cannot be argued. When I say I am angry, you can't tell me I am not—I am the final judge on my feelings but not on your character (i.e., in the last example, "selfish").

Unfortunately, most of us have been conditioned to respond immediately in the "you" tradition. Particularly for people who are used to dealing in directives and criticism, moving from the "you" mode to the "I" mode can be a difficult transition. It takes conscientious thought and practice to change old habits.

For practice, I encourage you to think of a situation that has recently caused you to feel anger, and then write it as an "I" communication. Remember that your message does not qualify as an "I" statement if you express your feelings while at the same time still accuse your child. The message, "I feel *furious* when *you keep forgetting to assume your responsibilities* because *I have to bring your homework to school*" may have the three components of an "I" message, but is in actuality a "you" message with an "I" trimming. The listener will respond defensively to the clear "you" message ("*You are irresponsible*").

To change this into a more appropriate "I" message, the corrected statement might be: "I feel *furious* when *I have to make a special trip to bring homework to school* because *it interrupts the activities that I have to do.*"

Similarly, the statement "I feel very angry when you only think of yourself and forget the important things I asked you to do for me" would be much more effectively expressed as follows: "I feel angry because I was expecting that the clothes I wish to pack for my trip would be picked up from the cleaners, and now I won't have what I need."

Being able to express your anger in the form of an "I" message does not guarantee that your child's offending behavior will immediately change. In dealing with children, the "I" message is only the first step in attempting to resolve a disturbing issue. If the behavior is not corrected by a clear understanding of the problem and its solution, you will then need to apply consequences as a form of discipline. However, when parents can talk to their children and express their negative feelings in this manner, they have the greatest possibility to resolve satisfactorily most types of problems.

Roadblock Six: Need for Control and Authority

High-achieving and powerful parents often speak to their children from the belief that they are the final authority on almost any issue and must always be in control. Even when a child presents reasonable arguments against a decision the parents have made, these parents respond by dismissing the child's opinion and feelings. Clearly, this kind of interaction seriously inhibits effective parent-child communication. It also makes many children timid about expressing an honest opinion to anyone.

I saw an interesting example of this situation at a dinner party. My host was a judge, admired for his judicial skills and his commitment to maintain steadfastly positions that he valued. At the dinner table that night were his two teenage daughters along with his wife and several guests.

During the course of the evening, the conversation turned to the judicial process, and a spirited debate ensued in which the guests challenged the host on several of his views. At no point was there any anger or sarcasm, merely a stimulating exchange of ideas. The teenagers did not participate in the conversation, and the younger one eventually excused herself from the table.

The following day I called my hostess to thank her for the evening, and was surprised to learn that their two children had been upset by the evening's events. The mother explained that they were not accustomed to seeing people disagree or argue with their father. The two girls felt that their mother should have even stopped this type of conversation.

This anecdote exemplifies a household in which father always knows best. Although I witnessed only a few hours of the parent-child interaction, it was clear that a "do not challenge Dad" message had been powerfully communicated to these children.

Without the freedom and the encouragement to express themselves fully and appropriately, children will either repress their feelings and opinions until they become passive, compliant, and
subdued, or angrily rebel. Neither of these extremes creates emotionally well-adjusted youngsters. As adults, such children will
often find themselves frustrated by their inability to demonstrate
leadership, creativity, and initiative. They may remain passive followers, individuals who go along with the crowd and are not able
to rise above it.

Another way in which the "don't challenge my opinion" perspective is experienced is in the frequently heard complaint, especially from affluent adolescents, that their parents have already
made up their minds before a discussion even begins. When the
teenager tries to make his case, the parents abruptly terminate the
conversation with such comments as "We are not going to discuss
this further," or "We already know what happened and why." Parents who react in this way night just as well say "We know everything and you know nothing!"

Affluent parents need to be aware of the serious consequences
of an authoritarian communication style. If you want your children to achieve independence and success in the world, you must
accept free thinking, disagreements, and debate. While parental
authority is an essential part of raising healthy children, it must be
supported by reason. Particularly regarding family decisions, parents should include input from all those involved in the outcome.

The next time you are conversing with your child, try to picture
yourself standing apart form the interaction and observe what is
happening. Monitor your interactions with your children. Are you
aware of their ideas and opinions? Are they free to express criticism? Do you know what your child thinks about various issues
and decisions? How might you respond if your position is challenged? Do you abruptly cut off the conversation, threaten punishment, or do you listen freely to the child's point of view?

It is often difficult to see ourselves in a completely objective
manner, but deep inside we have an awareness of our behavior patterns. You know what type of feeling you experience when you are
being challenged. When this happens, you as parents must learn to

control the defensiveness that you experience in these situations. Unless you can modify this attitude yourself, your child will not feel comfortable enough to open up to you when he or she needs to disagree with you.

Roadblock Seven: Bad Manners

If a friend were visiting your home, or a colleague were conversing with you in your office while he finished a cup of coffee and you suddenly realized that you were going to be late for an important errand and would have to leave immediately, how would you handle the situation? Typically, the conversation might sound something like this:

"I'm sorry to rush you, but I suddenly realized I have to be somewhere in ten minutes. I have really been enjoying our discussion and want to finish our conversation. When could we continue? I apologize for having to end so abruptly."

Contrast this gracious request with what might occur if your child were in the midst of an afternoon snack, conversing with you and you had that same sudden realization. Your conversation would probably wound more like (voice rising in irritation): "I don't have time to sit here while you dawdle over your food! Finish that quickly and get into the car before the store closes!"

That response may be a bit extreme, but from my experience in both my office and in clients' homes, I find that, without fully realizing it, many parents speak to acquaintances and even total strangers with more courtesy than they do to their own kids. But children are acutely vulnerable to the manner and tone in which their parents speak. If you speak to them with less regard than you would an employee, obviously they will feel demeaned. Additionally, their perception of your irritation is often greater than the reality of how you feel, and consequently they might feel total rejection when all you feel is a slight annoyance.

This is particularly true for young children (ages two to eight) who tend to view the world in simple terms. They do not realize that your bad moods may be caused by the events of the day, or that your frustration may have nothing to do with them. The young child thinks that when words are said in anger, he must have done something "bad" to cause such a response. And when the child cannot understand what he did wrong, he may turn his own frustration and anger inward, bringing on a sense of helplessness and depression.

Concerned parents acknowledge the importance of their children developing positive self-esteem, yet what comes from their mouths is often in direct contradiction to that goal. However, if parents learn to display their good manners consistently when speaking with their children, they will avoid roadblocks as well as enhance positive self-esteem. As David Elkind, in his book, *The Hurried Child* writes:

> Being polite to children is very important and may do as much for improving parent/child relations as many of the more elaborate parental strategies that are currently being proposed. The essence of good manners is not the ability to say the right words at the right time but, rather, thoughtfulness and consideration of others. When we are polite to children, we show in the most simple and direct way possible that we value them as people and care about their feelings. Thus, politeness is one of the most simple and effective ways of easing stress in children and of helping them to become thoughtful and sensitive people themselves.

When your child feels you show respect for him, he will feel safe with any type of information he wishes to present.

Who is Sorry Now?

Eric Segal's well-known novel, *Love Story*, gave rise to the popular expression "Love means never having to say you're sorry." Although Segal may have appropriately used this phrase to capture the image of devoted love, this philosophy is ruinous to healthy and effective parenting. Affluent parents must also learn to apologize when they are wrong, no matter how difficult this may be initially.

For many parents, there seem to be dual obstacles to being able to apologize to their children. The first is the capacity to recognize that one is in error. The second problem, shared by many powerful individuals, is the inability to admit an error in the form of a verbal apology.

Because they equate strength with being perfect, many parents believe that admitting an error is a sign of weakness. Of course, this is far from true. Criticizing others excessively and refusing to admit errors are actually symptoms of weakness and insecurity. Humility and admissions of fallibility are demonstrations of strength.

Therefore by admitting an error, parents can actually teach children about personal strength and integrity. If you want your children to learn how to acknowledge their mistakes, you are going to have to learn how to admit yours. If you want your children to apologize, you will have to show them that saying I'm sorry is another way to express love.

Another specious assumption powerful parents choose to believe, particularly with younger children, is that everything will blow over, and by the next morning unpleasant incidents will be forgotten. Children do not forget. Mental-health professionals can attest to the extraordinary ability of patients to recall the tiniest details of a traumatic event that occurred during childhood as if the episode had occurred only hours before. Most of us carry such memories of our own childhoods, and your children will, too, if you do not learn to help them forget with an admission of your mistake.

Recognize when you are wrong, admit your error, and apologize. Children want to believe the best about their parents and will be genuinely forgiving. But it is up to the parent to acknowledge his or her mistakes by saying those often difficult but profoundly beautiful words, "I'm sorry."

Whether you are working with your child to build positive self-esteem, set realistic expectations, develop quality time, encourage independence, or utilize the language of encouragement, the primary method for accomplishing these vital goals is effective communication. Thus, concerned parents must constantly be aware of the manner in which they are conversing with their children in order to avoid the major communication roadblocks of disinterest, discounting, negative expectations, vague and unclear messages, overreacting, closed responses, and "you" attacks. The more of these roadblocks in your path, the worse your level of effectiveness will be.

It is extremely important to keep the communication channels open so that you can comfortably initiate positive interactions rather than negative ones. If you accomplish this when your children are younger, it will be easier to maintain this contact through the more turbulent adolescent times. However, no matter the ages of your children, avoiding these roadblocks will greatly enhance your relationship with each of them.

Unfortunately, some families may already have developed such unhealthy communication patterns that mere sensitivity to these roadblocks will not solve the problems. If you find your child responding with frequent lying, defiance, verbal abusiveness, argumentativeness or withdrawn and depressed-appearing behavior, you would benefit from seeking help from a mental-health professional who can objectively evaluate your situation and assist you in putting into practice more effective communication techniques. This type of assistance is most beneficial if the family members participate in counseling, since all members contribute to the activity of the family system. Often the child who appears to be exhibiting the most distressing behavior is only the one who overtly exhibits the dysfunction of the family system. Without working with the entire system, the behavior of the problem child may become quite improved while the behavior of another family member begins to deteriorate. It's up to you, as parents, to recognize your need for professional intervention—and the sooner, the better.

The Business of the Family— Family Meetings

In the business world, effective channels of communication are maintained through the use of regularly scheduled staff meetings, even though the participants may spend casual and work time with each other all week long. These meetings allow important information to be shared, positive accomplishments to be noted and problems to be brainstormed by all participants in order to determine the most appropriate solutions.

Regular family meetings can also provide an equally effective process of communication. Prearranged times for discussion allow all family members to gather and, without anger or agitation, review pertinent issues. In the busy world of affluent families, parents may often be away, meal times may not be shared, and finding the time to operate as a family unit can be difficult, so family meetings to foster long-term emotional health are very important.

The family meeting should be a regularly scheduled event, taking place at your home, with a specified amount of time set aside for the process. In this way everyone is able to avoid conflicting appointments. The most effective rules to follow are:

1. Schedule meetings on a regular basis so that all parties will be aware of time and place and conflicts in schedules are minimized.
2. Set up a definite time for each session.
3. Discuss both positive accomplishments of family members as well as problems to be solved, e.g. sibling conflicts or issues requiring decision-making such as plans for an upcoming family vacation.
4. Every point of view must be heard without anger, belittlement, or interruptions.
5. Give every family member the opportunity to express an opinion, regardless of the age or articulateness of the family member. Don't let the most verbal members (including yourself) dominate.
6. Let every family member who can "chair" the meeting do so on an alternating basis. Make sure that everyone's agenda gets attention.

Although this is the ideal time for conflict resolution, family meetings should also address the positive activities of family members. Do not let these sessions focus exclusively on complaints.

The family meeting can help each family member handle issues that are important to the entire family system. It gives the family as a whole the opportunity to demonstrate in a concrete manner that all of its members count. Children feel validated because they are able to contribute to the problem solving and this serves to increase their sense of personal competency.

Finally, the family meeting enables parents to use their limited free time in a quality manner. Your children realize how complicated and hectic your lives are. By making a formal commitment to communicate on a regular basis, they feel that they are indeed very special and important.

A Pocket Reminder on Communication

Few affluent parents lead simple, uncomplicated lives and most, therefore, need not only to reevaluate their attitudes and habits, but also to remember on a daily basis the practical aspects of effective communication. The following thoughts, taken from *A Parent Workbook on School Discipline* by John Bon, summarize seven important secrets for effective communication:

1. The Six Most Important Words: I admit I made a mistake.
2. The Five Most Important Words: You did a good job.
3. The Four Most Important Words: What is your opinion?
4. The Three Most Important Words: If you please.
5. The Two Most Important Words: Thank you.
6. The One Most Important Word: We
7. The Least Important Word: I

The ability to communicate effectively with your children is one of the most important challenges for every successful, affluent parent. However, your limited time, your occasionally frayed nerves, and your desire to help your child as much as possible, can all get in the way of creating a healthy communication environment.

Remember, though, that when a parent and child can truly talk and listen to each other, every problem can be resolved. The added bonus is that your child will grow into adulthood feeling fortunate to be able to consider you not only a loving parent, but a valued and trusted friend.

EIGHT

Step Seven:
Brat-Proofing Your Child

The girl's voice was sharp with irritation as she held the cell phone to her jaw and rudely demanded to know exactly where her mother was: "Why isn't she answering her cell? Then try her on her private line," she shouted. "I can't wait any longer!"

After a moment of exasperation, she said, "Oh never mind," and hung up. "They are all so stupid," she angrily blurted as she sat down next to me on the bench in front of the department store where I was waiting to meet a friend.

"You seem so upset. Is there anything I can do to help?" I queried.

"Our housekeeper is such an idiot. She never knows anything. My mom should be here!"

"What time was she supposed to come?" I asked and quickly realized from the response that her mother was no more than a few minutes late.

Through our brief conversation, I learned that Alexsa was thirteen and had been dropped off by her mother to buy some shoes for school, but from the numerous packages she was carrying, she had satisfied more than her footwear desires. As we talked, she continually insisted that she had to get home in twenty minutes, and when I inquired as to why I discovered that her urgency had simply to do with wanting to meet a friend to talk about what she'd purchased and she needed her mother to take her there.

I suggested that perhaps her mother was delayed in traffic, but Alexsa dismissed that possibility: "She's just wasting time somewhere and she knows how I hate waiting."

A moment later her mother pulled up to the curb and stepped out of her Mercedes. She walked over to Alexsa, apologizing for her delay. Then, seeing all of the packages, the mother's face showed concern. She opened one of the larger bags, withdrawing a leather aviator jacket with a price tag of $450.

"Alexsa, you certainly don't need this. You have so many other jackets just hanging in your closet."

Alexsa exploded, berating her mother's insensitivity. "Everyone at school has one of these! I *need* it!"

The mother's feeble protestations were no match for the power of this little tyrant. With a heavy sigh of embarrassment and resignation—which suggested to me that she'd probably gone through this kind of public spectacle with Alexsa before—Mom silently picked up all of the packages and carried them to the car. Alexsa, meanwhile, charged ahead, opened the car door and jumped in, not even attempting to help mother load the packages into the car.

Unfortunately, behavior like Alexsa's is not an anomaly among the offspring of the affluent. While spoiled brats can exist at any socio-economic level, the problem is most acute at the top, because affluent families have the wherewithal, and often the inclination, to indulge their children with a plethora of material possessions.

Of course, affluent children are not predestined to be brats simply because they have access to money and goods. Your children can grow up with realistic and well-grounded values as well as genuine respect for their possessions if you understand the implications of instant gratification and indulgence.

Defining Indulgence

Like realistic expectations, the issue of overindulgence is one of the more difficult for parents. While they want to give their children the best that life can offer, it can often be confusing to find the healthy equilibrium between too much and too little. I have had many parents in my classes who speak quite emotionally of the discomfort, uncertainty, and frustration they experience when they are subjected to their child's demands for more toys, clothes, jewelry, and other possessions. I have also heard many horror stories about the highly inappropriate behavior children have exhibited if the parents refuse to buy a wanted item, or children who cause embarrassing scenes when they refuse to share their possessions with playmates. These parents are left wondering what it is that they have done to make their child develop in this manner, and what they should do about it. In my seminars, parents will frequently ask such questions as:

Exactly what is the difference between indulgence and overindulgence?

How can I tell if I am overindulging my child? I don't think I am doing it.

I feel like my kid is the one driving the issue. I try not to yield to his every demand, but he's the one who makes me indulge him. What can I do?

In truth, indulgence cannot be defined in quantitative terms. There is no general, authoritative rule stating that if a parent buys *x* number of items, or purchases *y* number of gifts, or yields to *z* number of consecutive demands from a child, that the child will become spoiled. Indulgence cannot be reduced to a formula by which a parent knows when to say yes or no to a child's wants.

However, there is clearly a difference between healthy indulgence and unhealthy indulgence, or what is considered overindulgence. Unhealthy indulgence occurs when parents teach their children, consciously or unconsciously, to place a major emphasis on external possessions and value, and on immediate gratification. At the opposite end of the spectrum, a healthier attitude toward possessions recognizes that internal qualities, such as creativity, cooperation, sharing, and empathy, are more important to a fulfilling life, no matter how much one owns or can afford to buy.

Our society as a whole has a tendency to emphasize external values, such as material demonstrations of success, over internal values. But affluent parents themselves have a far greater vulnerability to a confusion of values than people of lower socioeconomic status. Therefore, the first step to understanding overindulgence and avoiding it is to evaluate your own parental attitudes and behavior.

Like the principles of healthy communication and realistic expectations, the issue of overindulgence often stems from how parents themselves think and act. Since a child's values are profoundly affected by the way in which you view material possessions, money, and power, and in how you respond to gratification needs, the example you set is critical in establishing the type of environment in which a child will not become spoiled, regardless of how much or what possessions he or she receives.

It is therefore useful to examine the special factors that you, as affluent parents, must consider in setting the example for your children. In reviewing the tough questions that follow, you will need to take an honest look at your own attitudes and behaviors. The insight and awareness you will gain from honest answers can help you see your place in creating and ending the problem. In this way, you will be in a stronger position to take the necessary corrective steps.

Do You Indulge the Children to Replace Yourself?

Throughout this book, I have addressed the serious consequences that limited parental time has for children, and here again, limited time is one of the primary factors that motivates parents to indulge their child in toys and other possessions as a substitute for their physical presence.

Obviously, in many situations, this occurs in a natural or unpremeditated manner. You are with your child, shopping at a store. Your child sees a toy and indicates his desire for it. You buy it, thinking that it will be a good item to occupy your child for a Saturday morning while you are busy. Other times, affluent parents may give a gift quite consciously as a replacement for their attendance at a school function, sports activity, or birthday party.

The sad reality is that many parents believe that such "giftwrapped guilt relief" is a legitimate substitute for absence or lack of attention. I have even heard the following rationalization: "How can you complain about the long hours I spend working when you are enjoying all the luxuries it provides?"

I was recently shopping for holiday presents when an elegantly attired man turned to me, proudly displaying his recent purchase of a very expensive electronic toy. "My son is really angry that he is not going away with us during the holidays, but I figure that he'll be so absorbed in this toy that he won't really miss us. Don't you think this should do the trick?" he questioned, flashing a wide smile. Unfortunately, he picked the wrong individual to support his position, and by the time he left the store, he had received a far more involved reply to his question than he had bargained for.

Overindulging children with material objects to make up for your absence can lead to serious consequences. Unable to have the parental time and attention he truly hungers for, a child can become increasingly ungrateful, selfish and demanding. Eventually, the child may learn to resent the gifts that have been given as a replacement for attention and love, and this in turn can lead to a destructive cycle of guilt and hate in the parent-child relationship.

Do You Indulge the Children to Avoid Hassles?

Overindulgence sometimes results as a way to avoid a face-off between parent and child. When a child demands something and you refuse, the child's natural response to the thwarting of his desires will inevitably be to voice a protest. Some children do it in a controlled manner, others stage a major theatrical performance, but the effect is the same—stress.

As a result, many affluent parents would prefer to indulge their children than to manage the ill-will of an argument, especially when tranquility can be easily purchased in a new toy, electronic game, or a clothing shopping spree. Children quickly recognize this vulnerability and learn to increase their oppositional behavior to the point where parental capitulation is inevitable.

Unfortunately, one of the realities of effective parenting is con-frontation. While many parents find themselves intimidated by a strong-willed, manipulative child, it is important to remember that effective parenting does not exclude having an angry child. As your child grows and tests the boundaries, the limits you set will invariably cause moments of anger and frustration. This is healthy, and children must learn to deal with frustration appropriately when their wishes are not immediately fulfilled. When parents succumb to intimidation, they are making the first mistake in unhealthy indulgence. It is far better to have an occasional angry outburst than a lifetime of spoiled behavior.

Remember also that household staff is highly vulnerable in this area. They may believe that if they do not indulge the whims of a demanding child, they may run the risks of precipitating a major tantrum, which may then be interpreted by their employers as their inability to care properly for their charge. Parents must therefore take the time to make sure the limits they wish to have maintained are clearly understood by staff, as well as to assure them that some oppositional behavior from the child is to be expected.

Do You Indulge the Children to Be Fair?

Some affluent parents feel that if they are indulging themselves, they do not have the right to deny their children the same gifts. If Dad gets a new Italian leather jacket, everyone else in the family can have one, too. Many affluent children even learn to play into this kind of parental guilt and become brazen enough to verbally castigate their parents for selfishness if they are denied equal purchasing power.

The problem with this egalitarian purchasing approach is that for the parent there is generally a connection between the effort and the reward, but for children, there rarely is. Since they have not worked for the money to buy the possession, they do not correlate the cause with the effect. It is not, therefore, surprising to find affluent children well versed in the art of demanding without any sense of responsibility for producing. Fairness is appropriate to consider when you are buying for more than one child, but it is not necessary to supply your children with purchasing power equal to yours.

Do You Indulge Your Children to Reflect Your Success?

For many affluent parents, overindulgence is the result of their need to demonstrate their success to the world. With an abundance of disposable income, they eagerly satisfy the desire of their children, who contribute to the evidence that the family has "made it." Just as the correct address and the parents' membership in exclusive clubs are indicative of their wealth, so, too, do the children's designer clothing, jewelry, and extracurricular activities reflect to the community the financial status of the parents.

Several years ago, I was involved in creating a special fine-arts program to supplement the kindergarten class at a local school. The children participating in this program attended the regular kindergarten in the morning and then worked with an artist for several hours in the afternoon, exploring music, dance, and crafts. Because the activities often involved working with materials that could soil clothing, we advised parents to send their children to school in play clothing.

The day we sent the clothing advisory home, I received an angry call from one of the parents of a child in the program. In no uncertain terms, she informed me that she and her husband had not worked so hard to reach the financial and social level that they had now obtained to let their child come to school dressed like an "urchin." Her child would just have to be careful with her clothing or she would not be able to participate in the program. While this particular situation focused on clothing, it was clear that many other decisions would probably be made for this child based exclusively upon how this youngster would appropriately reflect the family's social status. Obviously, children are not decorative possessions, and indulging them materially as an extension of external parental values is extremely misguided.

Do You Indulge Your Children to Keep Up With the Competition?

You have just moved into an exclusive community. One new neighbor introduces you to a top designer who will supervise the interior furnishing. Another points the way to a superb caterer who can handle your next party. Soon you have fallen into the "right" routine, shopping in the recommended stores, enlisting the services of the appropriate florist, enrolling your children in the desired private schools and exclusive summer camps, marking their birthdays with festive theme parties coordinated by the most fashionable party planner.

In this environment, it is easy to become overindulgent. When living in an affluent community where everyone is able to afford anything and everything, it is a challenge for parents not to adopt competitiveness as the norm. Falling into the keeping-up-with-the-Joneses pattern can happen easily, but in so doing, parents lose a realistic perspective of what befits their own circumstances and tastes.

Indulgence should not be based on what everyone else has or does. When this occurs, your children will not develop into unique individuals, aware of their personal interests and desires, and unaffected by the crowd mentality. A child's peers can be a strong force, and if your own habits teach your children to yield to competitive pressure, they will learn to focus on external values rather than their internal voices.

Do You Indulge Your Children As a Result of Your Childhood?

Many affluent parents who grew up in financially privileged but dysfunctional families may indulge their children in the very same way they were indulged. They recreate the lavish birthday parties and holidays of their own childhood for their children and pamper them with clothes and jewelry just as their own parents had done to make up for an emotionally deprived family life.

Miriam knew well the experience of limited contact with her parents. Her glamorous mother always accompanied her father on all his travels and Miriam and her brother were frequently left for extended periods of time with the latest nanny while her parents were away. She often played alone in her beautifully decorated room, surrounded by mountains of toys, books, and a closet full of perfectly coordinated outfits, but wishing that she could magically appear at the place far away where her parents were staying. When they would return, there would always be many new presents, but even when they were at home, they were still inaccessible.

Miriam married a successful film director and when his numerous projects require prolonged location work, away from home, she willingly joins him, flying back to her home from time to time for brief visits with her children. She has several caregivers in her employ, and since she prides herself on hiring only European-trained help, she feels assured that her children are being given the best possible care. As an additional bonus, each Saturday the governess takes the children to the local toy store where they can select whatever toy they desire.

On the other hand, some affluent parents who grew up in financially deprived families may equally indulge their children to compensate for what they lacked.

Hank grew up in an impoverished section of St. Louis. His mother had to work two jobs in order to provide the basic necessities for Hank and his five brothers and sisters after their father deserted them. To this day, Hank can still remember his self-consciousness at never being able to have the toys, new clothing or the opportunities of the more financially privileged students in his school. He admits that the desire to have these luxuries fueled his ambition to achieve his present success.

"I still feel the painful memories," Hank told me in explaining his reasons for indulging his two daughters. "I'm not about to let my kids endure many of those indignities. I want them to have the finest of everything. They're going to have the status I never had."

In both of these cases, the parents are using material possessions to deal with their own childhood issues. Their emphasis on external stimulation and acquisitions derives not from positive self-esteem, but from feelings of emptiness or anger about their own families. This then becomes the model of behavior they pass on to their children.

The problem is that in trying to deal with one's own childhood, whether it was privileged or deprived, parents teach their children to value material indulgence more than strength of character and feelings of love within the family. It is clearly difficult to escape from one's past, but your children need to live in the present, within a healthy family system you establish for them. When parents overindulge their children to compensate for their own childhood, they are creating a risk of far greater pain for their children in the long run than the pain they may have previously experienced.

Do You Indulge Your Children to Win a Divorce Battle?

Although the divorce statistics are rising among all socioeconomic groups, the ability to buy the love and affection of children becomes far easier for the wealthy single parent. Especially when children are shuttling back and forth between two families, an undeclared indulgence competition can often be created. Without consciously realizing it, each parent may try to outdo the other in making his or her home the more desirable place to be. They create this lure with possessions, gifts, and indulgences. Sometimes the children even orchestrate this rivalry, pitting each parent against the other, by blatantly challenging: "If I can't have it here, I am sure that I can get it when I go to Mom's [Dad's]."

The tragedy of this orientation goes beyond overindulgence. The child's most urgent needs during divorce—meaningful relationships with parents who can offer genuine interest, good listening skills, understanding and encouragement—can be easily overshadowed by the who-can-top-this competition if parents do not respond to the underlying issues.

Amanda had been the object of a bitter custody battle between her celebrity father and her mother. Initially both parents vied for her attention with lavish expenditures, but the mother's divorce settlement did not permit her to indulge in the free-wheeling spending that she enjoyed with her former husband. The fear of losing her only daughter if she could not acquiesce to her material demands soon became a nightmare.

In this situation, Amanda's mother needed to regain confidence in the fact that the most meaningful gift she could give Amanda was her friendship and love. In working with this family, I suggested that the mother and daughter focus on spending quality time together rather than concentrating on what they could not afford. Through special discovery days together, in which they went to parks for picnics, visited museums and various exhibitions, or hiked in the mountains, both mother and daughter established a strong bond and a close friendship. The quality of the mother-daughter relationship thus mitigated any of the negative effects of the father's overindulgence.

Things do not create the greatest satisfaction for children involved in divorce. In these difficult circumstances, one should overindulge only in love.

The Consequences of Overindulgence

The quintessential spoiled brat is the most obvious result of materially overindulging a child, for whatever reason it was done. But there are more subtle, yet equally significant, psychological outcomes that develop as a result of an orientation concerned with external values rather than internal qualities.

The Development of a Narcissistic Personality

The first of these is the development of a narcissistic personality. The term derives from the myth of Narcissus, who was so enamored of himself that the gods changed him into a narcissus flower, living forever beside a pool of water that offered continual self-reflection. Psychologically, the term refers to an individual who is self-indulgent and self-absorbed. For the narcissist, the world exists exclusively to be manipulated to meet his own personal needs.

Young children are naturally narcissistic or self-centered. When the precocious three-year-old wants to entertain at a family gathering, he expects everyone to stop their conversations and give him their full attention; he feels that this is a very reasonable request, and for the most part, it is. However, as children grow older and experience the world as a friendly, nurturing place, they develop a sensitivity and compassion for the needs of others.

Pathological narcissism is the end result of denying the fulfillment of a child's basic emotional needs, although the child's external physical needs may be lavishly met. A variety of servants may
cater to both the child, as well as to the parents, on immediate
demand, while the internal world of the child is ignored. The
house may be filled with people, but in reality, the child is very
much alone emotionally.

In fact the parents are often so indulged themselves that they
expect everyone, including their children, to meet *their* needs.
They are thereby limited in their ability to respond to the needs of
others, particularly the young child. Such parents often put their
children on display in the most elegant attire to show off for others in order to make Mom and Dad look good.

The child who is deprived of important emotional support in
this manner will believe that the world is not really safe and nurturing, and that the significant adults in his life are not trustworthy. Thus the child may begin to reason: If I depend upon adults,
they will disappoint me, leaving me with a cold, lonely isolated
feeling. They don't understand what I really need; only what they
want from me. In order to survive, I must protect myself from their
demands.

The child therefore feels that the only trustworthy person must
be himself, and he elevates this Self to a grandiose position in order
to soothe the feelings of frustration, fear, and anger that result
from the lack of sufficient emotional support from others. Because
the majority of the narcissistic person's emotional energy is
directed inwardly, this person is generally unable to sustain any
type of meaningful relationship with others.

In her book, *Narcissism and Intimacy*, Dr. Marion Soloman
describes the lifetime personal adjustment problems these individuals face. Although they might function with great financial success
in a career, their lives lack any type of personal connectedness since
they remain emotionally isolated from colleagues and friends.

Of course, not every spoiled, self-centered child will grow into
adulthood with the clinically serious diagnosis of a narcissistic personality disorder. However, many will become adults with enough

of the general characteristics of this disorder to cause them to have continual difficulty in their interpersonal relationships. They may more commonly be described as being egotistical, selfish, self-centered, or demanding. The bottom line is that it is very difficult to feel emotionally connected to an individual who is so involved with his own needs and demands that the concerns of others are ignored or discounted.

It becomes difficult for this type of individual to parent success-fully since the effective parent must be able to invest considerable emotional energy in nurturing a growing child. Therefore a destructive cycle may occur: the narcissistic parent produces an emotionally damaged child who will then parent his own offspring in a similarly ineffective manner. We can thus observe several successive generations struggling with serious emotional issues.

Possessions Lose Their Value

For the child who has everything, possessions often mean nothing. During a family conference, a troubled father verbalized a typical example:

> "For days all my son talked about was an expensive new robot toy. Nothing else seemed to matter to him, so I bought it. Oh, he was excited for a very short time—then he lost interest. He played with it for the next few days, but by the end of the week I couldn't believe it: the robot was thrown carelessly in the bottom of the toy box."

Material possessions obtained too easily are rarely valued. What, after all, defines the value of an object if not the time and effort necessary to acquire it? If all a child has to do is to ask and receive, he is not being given the opportunity to learn the value of anything.

During a visit to a home of very modest means, I was befriended by a ten-year-old child who invited me to come to his room and see his car collection. His room was sparsely furnished; a small book case held his few toys and books. The prized collection consisted of four metal cars, which he excitedly presented; sharing with me detailed background information on each. He explained proudly how he bought the latest model with money earned doing yard work. After he had shown me each car, he polished them with a tissue and carefully put them back in their designed places. Having worked and saved for these toys, he had learned the priceless lesson of care and respect for his possessions.

Boredom Rules

The effects of overindulgence on the affluent child extend beyond this loss of valuing material possessions. With all his physical and material demands met, and lacking a sense of direction and poorly disciplined, the child does not stay with any activity long enough to develop a special proficiency or passion. The child caught up in this ennui may continually seek new and sometimes dangerous thrills in order to find something different to do. Substance abuse and delinquent acting out are often the end result of this search for purpose and meaning in life.

As an adult, this boredom can translate into a lack of satisfaction in work or careers. The term "idle rich" has been widely used to describe these kinds of individuals who move from activity to activity, searching for situations that will ignite their enthusiasm and passion. Life becomes quite monotonous for these people, and they never achieve the internal satisfactions they frequently seek.

Lack of Self-discipline—"Entitleitis"

Overindulgence can seriously undermine a child's ability to develop self-discipline. Conditioned to expect instant results, he or she will always be looking for an easy way out, a quick fix, a chance to get by with minimal effort. This attitude in turn can lead to a resistance to accept challenges that necessitate concentration, persistence, and perseverance over a period of time. Such a child may therefore develop little ability to plan for the future, and will be unprepared to make important long-range life decisions or to pursue long-term goals.

Robert Coles, in the last volume of his *Children of Crisis* series, discusses at length the concept of entitlement. The result of his research indicated that the majority of wealthy children feel entitled to certain privileges of possessions and status, merely by the luck of having been born into the right family. In its mild form, this attitude leads to no serious personality distortion. However, in many cases, the attitude appears to be carried to an extreme degree and we find young adults with basic ability who are unwilling to apply themselves in any constructive or purposeful manner. They do not feel that they have a responsibility to work in any manner for their benefits but can simply sit back and be served by the world.

Delayed Gratification and Risk Taking

Ask any successful entrepreneur how they felt when they first began their business and universally I hear responses such as "scared or worried". Often they admit that in spite of their obvious success, they are still fearful and will remain so until the day the business is sold. There is an important lesson in these statements, namely how important it is to be able to delay immediate gratification and be willing to tolerate the discomfort of risk-taking in order to achieve any significant accomplishment.

Being a risk-taker requires an individual to place himself for an extended period of time in a state of uncertainty, without knowing what the eventual outcome of his actions will be. The overindulged child who demands instant gratification therefore greatly limits his options in life.

Taking risks is a natural part of growth. This is not to suggest that every child must be prepared to abandon everything in order to reach a goal. However, it is this ability to delay immediate gratification that eventually enables entrepreneurs to succeed, artists to flourish, students to learn, and executives to manage. It is also a very basic quality that provides the opportunity for virtually all adults to make significant personal changes or to embark upon any new endeavor in which the outcome is unknown.

Inability to Cope With Adult World

For many parents, a serious problem of raising your privileged children like princes and princesses is that they will not become kings and queens. What a rude awakening the world will hold for them! The affluence that many children experience when they are growing up often represents years of hard work and sacrifice on the part of parents, but these children may have little recollection of that early part of their lives. They live with the fantasy that when they are grown and on their own, they will automatically continue the lifestyle to which they have become accustomed. The result of this can be children who become highly anxious and depressed when the financial reality of their independent adult life becomes evident.

Even if a family has not excessively overemphasized possessions and personal indulgence, the comparative luxury of their environment is still impossible to hide. The parents cannot pretend that they are poor and expect the children to believe them. They don't have the leverage to deny a child a specific possession because they can't afford it.

Whatever the reason, when a child is overindulged, a learning equation becomes established: Just ask and you shall receive. Unfortunately, this situation only exists within the family. In the real world, the operative system is: Work and you shall receive. But, obsessed with continuing their indulgent lifestyles, these youngsters may look for short cuts, legal and illegal, to recapture their gilded ghetto.

One tragic example of wealthy children being misdirected in this manner was the highly publicized case of the Billionaire Boy's Club. Several members of this group were the sons of some of Southern California's most wealthy and socially prominent families. In numerous interviews, these young men spoke of their strong need to impress their fathers and friends with their financial success. This was almost certainly a value they had learned from their parents, but it made them easy prey for the get-rich proposals that resulted in crimes including embezzlement and murder. The case may be extreme, but the path from overindulgence to a desperate need for the trappings of success is not a long one.

Brat-Proofing Your Child

It is my hope that the previous sections enumerating the underlying reasons for and the consequences of overindulging your children have raised your awareness. A heightened sensitivity to these dangers can go a long way in preventing a child from becoming spoiled, as well as in remedying a problem that already is out of hand. If, for example, you have recognized yourself as a parent who may have become caught up in the indulgent lifestyle of other parents around you, taking steps now to control your natural motivations can begin to modify your over-indulgent behavior.

There are also a number of specific and concrete actions you can take that will help protect you and your child against the perils of overindulgence. Implementing these actions immediately will allow you to change whatever environment you have already established into one that puts materials possessions and external values into their proper perspective. Even those parents, like Alexsa's mother, who may find themselves with a spoiled brat on their hands can "unspoil" a child if they consider the following steps seriously and implement them consistently.

Watch What You Talk About and Do

"When the going gets tough, the tough go shopping" is a phrase emblazoned on tee shirts, tote bags and other personalized items. While an amusing quip, it holds a more serious meaning when applied to overindulgent families. Children are very receptive to your influence, and it is therefore important for you, as parents, to set the example in all your discussions and actions about material goods.

To evaluate the situation in your household, I recommend that you monitor for one week the type of conversation that occurs among members of your family, particularly you and your spouse. How much of it revolves around goods and possessions? Are you frequently commenting upon the newest acquisition of a friend or colleague? Is shopping an important activity? Is an expensive purchase a quick pick-me-up from the blues?

When children hear these types of comments or see endless purchasing by parents, they will naturally incorporate this into their own value system, and possessions will then assume an unhealthy preoccupation in their lives. If this is not your goal, you will have to moderate your discussions on these topics.

When you do spend money for your children, put your emphasis on items that will enhance your child's education. Using your wealth to purchase extracurricular learning experiences, books, computers and educational software, and trips to interesting places (rather than on designer clothes, toys, and other material excesses) lets your child see you use money to increase internal skills rather than as a tool for extravagances.

Distinguish Between Wants and Needs

Parents can benefit by learning to think in terms of a child's *needs* versus his *wants*. While you may not be able to control your child's demands, you can, however, limit your response to them by recognizing the difference between these two categories.

Have you ever noticed how two and three-year-olds confuse wants and needs? The child will say, "I need a cookie." Or, "I need to watch TV." Their urgency feels as gripping to them as their basic biological necessities. Most children will continue to think this way unless parents teach them otherwise.

Needs include the basic biological needs—food, water, air— along with a reasonable amount of attention, affection, intellectual and physical stimulation, and opportunities to be competent. Your child's needs are a priority; they should be satisfied as quickly as possible. Delaying food from a hungry child or withholding a hug from a frightened child does *not* promote internal values and such deprivation can ultimately be harmful.

Wants encompass virtually everything else your child craves, be it a material object or the choice of what to eat or any opportunity to get his own way. Some wants should not be satisfied at all; every toy your child sees advertised on television does not have to become part of his collection. Other wants may be perfectly reasonable but need not be satisfied *on demand*. By making your child *earn* those wanted objects—or at least wait for them—you give him the opportunity to develop the ability to delay gratification and to focus on internal values.

One way to do this is to let your child create a wish list. All requests for wants are written down, and at those specific times when your child would receive a gift, you can ask the child to select from the wish list. In this way, your child will learn to prioritize his desires and learn that waiting is a necessary part of receiving.

This is not to suggest that parents cannot spontaneously award a child with a gift from the wish list from time to time. There is clearly a shared joy from which both parents and children can benefit after a particular achievement, with a reward such as a special trip to an unusual place.

It may also be appropriate for a parent to indulge a want when it is connected to a responsible activity, such as a child receiving a car because he can use it for an after-school job or summer employment.

It is up to parents to ensure that wants and needs are clearly defined. A crucial part of this process is for parents to clarify this distinction within their own thinking and then communicate the appropriate message to the child at every opportunity.

Focus on the Internal Issues

Many parents yield to a child's demands without thinking about what the child may really be asking for. Children will often want objects for a particular reason without recognizing that there may be a more important issue at hand. When your child becomes demanding, do not focus on the demands themselves, since this stresses external values. By looking into the child's underlying emotional dynamics, you will help your child to explore internal resources.

For example, if your young child is bored and requests a new toy, you might interest your child in a creative activity to solve the boredom rather than purchasing as the solution. With younger children, encourage them to build a puppet theater, make some puppets, and put on a show. Take some chalk out to the driveway and draw a mural.

Many toys inhibit creativity because they provide all the stimulation—much the way television does—without asking the child to stretch his imagination. Creative play not only provides stimulation but allows the child to feel that he has accomplished something. And this feeling then translates to a sense of competency, an internal gratification.

The same approach is equally true for teenagers. They do not need to spend weekends shopping at the mall for clothes, games, and stereo equipment because they are bored. Instead, parents should encourage them to pursue hobbies, sports, creative crafts, or to involve themselves in philanthropic or community service programs, or to obtain a job.

Of course, an adolescent is more likely to voice an objection and attempt to convince you, the parent, that he is the only such deprived child among his peers. But don't succumb to any feelings of guilt. By not permitting your child to focus on external possessions, you will be helping your youngster develop the type of internal resources that will result in greater lifetime achievement and satisfaction.

Set Your Limits and Learn to Say "No"

As simplistic as it may seem, brat-proofing your child depends on your ability to set limits and then to say one very important word: no. Children, after all, will want everything since they have little sense of prioritizing. Each new television commercial creates an immediate desire. If there is an adult around to handle a task or service a need, the child will take advantage of this individual.

However, while a child's demands might suggest a perpetual desire to gain the upper hand and defy your limits, what he is often doing is searching, in his own way, to find exactly where those limits are. After all, one does not inherently know where a boundary is without testing it!

Thus, in many cases when a child makes demands about wanting a new object or being taken to his favorite amusement park for the third day in a row, what he is really asking for is to know the boundaries of his world. He wants to know how many new toys it is reasonable to ask for or how many times he should expect to be allowed to get his way.

Only by being willing to establish and reinforce your limits can you give your child gifts far more valuable than any toy at any price: security, self-discipline and control. As a parent, you must remember that your long-term responsibility is to help your child develop appropriate limits on his natural urges for self-indulgence. Certainly there will be resistance, arguments, and at times, tantrums. But unless you are prepared to support your child for an indefinite period of time, when you remain firm and consistent in your positions, you will see the development of a thoughtful, responsible young adult.

Clearly the ability to say "no" is much easier in a home where money is indeed a limited commodity. I have seen many parents confused as to how to set limits since the retort, "We can't afford it" was the honest limit setting statement in the homes in which they were raised. You do not lie to children. How foolish it would be to say "we can't afford it", when a child is clearly aware of the extravagant lifestyle surrounding him. However parents can clearly and firmly reply, "We do not choose to spend our money in this way." This not only sets limits but additionally communicates to the child that there are always choices to be made in regard to spending money.

Focusing Your Child on the Bigger Issues

When parents are reasonable in their material indulgences, set consistent limits, and focus on internal resources rather than external possessions, children will naturally develop the ability to distinguish between indulgent behavior and necessary possessions. But learning about overindulgence needs to go beyond the issue of material possessions. Affluent parents need to encourage their children to take an active interest in the needs of other people and in issues outside of their own subjective experience. By so doing, parents can foster moral development in their children so that they will begin to become sensitive to the needs and feelings of others and develop sincere empathy for those who are less privileged.

Affluent parents can teach their children a valuable lesson in making them aware that not everyone has the privileges available to them and that money alone does not make them superior to others. You don't spoil your children merely by giving them things, but by giving to them without making them aware that they, too, have an obligation to give in return. Talk about your feelings of relationship to society as well as your child's and always let your child know how proud you are when he exhibits behavior indicative of kindness, sensitivity and compassion.

Involve your children in appropriate social-service projects so they have a chance to participate actively in making life better for those who are less fortunate. Encourage them to volunteer their time at an orphanage or a shelter for homeless children. Engaging in philanthropic activities and social services and involving your children in them is another important way to demonstrate your values. By being exposed to individuals less financially privileged, your child can develop a greater appreciation for his own situation. For younger children, this may mean collecting unused toys and clothing, and taking them to a shelter for needy children. Older children can get involved in community volunteering or in helping parents research and select charities for family contributions.

Finally, make sure that empathy training does not exclude a consideration for your household help and the simple understanding that all human beings are entitled to respect, that people are not objects, and that human feelings are *always* more important than material objects.

Because of the importance of personal values in the issues of overindulgence, the rules of parenting in this area can seem quite nebulous and perhaps difficult to implement. You have to give and withhold on a different basis, one that can be very difficult to maintain. It takes thought and a specific commitment on the part of parents and surrogates not to take the path of least resistance and indulge their children both materially and behaviorally. However, you now know how destructive the consequences of this approach can be.

Your children will look to your leadership for the development of a system of internal values that will enable them to enjoy life with or without material wealth. Help them to put affluence in proper perspective: a bonus and not a necessity.

NINE

Step Eight: Teaching Your Child the Value of a Dollar

In many affluent families, money is rarely discussed. Some parents who subscribe to the notion that if you have to question what something costs, you really can't afford it act as if money is simply too plebeian a subject for their children to concern themselves with. Others feel that money is a complex and sophisticated topic, inappropriate for discussion with their children. Some affluent parents struggle painfully with money prior to creating their current financial success, and find talking about expenditures reminds them of a difficult past they prefer to forget. Still others feel that, as long as they pay the bills, money is none of their children's business. People can be very peculiar and wildly irrational the way they handle their finances. It can drive them—and their kids—crazy.

Not long ago, a teacher in one of the schools that services a highly affluent community told me of a situation that typifies some parents' distaste for the topic of money. This teacher had developed a lesson in economics in which one of the activities involved setting up a family budget. The children were then asked to discuss this assignment with their parents to get an idea as to how this issue was handled in their home. One little girl returned to school the next day and told of her father's response. He informed her that he was not at all interested in discussing the family finances and that she was lucky that she didn't have to every worry about it. By protecting her in this way as a child, he was risking exposing her to serious money problems as an adult.

Unfortunately, what occurs in such affluent families is that children develop little understanding of money and its value, or the relationship between work and a dollar. In these homes, the new plasma television arrives at the same time as the sophisticated home theatre equipment is installed in the newly decorated family room. Mom's new car shares a place in the garage with a variety of toys and top-grade sporting equipment. The children spend weekends with their friends indulging themselves with their parents' credit cards while sharing accounts of the most recent family vacation to Aspen. Surrounded by money and the things it can buy, children become oblivious to its value and often are incapable of its management. When it comes to understanding budgeting or how to handle money appropriately, these children of affluence can be disasters waiting to happen.

Money has an entirely different feeling in homes of modest income. It can become an all-consuming issue, the cause of endless stress between husbands and wives, and between parents and children. When having enough money to pay for the basic necessities of food, shelter, and clothing is not taken for granted, children quickly learn the value of a dollar.

As a result, children from families of average means are constantly learning that money is a finite thing, which is difficult to earn and must be handled with care. When the family spends their entire weekend comparison shopping for the best-priced television, CD player, or automobile, a lot more is learned than which item is the best buy. With little extra family money for generous allowances, these children quickly figure out how to earn their own through after-school and summer jobs, and how to save for more expensive items. As these children grow into adulthood, they are likely to give serious thought and consideration to how they spend this precious commodity.

Clearly, money can provide special advantages and worthwhile experiences, but its use must be tempered with a realistic outlook on its value and purpose. The ultimate tragedy caused by affluent parents who employ the silent treatment regarding money is that their children grow up having a distorted idea about its availability, its place in a happy, productive life, and have few skills in managing or investing it. However, you cannot shield your children forever from the financial realities of life. The sad case of the Vanderbilt family fortune, chronicled in *The Fall of the House of Vanderbilt* by a present-day heir, Arthur Vanderbilt II, exemplifies the results of parental neglect in this area. Within two generations, the family had lost one of the outstanding American fortunes through gross indulgence and a lack of knowledge regarding the basics of money management. Smaller fortunes are even more rapidly lost. For this reason the adage "shirtsleeves-to-shirtsleeves in three generations" is well known universally. One generation works hard to create the family wealth which as a result of financial incompetence is squandered away by the next generation so that by the third generation little is left and wealth creation must again begin.

As affluent parents, you must be aware of the potentially dark side of your financial success, and make a strong commitment to teach your children about money and its management. By developing an active program addressing the issues of your monetary attitudes and behaviors, allowances and other money-management learning opportunities, and by the role you play in showing your children the relationship between work and money, and by the manner in which you untie the financial umbilical cord when your children are ready, you can provide your children with the skills necessary for both surviving and thriving when they become independent adults.

Examining Your Own Attitudes and Behaviors

As with many issues in this book, examining your own parental attitudes toward money is a necessary first step. Depending upon your own personal background, money can have very different meanings to you, many of which may operate on a subconscious level. Can you recognize what your money behavior may be saying to your children? Are you possibly giving money messages quite different from those you consciously wish to make?

To begin a self-discovery process, take a piece of paper and write out the answers to these questions. I am asking you to write out the answers rather than simply think about them because I have found that in the process of writing, people become more deeply involved in their subject and unexpected insights often emerge. Spend at least five minutes writing out the answers to each of these questions:

1. What was the attitude of each of your parents toward money, and how did it affect you?
2. What was said directly to you about your personal relationship toward money when you were growing up?
3. What did you learn about money from watching other family members, friends, and peers?
4. What does money mean to you now? What do you see as its greatest value? Its greatest danger?
5. What are the attitudes about money you would like to teach to your children? How are you doing that? What changes would you like to make?

After you have completed this exercise, ask your parenting partner to reply to this same set of questions and compare your answers. What are the similarities or differences between your attitudes? How might you demonstrate those differences in your home? What effect could they have on your child?

You may find this initial exercise difficult or even painful to do, but it can help to put you in touch with the past and present money models you may be bringing to your role as a parent. It may also suggest areas in which you and your spouse may be sending mixed or confusing messages to your children. Conscious reflection on these attitudes can help you to affirm those you wish to continue sending and eliminate those you wish to avoid.

A recent acquaintance, Lucy, described her struggle to achieve financial competence because of a poor money management model as she was growing up. Although her immediate family was not wealthy, her father had been raised in a family that lived on an inherited fortune. He therefore conducted his own affairs "as if" he were in fact affluent, although he didn't have the immediate resources to back up his actions.

Saving or budgeting was not a necessity in the family because the father knew that one day; a portion of the family fortune would be his. Even if he got into financial hot water, he would always turn to his parents for assistance. As a result of this attitude, Lucy's father was proficient in spending money on family indulgences but not a very successful financial provider.

As an adult, Lucy was unable to establish clear career goals and often found herself in disastrous financial situations. Since her father had not yet become an inheritor, he was unable to rescue her. Finally in her mid-thirties, and $125,000 in debt, she obtained some professional assistance to help her develop the money management skills she was greatly lacking. At this point in her life, she is just beginning to achieve some of her career and financial goals.

Don't be like Lucy's father. Being clear as to what money messages you give to your children and taking the time to teach them healthy money attitudes will be among the most important investments you will make in your child's happiness and security.

Actions Speak Louder Than Words

In our society, money talks and people talk about money, but children are more influenced by what they see parents do than by anything they hear their parents say. They are keenly perceptive of parental behavior. When parents forbid children to use expletives and then pepper their own speech with them, children will do as parents do, not as they say. The same principle is true with regard to money.

Therefore, affluent parents must also evaluate their money behaviors and try to eliminate or modify those that may unknowingly contribute to an unhealthy home environment for teaching your children about money. The following reflect the money attitudes that may unwittingly communicate problematic messages to children.

Money is Power. Will your children view money as the ultimate power tool? Do you use money as a means of controlling others or keeping them in a dependent position? Is behavior of which you approve rewarded financially, while choices not to your liking result in financial withdrawal? What will your children learn about human relations if this is the perspective they see and hear at home?

Example: John had been a star baseball player and was determined that his eight-year-old son, Adam, follow in his footsteps, although baseball was not Adam's sport love. In an effort to enhance his son's interest in the game, John made Adam's attendance at summer camp dependent upon his participation in the spring Little League season.

Example: Chelsea, a young professional, came to her parents to borrow money to begin a business venture on the East Coast. They applied tremendous pressure on their daughter to move back to their home city in California, offering her even larger financial assistance if she returned.

Money Can Reduce Guilt. Will your children see money as a means of excusing unacceptable behavior? Are gifts consistently used as an apology? What will your children learn about right and wrong actions if they think problems can be solved simply by giving a present?

Example: Zach's parents were too busy to attend even one of his soccer games all season. Feeling badly about their absence, they presented their son with a new racing bike when he finished the season.

Example: Francesca and Marshall traveled extensively and returned home long enough, it seemed, only to clean their clothing for the next business trip. However, each time they went away, they brought home a duffel bag filled with presents and souvenirs for their children.

Money Is the Ultimate Fixer. Will your children feel that solutions to difficulties in friendships, grades, or even legal problems can be purchased without having to develop resource? What will your children believe they can get away with if all their problems are solved for them with gifts, tutors, and lawyers?

Example: Lisa was uninterested in her fifth grade class and was consistently negligent in completing her homework. Instead of assisting Lisa to develop appropriate study skills and examine her general attitude toward the importance of school, her mom and dad hired a tutor to come to the house three times per week to help Lisa complete her assignments.

Example: David was involved in delinquent behavior and vandalism, which resulted in his arrest. Although this was the second time, his parents hired a top law firm to take care of the situation so that nothing would appear on David's records.

Money as a Sign of Personal Worth. Do your children hear you describe possessions rather than accomplishments or inner qualities as signs of your or others success? Is money used in a game of one-upmanship with others in order to feel good about yourself? What lessons in self-esteem are absorbed by a child who sees their own value measured in dollars and cents?

Example: Rick, Sr., was known as Mr. Gadget among his friends. Each time a new electronic product became available, he was the first of his friends to purchase it. If one of his friends acquired an item before Rick, he would joke at the dinner table about how Dan beat him to it this time, vowing to his children that he would get the same item the next day.

Example: Marissa's daughter Yvette was frequently invited to the birthday parties of her classmates. At each party, Marissa noted what gifts were given by other parents and pointed out to her daughter that their present was always one of the best.

Money Is a Men's Issue. Do your children see money as an issue only handled by Father rather than by both parents? Do you include your sons in financial discussions but not your daughters? In many families a sexual bias is at play; while sons are taught the basics of finance, daughters are instilled with the unrealistic fantasy that "there will always be a man around to handle these issues." But how will your daughter be able to function in a competitive world if she feels incompetent to take care of herself?

Example: Jane and her brother Steven were both interested in music while growing up. However, beginning in junior high school, Steven was encouraged to work in the family business after school rather than join the band, while Jane was allowed to participate in the extracurricular activity, being told that she was not needed.

In truth, there is no absolute right or wrong in many of the examples of these money behaviors. It will depend upon circumstances and the consistency of the action. However, if you now have an awareness that these attitudes about money are similar to your beliefs, you will be vulnerable to parenting in a manner that places your child at risk of not being able to develop an appropriate understanding of the value and importance of money. Changing your own attitudes and behaviors, therefore, should become a priority.

Allowances and other Money-Management Opportunities

An allowance is one of the first practical money-management tools affluent parents can give their children. Appropriately utilized, a weekly allowance teaches discipline, decision-making, delayed gratification and an appreciation for the value of money.

Parents can begin allowances by the time a child has reached five or six years of age. Even at this age, children can see that money is used to buy things. They can make a selection in the store and pay for it with their own money. They can begin to learn about exchange. Though a child under the age of eight years usually has difficulty understanding the concept of savings, he can still be taught to budget his money and prioritize his purchases, but only if a parent is willing to say, when the child wants to buy two items, "You do not have enough money to buy both. Which do you want to have?" Understanding limits is a lesson never too early to teach.

Around eight years of age, a child can begin to develop a realistic understanding of money. At this point, he is able to distinguish between coins, count change, and understand the relationship between varying prices and his ability to afford an item. He can also understand the importance of saving.

Allowances should be divided into three parts: one part for immediate spending, one part for savings (delaying immediate gratification) and the third for charity. By the time your child is in high school, ask him to submit the budget he feels he needs but over which you have line item veto rights. Then give the allowance in larger amounts to cover increasingly longer intervals as this encourages long-range planning when your child prepares to go away to college.

Teenage children should also be given an allowance that covers a majority—if not a totality—of their personal expenses. Make such expenditures as entertainment, presents for friends and even clothing a part of an allowance large enough to accommodate all of these responsibilities. In this way, your child will realize that money is a finite commodity, and he will put far more thought and consideration into spending it.

When a child prepares to go away to college, a single lump sum at the beginning of each semester (and later each full college year) is well within the planning capacities of a collegian. If, through poor budgeting, your child runs out of cash before the end of the term or school year, he or she can get a job to earn the required balance.

How Much Allowance is Enough?

Affluent parents are faced with a practical and fundamental problem: how much allowance should they give their children? There is, of course, no universal answer to this question. Determining the exact amount of allowance for your child depends on many factors, including the child's age, his financial responsibilities, and community standards. However, a general rule of thumb is that an allowance should not be so small that the child is always financially frustrated, but not so large that the child never has to make choices.

Discuss allowance with other parents in your community. Don't be pressured by choices that may well be out of line with what you feel is right. However, do take into consideration your child's allowance in relationship to peers. Too little can cause problems, just as too much can.

Don't tie an allowance to the child's doing ordinary chores or responsibilities within the family. Cornell's noted child psychologist, Dr. Lee Salk, pointed out that when children are given financial rewards for family chores, they lose the opportunity to participate as a family member. Children should handle regular tasks in the home (keeping their room in order, helping in the kitchen, etc.) not because they will receive money but because they are a contributing member of the family.

Children should be given at least some of these tasks for two important reasons: first, to feel that they are truly a contributing, not merely dependent, member of the family, and second, to have opportunities to enhance their sense of competency. Having chores means being responsible for something important. When a child has performed a task, he should be recognized for having fulfilled the obligation.

Of course, in many affluent homes, finding chores for children may be difficult with housekeepers, gardeners, and other outside help paid to perform such tasks. Parents should develop a list of special chores—such as washing and detailing the family car, cleaning the basement, garage, or attic, domestic repair work, or babysitting—for which they can pay a child. If your child has spent his money by mid-week and needs additional cash, these jobs provide the opportunity to earn the needed amount.

As soon as they are of an appropriate age, children should be encouraged to work to earn money as a supplement to their weekly allowance. Having the opportunity to work gives your child a greater understanding of the value of money since he will be able to equate it with time and effort. Working will increase your child's feeling of competency and control over his life. Above all, he or she will receive an early lesson in the realities of work: that it can be rewarding, stimulating, challenging, and most importantly, that it can provide a lasting and satisfying sense of purpose that makes it worth the effort.

Should an Allowance Be Withheld As Punishment?

In order to utilize an allowance as an effective and ongoing lesson in money management, the allowance should not be tied to your child's behavior. When parents tie money to behavior, it not only equates displeasure with a smaller cash flow, it also conveys the opposite message: that the child can get more money by behaving well. This puts a price on, and thus emphasizes external values rather than developing internal standards. As I will address in the next chapter, inappropriate behavior should be handled by consequences. But withholding the allowance is not an appropriate consequence. Money should not be the controlling element, because when it is, you are not teaching your child a healthy view of the use of money.

This does not mean, however, that a child's irresponsible actions cannot cost him money. If your child disregards the household rules by playing ball in the house and breaks a window, letting him pay for it out of his allowance is a logical consequence and a lesson in financial responsibility. Similarly, if a child is delinquent in assuming household responsibilities, the parent might inform the child that if he does not complete the task himself, someone will have to be hired to handle the job and the responsibility of paying for this service will be placed on him. Realizing that not cleaning up one's room will cost five or ten dollars in housekeeping wages can quickly teach that responsibility to a lazy child. The loss of money should not be a punishment but should take place only if it is a consequence directly related to what the child does or doesn't do.

From Financial Literacy to Financial Competency

While allowances represent the most universal means for parents to teach children about the value and the appropriate use of money, there is much more work to be done to prepare your child for financial self-sufficiency. It begins with a greater understanding of the financial landscape. I call this financial literacy. But it continues with developing specific practical skills and experience, which I call financial competency. Affluent parents have the responsibility of preparing their children for the responsibilities of earned income and inherited wealth. It is just another one of those tasks they forgot to mention to you when you signed up to be a parent.

When and how do you start?

If you have learned the lessons described earlier in this chapter—openly discussing money with your children, teaching early principles of money through allowances, and holding children accountable for failures of responsibility—you've already begun the journey from financial naiveté to literacy to competency. Children learn at different speeds, different ages, and in different ways. So, keep your eye on the goal, but adjust the timing and process to fit the talents and limitations of each of your children.

Bank Accounts. One of the first steps in this journey is banking. When your child is approximately eight years old, you can introduce him or her to the process of banking by opening a savings account in the child's name, and encouraging the child to make regular deposits. In this way, the child can follow the growth of the account, the compilation of interest, bank charges, and other financial transactions that will become more and more meaningful with time.

But, don't just open the account, fill out the paperwork, and then tell your child what you've done. There's little learning in that. Take the time to talk to your child about which bank, how much they charge for various services, whether they offer on-line banking, whether they answer your questions politely and respectfully, and anything else that in your experience has affected where and why you have selected the specific bank. It's this critical thinking and series of questions that is the real learning experience for your child. You might be amazed at how much of this will stick. The most valuable lesson is that you have shared your insights with your child, engaged him or her in a dialogue, and initiated a real teaching environment.

By age twelve or thirteen, your child should be ready for a checking account and maybe even the first credit card. With this new freedom, however, come new responsibilities and new learning opportunities. With every checkbook comes a check register. Follow the simple rule: if you don't balance the checkbook every month, no more money will be added. This may seem like heresy, since many parents don't balance their checkbooks either, but there's no time like the present to change bad habits. Don't forget to calculate in the expenses and bank fees. If you've done your homework at the front end, there won't be much. But, if the child has overdrawn, or used other banks' ATMs, or any number of other activities, there will be a host of added expenses. The child must learn to minimize or avoid the costs, and then to appreciate its significance.

As a parent, you probably learned to balance your checkbook by lining every cancelled check up in a neat pile and comparing them with your register. But your children will learn their banking on-line. Better join them, if you haven't already. Some of the banks, and more will follow, are converting to strictly on-line reports and reconciliation. No more cancelled checks and no more lengthy printed reports. Sign your child up, and start the process early.

Children learn by watching and by doing. Share these tasks with your child, but don't do them yourself. The goal of financial competency can only be attained through practical experience, trial and error, and learning from mistakes.

Credit. Perhaps the greatest challenge to you as a parent, and to your child as a new entrant into the financial marketplace, is to understand and manage credit. It's so easy to come by, and so easy to use, yet so complicated and confusing that it will be our first roadblock to financial competency and will continue to challenge even the most prepared for the rest of his or her life. Many children (and adults for that matter) believe there's money to spend as long as the credit limit hasn't been reached. So, if one credit card is good, two must be better. As you begin this experience, here are some basic principles to instill in your child:

1. Pick the right card. Learn how to pick the best and most flexible card. Maybe you're interested in frequent flyer benefits, or maybe you want to help your local school or other charity. Look at the choices with your child and make the selection together.

2. No more than one credit card. It's hard enough to control one card. Don't compound the difficulty with more than one.

3. No unpaid balances at the end of the month. Most credit card users don't realize that if there is <u>any</u> outstanding balance (even $1.00) at the end of the credit cycle (which isn't necessarily the same as the calendar month), then <u>every</u> dollar of credit in the following month will be charged interest (rates are as high as or higher than 18% with some card companies). If you can't pay it off through your allowance or work, you can't afford it. While this principle is violated by mature working adults because of the nature of their financial obligations offset by reliable sources of income, it's not a habit that is good to teach your child. Financial discipline is the bedrock of financial competency.

4. Debit versus credit. You may even want to start with a debit card, instead of a credit card. This is a substitute for a check book, since it pulls money directly out of the checking account. No money in the account, no withdrawal on your debit card. However, watch for expenses and fees, and be sure that your child is balancing the checkbook monthly, whether on paper or on-line.

5. Credit rating. By the time your child reaches age 18, you should have gone through a credit check and rating with him or her. There are three credit agencies that do this

work. (See Resources for Parents at the end of this book for more information). Each agency will calculate the individual's "FICO" score. FICO is the abbreviation for the company that actually devised the formula (Fair Isaac Corporation), but this score is widely used by virtually every vendor and lender in the country. Every time you apply for a credit card, purchase an item over time on installments, or even apply for a job, you're likely to have this score checked. The higher the score, the better you look. The lower the score, the more expensive your purchase will be, because the interest rate the bank or vendor will charge you (if they accept your credit at all) may increase. Your prospective employer or maybe even your school admissions officer will be influenced by this score. Learn the system early and learn it well. Go to the FICO webpage for more information (www.myfico.com).

Budgets. Without a budget, your child will fail to learn limits. I remember the story of a client who told me that his wife was given an unlimited spending budget . . . and exceeded it! If discipline is the bedrock of financial competency, then the budget is its physical outline. The use of the budget is a powerful way to ensure that your child not only learns the value of money, but also the necessary survival skill of being able to prioritize.

Children should learn as early as possible to be accountable for all of their expenses. For example, children should be required to keep detailed records of all their purchases so that they can look back and discover where their money goes.

The process of building a budget is one which should get your attention. It's a wonderful learning experience for everyone. Just how much is needed for personal items, like extra clothing, or that special hairdo? What should be available for school trips, or gasoline for the car, or computer programs or peripherals? Should some portion of every allowance be set aside for charitable purposes? How much should be saved and invested? Just the discussion about these choices is healthy and educational.

Discipline in not always easy. Ian had a budget. His revenue came from his parents, with allowance, birthday and holiday presents, and a modest after-school job. The budget included personal purchases, as well as special occasions. Then came the new combo CD player/tuner. Although he had an adequate system in his room, he was lured by a more sophisticated model—the new, "cool" version. It was beyond the budget, but Ian decided to use his money to purchase it anyway. When the unforeseen spring ski trip with his friends came up, there was no more money. Ian's parent's had three choices.

1. Bail Ian out. Help him out "this time", so he wouldn't be disappointed. It's hard to see your child distraught. Spring breaks are only for the young. His friends would never understand. He'll do better next time.
2. Lecture him. You could hope he learns from his mistake and warn him that bad decisions in the future will result in even more serious consequences.
3. Let the chips fall. You could discuss the dilemma with Ian, but don't try to change the consequences of his action.

I have no doubt what is appropriate. Bailing out a child destroys any potential for learning. When parents continually fix an offspring's financial mistakes, the child will never learn to how to solve the problem himself. Lecturing a child on his mistakes only adds insult to injury, focusing the child's attention on defending his mistakes rather than learning from them.

Permitting your child to learn by the natural consequences of his actions is the single most effective educational tool. When a child is allowed to experience fully the impact of a poor choice, he will be more astute or least more cautious in his future decision-making. Parents must therefore focus not on the suffering their child might go through with a broken toy or an empty wallet, but on the lesson the child will have learned.

Major purchases. Parents should involve older children in major family purchases by giving them the responsibility to research the price of competing brands and the quality of the products the family intends to buy. You may be surprised how much more your teenager will know about your choice for a new car, television set, computer, or stereo than you may know. The Internet has more consumer information and helpful analysis than any one person could possibly gather through experience. The kids know the Net. They toggle between PriceGrabber.com and Buy.com with ease. What they don't know about a product, they know about how to research the product. If they don't know, get them started. The team effort this encourages helps reinforce the notion that each child can add value to the decision-making experience. It's no longer "dad knows best", but the "family knows more". This inter-reliance and shared respect creates self-confidence and self-esteem, and it's fun.

Investments. Financial competency includes the ability to manage accumulated wealth. The stock market offers an excellent opportunity to expand the child's understanding of investment. By using a portion of his or her savings to purchase even a few shares of an inexpensive stock or mutual fund, the child will be motivated to take a serious interest in following its changing market value, learn about the company's business, and become involved in the decision on when to sell or reinvest. The process of learning, selecting, and investing in a particular stock or fund is even more important than the financial results. The child must understand that the newspaper is more than a listing of movies, concerts, and sports scores. It has the information the child will need to understand the investment and track the results. Many of our kids today are more comfortable getting their information off the Internet. This is not necessarily a bad thing or a lazy decision. The Net can help you research a stock, compare it with others in the industry or within amongst industries. It can automatically track the stock for you and report back regularly. There are so many choices available in this area, that you need only go on-line and "Google" it by typing in "stock research". You'll be taken to such hot spots as MSN Money or Yahoo Finance. The most important message here is to begin the process early, do it as a family, be disciplined and consistent, and use this experience for everyone to learn together.

The Work-Money Connection

Mental-health professionals are in general agreement that in order to have a fulfilling life, a person needs two things: love and meaningful work.

In most affluent families, the children have a tremendous potential for achieving satisfying life work. Through their own efforts, and perhaps utilizing family resources and connections, most children are able to pursue, first, after-school jobs and, later, careers of their own choice. The affluent child will not need, as so many children do, to quit school and work at some tedious, unfulfilling job in order to assist the family's economic survival.

Yet, in some families, affluence becomes an obstacle to the desire to work, often due to the parent's role modeling of what work means. Particularly in families with substantial inherited wealth, a child may see his parents as the classic "idle rich," drifting through life, socializing with friends, and constantly traveling for pleasure. This ethic can create the dangerous illusion that life is a series of indulgences, filled only by activities to amuse and entertain. In this environment, a child will almost inevitably grow up with a lack of focus that could ultimately turn to disillusionment in adult life. In this era of exploding wealth, especially among very young entrepreneurs, by the time the child of the wealth creator is old enough to understand, the working parent has retired. The age of "retirement" for many first generation wealth creators has moved down so far that the child may never have actually seen the parent working.

Alternatively, in the world of the obsessive workaholic, the child may be given a very negative picture of work. If you frequently complain about the problems and pressures of your job, are tense and fatigued every night when you return home, and fail to focus on the qualitative aspects of your family life, your children may not view work as a positive and stimulating experience, but rather a competitor to a good family and something to be avoided. You may not remember the school open houses you missed, the Little League games you didn't attend, the school play with your daughter to which you came late, or the homework assignment that could have been so much more successful and fun with your input and oversight. But your child undoubtedly can. I have talked with more than one affluent teenager who questions attending college, saying something like "What's the point? I don't want to end up miserable in the rat race, like my Mom and Dad."

Balance in Life and Work

Finally, you may be undermining the atmosphere of a positive work ethic when you say to yourself and to your child that "I don't want you to have to work as hard as I did." Working hard is how you achieved your success. That wasn't the problem. It may have been the lack of balance between work, family, and play. It may have been the mistakes of inexperience that you suffered through. It may have been the lack of capital that held you back. But it wasn't working hard. The signal that you send when you say don't work so hard is that it's okay to kick back. Life will come to you. I will make your life so easy that you can consume, instead of contribute.

If you have been successful in your business or career, you will have enjoyed the sense of accomplishment that is essential to personal fulfillment. If you do not encourage the environment in which your child can achieve, to whatever level or extent that child is capable, you will have deprived your child of one of life's greatest rewards. It's not too trite to remind us all that life is not about the destination, but about the journey.

Cutting the Financial Umbilical Chord

Perhaps the most difficult transition period for any family occurs when a child must leave home and establish financial independence. Affluent families often have a more difficult time in making this transition because they have the resources to prolong the period of dependence. But postponing independence and financial responsibility is almost always destructive. The following story illustrates not only the potential problem of postponement, but the ultimate benefits of squarely facing the challenge.

After graduating from a prestigious university without any focused career goals, Kristen returned to her beautiful decorated bedroom in the family home to consider her options. For the next two years, she enjoyed a luxurious life, paying little attention to her parents' suggesting that she begin looking for a job and moving out on her own. She made a few brief forays into the job market, but within a few weeks in a new position, she would quit, complaining of unsatisfactory working conditions, entry-level pay and no opportunity to move up quickly. When even her friends suggested that she might have to tolerate hardship at a job long enough to advance to a position of greater authority and better conditions, Kristen made it clear this would not be necessary for her because if she really had to, she could always work in the family business.

Her mother and father voiced concern about Kristen's indecision to each other as well as to family and friends, yet they continued to indulge her. They not only permitted Kristen to live at home, but they gave her unlimited use of charge accounts and credit cars, hoping that things would soon work out and not wanting to make the situation any more difficult for their daughter than it seemed to be.

After the first year, however, Kristen's parents observed a notable change in their daughter. Her weight increased. She had insomnia and began sleeping away the morning and sometimes part of the afternoon. She became increasingly sullen and withdrawn.

When Kristen's parents finally sought professional help for her, they were surprised to learn that the recommended therapeutic intervention consisted of immediate termination of all financial support and the insistence that this young adult become self-sufficient. They were advised not to permit Kristen to work within the family business until she had proven responsible work habits in another job.

Kristen resisted these recommendations and tried to enlist her parents' sympathy and concern, insisting that she did not possess the resources to make it on her own. While the situation was painful, the parents held firm. Soon, Kristen moved into an apartment with a friend and within a few weeks landed a job assisting the owner of a photography studio. Two years later she has made impressive career growth, and now manages the studio herself.

Kristen has become a self-confident, energetic, enthusiastic young adult, who now describes the period when she lived with her parents after college as her "adult infancy." She acknowledges that she had no real concept of the value of money. She assumed that it would always be there and that she was entitled to whatever she wanted or needed. Fortunately, Kristen also recognizes that beneath this feeling of entitlement was an unjustified fear that she really lacked the competency skills to support herself. She is grateful now to feel that she can independently meet her own needs.

Many affluent families face similar circumstances, particularly in today's job market where college graduates often need several months to find an entry-level position. But cutting the cord does not always require the sudden abrupt cessation of any and all financial support. If your child is taking observable action to become self-sufficient, this should be encouraged. You can then negotiate a gradual move toward his independence, with decreasing financial assistance, and still serve your ultimate goal of helping your child take responsibility for himself.

In cutting the umbilical cord, the goal for parents is to be very careful about giving a dangerous double message: You should be financially responsible—but we will actively support your financial dependency. Independence gives an individual a powerful sense of personal control and self-esteem. While your children are fortunate to have a financial safety net that will generally protect them from having to deal with real poverty, responsible parents must be sure this safety net psychology does not become a source of incapacitation.

Several years ago, Los Angeles Magazine featured a cover story with a headline that read "Ugh, they're back!" It focused on the dilemma of the once "independent" adult child, now in his or her mid-twenties, who has come home after a few years of bouncing around and not making enough money to live the way the young adult had experienced as a child. For a while, the pleasure of having your child back home compensates for the messy room, food demands, and renewed invasion of your privacy. Then, the pattern becomes troubling, as the child substitutes your providing food and lodging for his or her own financial responsibilities. The longer you wait to make the decision you have to make, the harder it will be on everyone. Your task as a parent was to provide the environment, education, and opportunity for your child's independence. You did your job. Now it's time for your child to do his or her job.

Anything given is not nearly as precious as that which is earned. So, let your child go and give him or her all the encouragement, insight, and assistance he or she may need. But don't try to prevent the hard knocks of life for your child. It will only make it tougher in the future if you do.

Finish the Training

If you missed the chance to prepare your child for financial competency before the child went off to college, don't despair. There's still time. Lifelong learning is not limited to seniors and retirees. Young adults, between the ages of 18 and 35, are often very ready and eager to finally learn the skills that should have been acquired years earlier. But the educational process is somewhat different for a 25-year-old than for a 15-year-old. Adults learn more from peers than from parents, and they learn more by doing than by listening. Financial training for adults takes on new and greater relevance. The mistakes are costlier and the stakes are higher. Beyond the skills of banking, credit, and basic investments, a competent adult will have skill in:

1. Risk management, including protecting against the risks to yourself, your family, and your business;
2. Investments, from securities, to real estate, closely held businesses, and commodities;
3. Major purchases, including a car or home;
4. Marital property issues, including premarital agreements, and the consequences of divorce, child support, and alimony;

5. Estate planning and inheritance, including wills, trusts, and the rights as well as responsibilities of trustees and beneficiaries;
6. Tax planning, including income, gift, and death taxes;
7. Business structures, including corporations, limited liability companies, and partnerships;
8. Acquiring, running, and growing a family business;

Financial skills will not be enough, however. It will require competency in critical life skills that enable the adult to be successful in business, profession, and family. The competent adult should have skills in:

1. Communication
2. Leadership
3. Consensus building
4. Negotiating
5. Problem resolution
6. Team building

Encourage your young adult to continue this process until these skills are acquired, experienced and employed.

Trust Fund Syndrome

To most people, a generous trust fund appears to be a fantasy come true, a carefree existence with the freedom to indulge one's desires and impulses without concern for such mundane details as budgeting or bill paying. In reality, however, the lives of many trust-fund beneficiaries are more pitiable than enviable.

The stories are endless. Barbara Hutton, one of the most chronicled heiresses of the twentieth century, stated, "I was gutted with privilege, softened by luxury, weakened by indulgent nannies. When you inherit as much money as I did, it destroys whatever incentive or goal you might have." The tragedy of her life seems to support that statement. And if you think such stories are vestiges of older times, check out Johnson & Johnson heir Jamie Johnson's searing documentary *Born Rich*, which captures similar sad and dissolute lives of young heirs in the twenty-first century. The problems of excessive wealth will, it seems, be with us for the foreseeable future.

Of course, not every affluent child who receives a trust is destined to end up a tragic figure. But after years of experience with families of wealth, and working with the best financial and estate planning professionals available, I have recognized the patterns and themes. They are self-evident to anyone who is paying attention.

How Much is Enough?

The accumulation of wealth in America over the last quarter century or more has exceeded anything in previous history. According to a well known study conducted by John Havens and Paul Schervish at Boston College Social Welfare Research Institute, over the 55 year period from 1998 to 2052, the wealth transfer will range between $41 trillion and $136 trillion. The mid-level estimate is $73 trillion, and this assumes a maximum real growth rate of 3% over the next 55 years. Even with a substantial portion passing to the government in taxes, and more passing to charity or foundations, there is substantial wealth passing to children and other heirs.

This has a led a number of prominent wealthy individuals, from Warren Buffet to Bill Gates, to warn against the excess of affluence. Buffet is reported to have said on more than one occasion, "I want to leave my children enough to do anything they want, but not enough to do nothing."

There is a great debate amongst estate and financial planners regarding how much is enough and when is it too much. The real question you need to answer is what is the money for? Is it to support a lifestyle that you have created for yourself, and which your child expects to continue using your resources? Or is it to enable your child to have the resources with which to choose how to be productive and fulfilled? Ask yourself this question: do you want your child to retire on the date of your death? Before jumping to the answer, consider the implications for your child.

Perhaps the most obvious problem with a trust is that when a child knows he will always receive sufficient money to live comfortably whether he works or not, he may lose motivation to do something constructive with his life. I have seen too many such beneficiaries drifting through life, moving from one activity or vocation to another, leaving unfinished business and unmet ambitions along the way. Particularly for those individuals who will inherit considerable wealth at an early age, money is a challenge to both their character and ingenuity. It is easy to do nothing risky, to take no chances, but the consequence is a life not fully experienced.

In a culture that prizes self-made individuals over those who were not, the young inheritor is often regarded with both contempt and envy. Even worse, however, is that our society tends to define its members by what they do, and a wealthy youngster who doesn't have a purposeful activity loses an important criterion for self-identity.

Guilt is another common problem among trust-fund beneficiaries. Without a sense of having participated in creating the family fortune, the beneficiaries may feel undeserving of this unearned money. The result is that they are denied the feeling of achievement that is so important to their sense of competency and self-esteem. They grow up as adults who are bored with their existence and depressed by a lack of personal self-worth.

Prepare your child. The trust-fund beneficiary may also experience dismay at suddenly being thrust into such a position of financial responsibility. Many affluent children confess that, despite knowing in advance of their trust fund, they had little understanding as to the extent to which this new income would disrupt their lives. They often admit they were totally ignorant of their financial situation, until the actual day when the money was transferred to them, at which point they were traumatized by the myriad details and decisions with which they were confronted.

If your child is going to be the recipient of a trust, you do him or her no favors by hiding the reality and ignoring the consequences. When your child is a teenager, it is perfectly appropriate to let the child know that, should anything happen to you, as parents, you've taken care to be sure that there will be enough to get him or her started in life, including college and graduate school, and maybe some help to buy that first home. This is an easy way to begin the discussion about what a trust is, who will be responsible as a trustee to take care of the funds, and what's expected of your child. It enables you to break the ice and to talk about the realities of death.

As a young adult, your child should be given even more instruction and exposure, including meeting the advisors with whom you are working and to whom you have entrusted your planning. At some point, these professionals may be called upon to interface directly with your child. It would be very healthy to begin that relationship early and continue it throughout your life.

Design the Trust to Empower, Not Disable. A trust does not have to undermine your child's efforts or enthusiasm. Designed well, it can facilitate, encourage, and reward hard work, self-sufficiency, and good character. Designed improperly, it can create dependency, indolence, and frustration. In part, the task is to manage your child's expectations. You don't want the child to grow up with the belief that you are merely holding on to wealth that belongs to him.

During the school years, the trust should provide the resources needed to support the child, whether for basic necessities or to maintain a comfortable lifestyle, which is the least disruptive and most reassuring. But should the child choose to leave school before finishing, or to use the school as a crutch to maintain a steady income, without reciprocal effort, the promise of support can be revoked just as quickly.

When school is over, and this could include graduate school technical or vocational school, or special education, the trustee should be encouraged, perhaps required, to curtail the distributions. There's always a need for some transition or "bridge" between the school years and the work years. But the time for transition should be limited and defined. No one should be able to coast for very long.

Avoid the temptation to start the regular flow of income or regular distributions of principal at age 21, or anytime during the early career building years. This may mean up to age 35 or 40.

These early years represent a critical period for the young adult to create financial autonomy apart from the family, and to establish a career and business path.

There are important exceptions to this principle, of course. The child could really use help with a down payment on a home, but the home should be one that the child can truly afford. This usually means that, after a down payment of 25% or 30%, the child is able to service the debt of a home loan from his earned income. The child should not depend on the trust to provide the income, or it will simply shift the responsibility for maintaining the lifestyle of your young adult from himself to you. Your child should not expect to move into the big house on the hill, just because you lived there. A dangerous expectation is that they will begin their lives where you left off.

Other exceptions include funds to help the child go into business, or to assure adequate funding for emergency healthcare. You may even want to supplement the child's income for very good reasons, such as the child is or becomes physically or mentally incapacitated, or perhaps has gone into a worthy public service, such as teaching or charitable work, and cannot afford to live comfortably at the salary that such important and noble efforts are able to pay. This type of help certainly won't undermine the child's character, but rather will reward him for effort that you believe is worthy and appropriate.

Some parents want to encourage financially productive work by creating matching funds through the trust. Earn a dollar; receive a distribution of a dollar. But be careful, don't put too much emphasis on how much the child earns. Rather, focus on the child's efforts, energy, and passion. These are the qualities that assure personal fulfillment, not the size of the W-2 at the end of the year.

At some point, perhaps by age 35 or 40, the child will be ready for distributions. Start gradually, distributing a portion (maybe 25%) at the first round, so that the child becomes familiar with the size of the unrestricted wealth. More can come over time.

Remember that a child unprepared to manage wealth at 25, with no further training or experience, will not become automatically smarter at 35. So, use the interval to continue the financial

competency training we talked about earlier. Require your trustee
to use some of the funds for this training. Give your adult child the
right to co-trustee with a professional or other experienced fiduci-
ary, who is serving as trustee. This is the best way to groom the
child for this responsibility, and will be your best assurance that
unrestricted access to the trust principal will not be wasted or
dissipated.

Encourage Social Conscience and Family Philanthropy. The wealth
creator is often concerned about creating family legacy. How will
he or she be remembered and what will this wealth say about the
family through the generations? It seems clear to most observers
that how you spend your wealth tells more about you than how
you earned it. If you ask most people what they remember about
Andrew Carnegie, they would likely tell you "libraries". Few today
remember the tough capitalist that owned steel mills and fought
against the unions. Carnegie's legacy is assured through his
thoughtful and perpetual philanthropy.

Affluent parents can also help their children overcome the
potential of "trust-fund guilt" by encouraging philanthropic activity. The Vanguard Public Foundation's publication, *Robin Hood
Was Right*, describes the feelings of guilt, embarrassment, and fear
of other people's envy shared by many young inheritors. This particular foundation and others, such as the Haymarket and Liberty
Hill Foundation, are comprised of groups of young, wealthy inheritors who are dealing with creating a positive sense of self by involving themselves in giving to what they describe as alternative philanthropy. These represent organizations dedicated to increased
social justice and a fairer distribution of wealth and power.

The dramatic rise of private foundations, often called family
foundations because of their control by family members, is only
partially a function of the growth of accumulated wealth. It also
reflects the growing recognition that an important family value is
philanthropy. A foundation can become the platform from which
the wealth creator, children, and future generations, express their
core values, their most passionate concerns, and their sense of

community. It can serve as the family enterprise through many generations, functioning in some respects like the family business. Unlike most family businesses, however, that last for one or two generations, the family foundation and the tradition of family philanthropy can and should last forever, or as long as family members care to respect their heritage, and have the interest, time, and training to work together.

Maintain an Attitude of Openness

Jamie Johnson, the 23-year-old great-grandson of the founder of Johnson & Johnson we spoke of previously, observed in his documentary *Born Rich* (which aired on HBO in November, 2003):

"My parents never sat me down and said, 'you're rich'". I was 10 years old. I was in fourth grade. During a free reading period in the library, a kid in my class found my dad's name in a copy of *Forbes* magazine with a list of the 400 richest people in America and my name was found. The kid read the article aloud to the whole class. Everyone including my teacher ran over to check it all out for themselves. It was strange, all my friends and me finding out at the same time how rich my family was. I felt like I was learning a secret I wasn't supposed to know."

Many parents try to hide or deny their own wealth, and don't want their children to know that there is substantial wealth set aside for them. They fear the effect of such information on their effort and work ethic. If they don't tell the kids, they delude themselves, maybe the kids won't know. They accept this premise, despite the fact that they have several expensive homes, no one is working, the private jet is always available, and vacations end just before the next one begins.

Researcher, John Levy, who spent five years interviewing wealthy parents, heirs, and psychologists for his study, "Coping with Inherited Wealth," has noted one experience that seems to distinguish those who function well with inherited wealth from those who don't: the parents have dealt with money issues openly and straightforwardly with the children.

Unfortunately, Levy's research found that few inheritors actually had the benefit of this openness with their parents. "If the wealth and its eventual transmission to the children are dealt with covertly by the parents," Levy warns, "children are apt to sense the money as something dark and shameful. This makes it more unlikely that they will ever be comfortable about the money itself or about themselves as inheritors."

As Levy suggests, "Parents should keep their growing children aware of some of the pitfalls and problems associated with wealth, particularly by drawing their attention to individuals and families who are handling their money and position especially well or badly."

An important aspect of this openness also includes, as your children become more able and interested, discussions with you on the kinds of obligations and ethical issues that accompany affluence. This will allow them to see their capital as carrying with them certain responsibilities in the society in which they live.

The ability to deal successfully with money is one of the primary survival skills that a child needs to master. Whether one day your child will earn his way or will be in the position to make important decisions about handling inherited funds, learning to manage finances is critical to responsible adulthood.

Effective parents develop a systematic program for educating their children in the area of money management. In these families, money will never become the root of all evil but will be regarded as a valued asset.

Step Nine: Practicing Effective Discipline

Learning how to discipline intelligently, firmly, and compassion-
ately is one of the great tasks of parenting. The challenge of this
task is heightened by the personal involvement that each parent
brings to discipline. Questions such as, Will I destroy my child's
love for me?, Can I cause deep-seated emotional damage?, How
can I keep my temper under control?, and, What kind of parent
must I be if I permit my children to behave in defiant, insolent
ways? are but a few that parents are forced to answer. Additionally,
this subject often brings back painful memories of how discipline
was handled in the parent's own family.

For many generations, the well-known adage, "spare the rod
and spoil the child" gave parents a very specific guide to discipline.
This philosophy had its roots in the view that people possessed
some inherent badness that could most effectively be removed
through physical punishment, by literally beating the devil out of
the person. Thus, the theory went, if one could get rid of all the evil
during childhood, boys and girls would grow up to be conscientious, responsible, law-abiding citizens.

Some parents took this to the extreme—the more punitive the
process, the greater the cleansing of the soul. As a result, many
youngsters spent their childhood years enduring fear and pain.

Later, as parents, they inflicted this same harsh treatment upon their own children, and so the cycle was perpetuated.

Fortunately, today we have come to place greater emphasis upon the power of human beings to make positive choices through encouragement and support. The parental goal has thus shifted from beating to helping children develop a sound foundation of self-esteem with which to facilitate their maturation into responsible, self-disciplined adults. Although our culture has yet to eliminate completely the paddle-happy philosophy of child rearing, this type of discipline does not have the social support that once existed. Child-protection laws now protect most children from brutal physical abuse.

The paddle had, and still has, a strong attraction for parents because it's an easy answer. Without a rod, many parents feel at a loss for a workable system of discipline. In fact, the discipline issue is one of the most frequent concerns in my parenting programs. And yet, knowing the widespread interest in this subject, I have purposely saved this chapter for the end of the book. If you have been able to apply the techniques of the preceding chapters and are:

- Actively involved in enhancing your child's self-esteem
- Taking steps to insure your limited time together with your child is quality time
- Ensuring that others involved with your children follow the same rules as you have set
- Looking continually for ways to be encouraging
- Listening and communicating effectively
- Avoiding rudeness with your children as you would with a friend or colleague
- Resisting the temptation to take the path of least resistance by overindulging your child
- Setting realistic limits and being consistent about enforcing them
- Looking for ways in every aspect of your child's life to make that child feel competent and responsible

Then, I know you will be able to maintain the "house rules" without discipline becoming a major problem in your home. Still, for those times when the behavior of your children remains unacceptable, we will examine the issue of discipline and determine what are the most effective techniques you can apply.

Defining Enlightened Discipline

The word discipline comes from a Latin origin meaning, "to make a disciple of"—that is, a pupil who is being instructed. The majority of dictionary meanings refer, in fact, to the instructional and training sense of this word. In this broader context, discipline becomes a method for teaching children proper social conduct, and not, as it is more frequently used, to refer to methods of punishment and means of control.

The true goal of discipline should be for children to internalize a code of personal ethics in which they choose for themselves not to engage in unacceptable or inappropriate acts because they realize the value to everyone of thoughtful and compassionate behavior.

The Importance of Family Rules

The family is the starting point for learning discipline in the sense we have defined it. Just as every social organization needs rules to govern the behavior of the members of its group, effective families are no different; they need to establish rules to guide their children's behavior within the home and outside it. Discipline can not occur in a vacuum; without rules, your house of discipline lacks a supporting structure. You cannot discipline your children without having them first know what the rules are.

I won't presume to tell you specifically what your family rules should be. Whatever rules you establish, however, should serve the purpose of helping your child to learn self-regulatory behavior. Young children do not naturally impose controls on themselves. They are driven by an infinite curiosity and must be taught what can be harmful to themselves and others and what pleases as well as displeases the adults around them. They must learn to deal with the frustration of not getting their way and how to express anger in an acceptable manner. Even when children openly do not agree with your rules, they must accept certain regulations as a cooperative member of the family system.

Although you may have been brought up to believe that fear of parents can control behavior, fear is not an emotion by which parents should regulate their children's actions. Effective discipline occurs when the child himself makes the choice to behave in an appropriate manner rather than merely responding to the parental threat "Do it just because I said so!" or "Do it or you'll be very sorry!" Instead, the child must feel "I choose to do this because I understand the rules." Furthermore, the moment a feared adult is out of sight and out of mind, children will resume an unwanted behavior.

As children grasp the regulations of their home environment, they will begin to feel increasingly secure and able to control their naturally impulsive behavior. Throughout childhood development, these initial rules then become the foundation upon which the child continually builds. These internalized rules and regulations allow a child to function successfully in the larger world outside the immediate family.

Without rules and balanced guidance from parents, a child can suffer traumatic consequences. On one hand, the undisciplined child will constantly create stress, frustration, and anger in relationships with the adults in his life, and may grow into adulthood at risk for serious behavioral problems. On the other hand, the overly disciplined child may interpret constant parental punishment as rejection and the loss of love, which in turn may cause the child to increase what was previously only a marginally unacceptable behavior. For this child, if a vicious cycle of acting-out, punishment and more acting-out persists, the child will ultimately develop a very low self-esteem and be equally at risk for serious behavioral problems.

Affluent children who have not learned to conform to the rules of the family will have little respect for the rules of the world. These are the children I saw in the school environment with a chip on their shoulder, continually trying to manipulate the system for their own benefit. They constantly have excuses and justifications for operating outside the system. Rules, they seem to believe, are made for others. Lacking a respect for the rights of others, poorly disciplined children are often rejected by other students and become isolated and lonely, thereby intensifying their selfish and egocentric feelings. Defying the legal rules of society can become a logical next step, placing these youngsters at risk for involvement in delinquent activities, both as teens and as adults.

In affluent families, certain personality characteristics can significantly influence the manner in which discipline is handled. Many individuals have reached successful positions in their lives because they were not conformists. They were the risk takers, mavericks, rebels—those individuals who were not above breaking or at least bending the established rules of society in their drive toward personal success.

Although this type of parent may verbally acknowledge a desire to have his or her children behaving in the most socially appropriate manner, at an unconscious level this very parent will reinforce the more nonconforming actions of his child. When I conferred with parents regarding problematic behavior on the part of a child, such as challenging the authority of school personnel, refusing to complete certain school requirements, and aggressively dealing with peers, I often heard a parent admit in an overly apologetic manner, "I can understand what is happening because I was just like that when I was a child." The message that is revealed in this admission is that in some way, often without the parents' awareness, this problematic behavior is being positively reinforced at home since the parent identifies it with his or her own success. In order to help the child make the appropriate changes, it is necessary for the parents to become more sensitized to the messages that are being communicated.

On the other hand, many affluent parents have achieved their position because they took control of their lives as well as the activities of those around them. These individuals will deal with their family in the same manner expecting unquestioning compliance to all the rules that they establish.

Establishing an effective discipline system necessitates sensitivity to these personality characteristics. Additionally, it requires parenting time, consistency in application, patience, a sense of mutual respect between parents and children, and the ability to not overreact to an unpleasant situation. If affluent, high-achieving parents do not assimilate these important characteristics, their ability to utilize discipline as a successful teaching tool becomes seriously weakened.

Discipline Styles

The methods by which a parent ensures that a child will learn the family rules can vary considerable. These differing approaches fall under three generally recognized categories: autocratic, permissive, and effective.

The Autocratic Parent

Very few people wish to recognize themselves in the following scenario; unfortunately, in only slightly modified versions, I see this style of discipline all the time.

As the clock approaches 6:30 P.M., the tension can be felt in the Harris family as the mother and children scurry about to make sure that everything is in order before Mark Harris's return from a hectic working day as CEO of a rapidly expanding manufacturing corporation.

This father has very decisively indicated what he expects of the children. Both Jessica and Todd know that the evening will begin with an inspection of their homework and probably an angry tirade if it has not been completed to their father's satisfaction. Mark's wife, Susie, is hoping that today was a good day at the office, because Mark's temper is always more volatile when the day has been stressful. She is anxious to avoid the angry abuse that often occurs with even a minor infraction of the family "rules." She is also worried about the information she received from Todd's teacher today during their parent conference. Should she discuss it with her husband and deal with his reaction, or just say nothing and try to handle the problem by herself?

Susie wishes that Todd felt closer to his father so that they could mutually discuss the difficulties he is currently experiencing. However, she is well aware of her children's ability to keep busy with their activities in order to limit their interaction with their father when he is home. Frankly she cannot blame them. Mark's controlling attitude and punitive behavior make everyone feel stressed and anxious.

Parents who have experienced success and financial rewards in the world often use this autocratic approach to discipline, believing that they are the ultimate authority of what is best for the lives of others. In this approach, a child's duty is to obey—and as quickly as possible. The autocratic parent is never wrong, and any challenge to his position provokes anger and reproach. Physical and emotional punishment is the autocratic parent's most readily used tools.

The autocratic parent does not feel comfortable unless he is in control of everything. Since such total control is virtually impossible to maintain all the time, this type of parent frequently feels frustrated and irritated, and often functions in an agitated emotional state when things aren't going well.

Interacting with children from a controlling frame of mind puts the autocratic parent in the position of reacting rather than acting. This type of spontaneous reaction precludes the time for thought and planning and will never render the most effective parenting approach. This parent finds himself lashing out at even the slightest infraction of the rules, and behaving in a manner that creates unhappiness in the family and guilt in himself.

Autocratic parents are individuals who are accustomed to relating to others with a win-lose mentality—and they must be on the winning side. Winning, in their mind, means maintaining control and satisfying their own demands, and they constantly push others until they get their way.

But the win-lose mentality, which may work in the market place, does not translate well to parenting. Autocratic parenting produces an outcome in which everyone loses. The effect of this kind of discipline on the child can be gravely detrimental and its punitive response frequently reinforces the unacceptable behavior it is meant to discourage. While a spanking might temporarily cause the behavior to stop, parents with an autocratic style often report having to repeat the spanking over and over because nothing seems to work.

In the end, autocratic discipline not only fails to teach children to understand the logic of rules, it may also teach that violence is a way of dealing with conflict. Countless studies have found that children who are disciplined with physical force have a far greater propensity for violent behavior than children who are not. In extreme cases, the children grow up to retaliate against their parents.

One of the greatest fallacies in all relationships is the belief that we can control someone else. Psychologists who are privy to the otherwise untold stories of their clients hear again and again of the extraordinary deceptions of which people who feel themselves to be overly controlled are capable. Except in rare cases, trying to control is a dangerous mistake leading, in marriages, to affairs and divorce and, in child-rearing, to animosity and revolt.

The Permissive Parent

Life in the Smith family is quite different than at the Harris's. Both Mr. and Mrs. Smith are successful professionals, and when they return home, they do not want to be disciplinarians, but prefer to enjoy their children.

Tonight, fifteen-year-old Liz wants to go to a party at her friend's house. Since it's the middle of the week, her father tells her that she will have to save her socializing for the weekend. But Liz is familiar with her parents' weak resolve, and so she immediately begins badgering her father to let her go out "just this once!" Without much effort, she changes her father's mind, promising to get up early in the morning to do her homework.

Seven-year-old Mikey has been glued to the television set most of the evening. Although it is now his designated bedtime, he begs to watch one more program, and here again rather than argue, the Smith's give in.

The permissive approach to discipline is characterized by both the lack of clear rules and the lack of consistency in enforcing them. Just as autocratic discipline can create negative repercussions, children raised in homes that operate with inconsistent discipline will also experience problems.

When rules are not consistent, children respond in a variety of ways. Some become fearful and anxious because they do not know what to expect or what their limits are. Frightened of their own impulses, which they are struggling to control, they may become angered at the adults in their lives who do not seem dependable and protective.

Other children, discovering that they can change the rules if they badger enough, will develop the skill of argumentation into an art form. I have heard permissive parents complain, "My kid won't take no for an answer." But why should they? Permissive inconsistency has taught these children a clear message: If you put up enough of a fuss, Mom or Dad will become worn down and capitulate to your demands.

Parents who operate in this discipline style often find themselves talking and talking to children who appear to have hearing problems. I have observed many intelligent adults lecturing, directing, and advising but getting little if any response from their children. There's nothing wrong with the ability of these children to comprehend the English language; they have simply learned from experience that there will be no consequence if they do not follow the rules.

The inconsistency of permissiveness is often seen in affluent homes where there are or have been many caregivers, each with his or her own disciplinary philosophy and without guidance from a definitive set of household rules. The child in this situation, unable to adjust to the ever-changing sets of rules, eventually stops trying and acts on his own volition.

A family system that may create the similar effects of inconsistency is the existence of strong disagreements between parents. For example, Dad makes rules that Mom feels are inappropriate, and so they undermine each other's authority by creating a double standard: one for when Dad is home, the other for when he is not. Or, conversely, Dad may feel that Mom is too strict and openly criticizes her in front of the children, thereby letting them know of the conflict and hinting of their ability to take advantage of it.

Like the autocratic style, the permissive approach to discipline seems to be that of a win-lose situation. In this case, it is generally the child who appears to be winning by getting his way, while the parents have lost in their ability to maintain family rules. But in fact, the child has lost the opportunity to develop internal controls and the ability to deal appropriately with the rules of society. This is more appropriately a lose-lose scenario.

The Balanced Parent

It is Thursday night and the Ryans have just convened the weekly family meeting. Sixteen-year-old Tessa Ryan wishes to discuss her curfew time, which she feels is too restrictive. Tessa has been involved in numerous school and social activities, and she has compiled a list of upcoming events for which she feels a change in her predetermined curfew time is necessary.

Acknowledging that Tessa has been responsible in meeting her curfew obligations for the past six months and that she has presented a logical justification for additional privileges in a mature and responsible manner, Mr. and Mrs. Ryan agree to extend the time on those evenings that involve a special activity. They agree as well to give her an extra half-hour on Saturday nights. Tessa will still be responsible for informing her parents of the location of the events she attends as well as all transportation arrangements.

This type of approach is indicative of effective discipline because it is a win-win solution for everyone. Tessa feels like a winner because she is able to communicate in an honest manner and is involved in the decision-making process. The Ryans also feel they have won; they have communicated with their daughter in a calm, unemotional manner and still have been able to establish rules for behavior that they are confident will be followed.

In short, effective discipline occurs when parents trust and respect the ideas of their children and allow them to participate in establishing the family rules. If a child feels respected for his contributions, and knows that he participated in the formation of the rules that will guide his daily life, he will likewise respect those rules with a minimum of anger or defiance. The mutuality of effective discipline enables the family system to operate in a more harmonious manner.

Of the three discipline styles, this balanced, cooperative approach is obviously the model conscientious parents should utilize. To make the first step in changing your past behaviors, the following guidelines will help you develop a more effective discipline program. This program will involve establishing clear rules for the operation of the family after having received as much input as possible from all family members involved. Once the rules have been determined and articulated to everyone, both parents must then agree upon what action to take if the rules are broken. This action must also be clearly spelled out to the entire family as well as to any surrogate child caregivers so that everyone will respond in the same manner.

Distinguish Between the A and B Rules

Many parents tend to treat rules as rules, and enforce every regulation in the same strict manner. However, effective discipline involves recognizing two different levels of family regulations. One level may be considered the A rules. These are the absolutely essential rules about which there is no negotiation. The second, or B level, might be considered "wants." These are behaviors that you might want your child either to do or to not do, but on which you have some flexibility. These B rules actually serve a purpose. Because part of a child's development process is the testing of their actions against some parental regulations, this area of wants allows you to maintain discipline without unrealistically expecting your children to behave perfectly.

For example, there is a vast difference between playing football near the flower beds versus playing near the swimming pool, although you may certainly want neither. But the latter is a potentially dangerous matter, and therefore needs to be emphasized and enforced as an A rule. You might not respond as strongly to an infringement of the rule regarding playing by the flowers, and thus this becomes a B level request.

Another example of an A rule might be coming home right after school unless other arrangements have been agreed upon. A B request may be keeping his or her room neat and tidy at all times.

Parents who have not differentiated in their own minds between A rules and B rules will find themselves in conflict with their children too much of the time. To avoid this, concentrate on your A list and maintain consistency on these points. You can then be more flexible with the B list, permitting some negotiation in these areas. Such give and take with your child can help immeasurably in eliminating continual power struggles.

Differentiate Feelings from Actions

Effective discipline also requires that parents understand the difference between their child's feelings and actions. Parents frequently try to discipline a child's feelings when they run counter to their own wishes. But feelings, whatever they may be, are a natural part of human experience. Since we do not want our children to feel ashamed of their feelings or to repress them, no matter what they are, they should be acknowledged and accepted as being real and valid, not punished.

Negative actions, however, should not be accepted. By making your child accountable for what he does, while at the same time demonstrating respect for his feelings, you will teach him to control his impulses and to understand that he can feel anger, jealousy, and other emotions parents would often like to deny in their children (as well as in themselves) without acting it out by hurting others.

An example of this would be permitting a young child to verbally declare to his parents, "I hate you!" Parents in my workshops admit that this statement often causes them to have a strong emotional reaction, resulting in a punishment for their child. However, this statement should be accepted for what it actually represents to a young child: not a deep feeling of hatred, but merely a response to the feeling of being angered and frustrated in some manner by his parents. This and similar verbal expressions should be accepted without punishment. But if a child then tries to act out the feeling by physically assaulting the parents or a sibling, such actions must swiftly be curtailed and a consequence forthcoming.

Another example is the child who does not like school and verbalizes his feelings about it. Here too your child has a right to express his feelings without retaliation or a sarcastic retort from you. In this type of situation the use of reflective listening would be useful to help determine the specifics of why the child is unhappy. Following this clarification, you can then proceed to try active problem-solving, outlined in Chapter 5. But whatever the child's reasons, parents have an equal right to insist that the child must still follow the rules of a conscientious student and participate within the classroom in an appropriate manner.

Remain Focused on the Problematic Behavior

Effective discipline focuses on inappropriate behavior, not character assassinations of the child's person. Excluding those cases of severe physical abuse, the most significant, long-lasting damage that occurs to a child is in the form of psychological and emotional abuse. When a child is continually told that he or she is horrible, stupid, lazy, bad, miserable to be around or some other such personal insult, the child will eventually come to believe that these character assassinations are, in fact, a basic part of his or her character and may then even begin to act out that assigned part. An occasional physical spanking will not have the long-lasting harmful consequences of the repeated verbal spanking.

This is the reason it is important for parents to stay focused on the specific action of which they disapprove and completely avoid character commentary. Instead of berating the sloppiness and stupidity of the child who has spilled cereal on the living-room rug, effective discipline would focus upon the unacceptable behavior: eating in the living room when the house rules stated that food could not be taken from the kitchen. In this case, a consequence would be appropriate, such as making the child thoroughly clean the carpet.

Say Yes As Often As Possible

Parents tend to be quicker to reply to their children with the word *no* rather than *yes*. This pattern of response can often *cause* discipline problems rather than solve them.

Imagine you are busy making dinner when your ten-year-old runs in to ask if he can ride his bike down the street to visit with his friend. Glancing at your watch, you realize that dinner will be ready in half an hour, and so you quickly say "no". Your child then pleads his case, promising to be back in twenty minutes, and so you find yourself struggling to maintain your original position. Your child will then increase his verbal argument, probably wearing you down until you finally agree to let him go.

The trouble with frequent "no" interactions is that you are in danger of conditioning your child to be argumentative and difficult. When a parent denies a child's wishes too often and too quickly, the child will soon learn to present challenges, which are often quite logical, to the parent's authority. Encouraging your child's reasoning abilities is important, but the context for this should not be at the expense of discipline. When children learn that they can argue and carry on enough to wear you down to the point of capitulation to their demands, they will not respect the rules. Saying yes to their requests more often in fact allows you to avoid such no-win interactions.

For many parents, of course, saying yes often means breaking a longstanding automatic habit. In my seminars, I advise parents that whenever they receive a request from their child, they might counter their natural tendency by silently counting to ten while asking themselves: "Is there any possible way that I could say yes to this request?" Anytime you can say yes (either to an entire request or to a part thereof), do it.

In fact, by saying yes whenever possible, you strengthen the authority and validity of your no's. When your child realizes that you give considered thought to your responses, he will be less likely to argue or try to change a no for which you now have sound reasons. This simple change will go a long way in helping you set limits in a fair, firm, and consistent manner, demonstrating some of the basic tenants of effective discipline.

Avoid the Question "Why?"

Josh and his younger sister, Lindsay, are sitting on the couch watching television. Josh suddenly leans over and pinches Lindsay, who bursts into tears. Within moments, Mom angrily hovers over the boy, asking the most common first question—Why did you do this?—supposing he has a reason.

The fact is, children often do not know exactly why they have misbehaved, and the reasons can in fact be quite complex. Like adults, children react to various situations based on previous experiences, many of which have been completely repressed into their subconscious. They are aware of what they are doing, but can seldom identify the real motivation behind an action.

In this case, it might be that Josh was unhappy about something that had happened at school—a teacher's scolding or perhaps he was excluded from a game at recess. Whatever the reason, it is unlikely that Josh will be able to correctly articulate the real reason for his aggressiveness. Asking him to do so is almost guaranteed to make him and his mother increasingly frustrated. It is likely that Josh will silently sulk while his mother will interpret his reaction as defiance and intensify her anger.

Some parents, unable to drag a response out of their child, become so unnerved that they not only supply the question but also the answer, as in the following example:

MOM: Why didn't you finish your homework assignment last
night?

CHILD: (Shrugs shoulders in silence.)

MOM: Was it because you still think the teacher is picking on
you or are you still angry because you got benched during your recess yesterday?

CHILD: (grateful for an explanation that will appease his
mother) Yeah, she's always mean and unfair to me.

MOM: I know she has her favorites and that would make me
mad, too. But just try a little harder and maybe she will
change her attitude toward you.

Answering your own why question doubly intensifies the problem. In this case, the parent has not truly verified whether or not
this child's teacher has in fact been picking on him. The child has
learned, however, that blaming the teacher is a good vehicle for
gaining the sympathy of his mother and diverting her from the real
issue, the fact that the homework was not completed.

Effective discipline does not require a parent to know or understand the exact reasons that may have caused a child's misbehavior.
You are not required to play amateur psychologist. What you need
to be concerned with is the specific inappropriate behavior. This is
not to say that a child should not be permitted to verbalize an
explanation if such a causal relationship is clear to him. And in
such cases you will not have to ask for one. Children immediately
present their defenses; they don't have to be asked.

In the above example, Josh might immediately defend his action
by stating that Lindsay kept kicking him and would not stop when
he asked her to stop. Even if this was in fact true (and in most cases
it is one child's word against the other's), does *why* solve the problem at hand?

Since discipline should also help establish a method whereby
the child will learn to make more appropriate decisions and
choices, regardless of how he feels at the moment, parents should
focus on the unacceptable behavior that occurred.

Operate As a Team

Effective discipline requires a unified approach on the part of both parents and surrogate parents. While parents frequently have differences of opinion on issues concerning child-rearing, they must strive toward cooperation when it comes to setting overall goals and creating family rules. When each parent has a different game plan, the child will end up very confused. In order to achieve a unified approach, I recommend the following strategies.

Establish a discipline plan when you are calm and unemotional, well before a crisis has the family in a volatile state. Formalize your system so that it can be executed by employees as well as parents, thus creating greater consistency for the child.

Consider the discipline models of your own childhood. Each parent invariably is a reflection of his upbringing. For example, adults who were physically punished as children have a high risk of being abusive parents themselves unless they undergo psychological counseling and learn alternative discipline techniques.

Examine the general state of your family system. If you and your spouse handle discipline in opposite ways, rather than arguing over whose approach is superior, search together for an acceptable compromise. As mentioned above, if you feel that the approach of your spouse is either too easy or too harsh and therefore respond in the opposite manner to even out the effect, your child will only end up frustrated and very skilled at playing one parent against the other.

Arriving at a compromise is often easier said than done. Compromise over such issues often necessitates the use of a neutral mental health professional who can help you develop an effective program by objectively incorporating the strongest features from both of your approaches. This type of help is readily available from community mental health clinics as well as through the use of private practitioners. Your family physician and local school are excellent referral sources.

With or without a neutral third party, it is of paramount importance for each parent to listen as nondefensively as possible to the ideas of the other. If either spouse feels conspired against in any way, he or she may act, without even fully realizing it, in a manner that sabotages the established discipline plan. Only through compromise can you create a win-win situation in which each partner feels validated because their points of view were considered in developing the overall plan.

In cases where parents are in disagreement over disciplinary action, one should not interfere with the action of the other in front of the child—unless not intervening will cause the child to suffer serious physical or emotional harm. In general, the time to resolve differences in how a disciplinary action is enacted is during a calm and private discussion after the heat of the battle has dissipated and emotions have had a chance to subside.

Communicate often and extensively with your spouse. Be alert to the technique children may use of going behind the back of the more restrictive parent to obtain permission from the more lenient one. Decisions made by one parent should be respected by the other—unless one parent is acting in a destructive and inappropriate manner.

The Key Tool to Effective Discipline:
Consequences

Currently, the most typical method of discipline involves punishment and reward. When a child disobeys the rules of the family, some type of punishment will occur, often, unfortunately, in a physical form such as hitting, slapping, or spanking. When a child behaves in an outstanding manner, he is rewarded. Sometimes parents may wish to encourage a specific behavior and so offer rewards in the form of a bribe: if you do this you will receive that. A common example of this is the practice of paying children a specific sum of money for the number of A's they receive on their report card.

However, this traditional reward-punishment approach has many drawbacks. Punishment implies a situation in which the parents are overpowering the child. But children today are being raised with a greater sense of their importance and power. Even if this message is not directly communicated within the family system, the child's importance and independence is encouraged in school as well as being represented in the television and film media. They will be more resistant, therefore, to the position of "obey me or else." Effective discipline needs to incorporate mutual respect and cooperation.

It is widely recognized in both academic circles as well as within the business community that the greater the degree of participation in an activity or decision, the more effective the learning and the more committed the participant will be toward supporting the process. A traditional system of arbitrary rewards and punishments places the child in the position of being merely the recipient of either the parents' favor or displeasure. However, it is possible to create a discipline program that permits the child to become involved in establishing family rules as well as determining what will happen if the rules are broken. The child will then be in the position of making choices and knowing objectively what the outcome of a positive or negative choice will be. In this way, the end result is not unilaterally imposed by a dominating parent. The child learns to assume responsibility for the outcome since it was his or her own choice of behavior.

The traditional punishment system is also quite limited, as parents generally use only a small repertoire of available punishments (restrictions, spankings), and these are usually not specifically related to the problem behavior. The child, therefore, does not truly experience a natural and meaningful cause-effect relationship between the behavior and the result of the behavior.

Punishment is usually done in anger, using either character assassination, such as name-calling, or the threat of loss of love. The effects on a child's self-esteem can be devastating. When parents demand compliance from their children without their understanding, they are implementing an authoritarian style of behavioral control.

A system of rewards and punishments also dictates that positive behavior will automatically receive some type of external reward. This attitude fails to recognize the basic desire of most children to please the important adults in their lives and to feel that they are an important part of the family, and that the ability to be competent and useful is its own reward. Children, who learn to exhibit appropriate behavior only because there is a tangible reward in it for them, are denied the feeling of a sense of worthiness by being a cooperative and contributing member of the family.

Our changing culture calls for corresponding changes in discipline. Although parents still have the responsibility for setting limits and controlling the inappropriate behavior of their children, and although the means for doing so may be much harder to apply than a simple punishment-reward system, they must nevertheless adopt a more enlightened and effective system: the use of consequences.

The Power of Consequences

A consequence differs from a punishment in that it is directly related to the action in either a natural or a logical manner. Consequences permit children to assume the responsibility for their choices, to learn form both their successes and failures, and to cultivate techniques for regulating their own behavior. When parents use this approach, there is no need for angry expletives, threats, or character assassinations because their disciplinary actions flow directly from the misbehavior. Though its implications are quite profound, this principle is, on the surface, very simple: a child must learn that every action produces a response, or consequence, which may be positive, negative, or a little of both.

When an adult is about to take an action, he or she will generally try to imagine its potential consequences, using common sense and prior experience. By analyzing these possibilities, the adult is able to decide whether the positives sufficiently out-weigh the negatives, and then, based upon that equation, whether or not to take the action.

In the same way, children can learn a great deal about behavior by experiencing the consequences that result from their actions. If they are rude, they will learn that they can provoke anger or even the cessation of a relationship. Similarly, not studying for a mid-term examination is likely to result in a poor grade.

Unfortunately, in families of considerable affluence, money often buys away the consequences. If the child breaks a toy or loses something, the parents may simply buy another one. If he is failing in school, the parent may hire tutors to spoon feed answers so that the child passes. If the child commits an act of delinquency, it is often taken care of by attorneys so that no criminal charges are pressed. As a result of such parental intervention, many affluent children can grow up without a healthy exposure to the cause-effect relationship so fundamental to human life. To avoid this trap, you need to understand and apply two different kinds of consequences, natural and logical, which can help you make the transition to a meaningful disciplinary style that will allow your children to grow up into responsible, competent, and respectful adults.

Natural Consequences

Natural consequences are the result of the natural evolution of a situation. If you go out in the winter without a coat, you are cold. If you do not eat, you are hungry. If you do not get enough sleep, you are tired. If you put your hand into a fire, you get burned.

While parents must protect their children from some natural consequences—such as putting their hand on a hot stove or playing on a busy street—there are many natural consequences you should allow your child to experience even though you would prefer that the child never suffer the pain involved. An example follows.

Mealtime in the Brown family had become an unpleasant, stressful experience. Both children, Haley and Ryan, were fussy eaters, complaining about everything that was served and barely eating anything. Throughout each meal, their mother urged them to clean their plates. When they did not obey, they were physically punished or banished to their rooms for the remainder of the evening, or their father became furious and left the table in a rage.

In this same situation, Mr. and Mrs. Brown could more calmly utilize natural consequences with their children by giving them the following choices:

- They may join their parents at the table if they do not complain about the food and can eat in an appropriate manner.
- Or they can leave the table and wait to eat until the next meal.

The Browns would have to ensure that their children do not snack so that they experience the natural consequence of their non-eating choice—hunger. Once experienced, the children almost certainly would make the choice to return to the table and behave appropriately. Mealtime then would become a positive family experience.

When applying natural consequences, parents should remain calm and controlled. Adding negative commentary or character attacks will only make their children experience the consequences as if they were punishments. In the Browns' case, if Haley and her brother complain later that evening of hunger, their mother and father must resist the urge to say "I told you so." They must simply express an understanding of their children's hunger, and remind them that they have choices to make. If they are not feeling hungry, they can make a better choice for themselves at the next meal. The key element in applying natural consequences is for parents not to intercede and protect the child from fully experiencing the effect of his behavior.

Logical Consequences

In some situations, natural consequences are obviously not possible. A parent cannot, for example, let a child learn about the natural consequences of playing in the street by permitting the child to become injured by a passing car. Logical consequences, however, *are* appropriate here, in that they likewise follow a cause-effect relationship. If your child is expected to play in the yard but has gone into the street, the logical consequence would be that he loses the privilege of play outside and must play indoors until he chooses to refrain from the inappropriate behavior. The following are three examples of instances in which logical consequences would be appropriate and effective.

Toddlers. Kelsey's over-abundance of toys is scattered around her room as well as cluttering up the family room. Though her mother has continually reminded Kelsey to put her things away, Kelsey has not. Kelsey knows that every morning the housekeeper will put everything back in its proper place. Thus there is no consequence.

It is up to Kelsey's parents to create a logical consequence so that Kelsey can learn to take care of her possessions. The mother can explain that since toys need to be put away after they have been used, she will assume from now on, any toys left in the family room or on the floor of Kelsey's room are items she no longer wants and they consequently will be given away.

The next day, Kelsey's mother finds several toys on the floor of the family room. She collects them, puts them in a box and, despite Kelsey's protestations, and takes them to a shelter for homeless families. Kelsey has learned a valuable lesson about the consequences of her actions or, as in this case, inaction. While she might not immediately assume a greater responsibility for her possessions, she ultimately will learn to do so.

School Children. The morning routine is a daily hassle in the Lieberman's household. Eight-year-old Michael never gets out of bed without constant reminders, and even then he is often late getting dressed and downstairs in time for the car pool. Even with the housekeeper helping him, Michael manages to enjoy his morning game of "slow down" and by the time he leaves, the parents' tempers are already running high.

The natural consequence of this situation might be simply to allow Michael to be late for school, but this is clearly an inconvenience for the parents who would have to drive him, and would certainly be unacceptable to his teacher. In applying the technique of logical consequences, however, the parents would inform Michael that he will be awakened at a reasonable time, but only once and that he is responsible for getting himself ready for school. When the car pool comes, Michael will have to get into the car in whatever state of readiness he finds himself, even if that means riding to school in his pajamas.

The next morning the parents awaken Michael once with a cheerful good morning, but they do not return to his room. Even when he is barely able to find time to gulp down a quick unsatisfying breakfast before having to leave the house holding his comb and brush and shoes and socks, running over the cold ground, the parents do not help him avoid the embarrassment of having to finish dressing in the car or manage the teasing of the other children. Following this experience, Michael is more than likely to be motivated to make the decision to get himself ready on time.

Teens. Prior to receiving his official driver's license, Jordan decided to go for a drive in a friend's car. While he was at the wheel, he collided with the front fender of a parked car, causing damage to his friend's auto.

There are two logical consequences Jordan's parents can implement for his irresponsible behavior. First, he will have to earn the money to pay for car repairs. Secondly, since he broke the law by driving without a license, he will have to wait an extra period of time before he will be permitted to apply for his license. Just as with natural consequences, the key element in creating logical consequences is for parents to allow their child to experience the problems, disappointments, or embarrassments that logically follow the misbehavior.

The Denial of Special Privileges as Consequences

In some situations, there are admittedly no natural or logical consequences for a child's behavior. In these circumstances, however, parents can use the denial of privileges in order to maintain a consistent consequence approach. A child who has acted irresponsibly is denied these special considerations, but a responsible child receives them.

In this approach, the key element is for parents to try to make a logical connection between what they consider responsible behavior and being given special privileges. To do this, it is important that you first begin by clarifying the privileges your child may currently take for granted and so thinks of as necessities. Children from affluent families often grow up believing that having been born somehow entitles them to such items as:

- Designer clothing
- Private bedrooms
- Expensive lunches, dinner, and parties
- New cars or motorcycles
- The latest in sporting equipment
- Personal MP-3 players, cell phones, HD-televisions, DVD players, computers
- Expensive toys
- Extravagant family vacations
- The freedom to invite friends to spend the night or weekend without permission
- Specialized instruction such as music lessons, tennis lessons, dance lessons, and martial arts lessons

By establishing that these are luxuries, not necessities, parents can make having such privileges the consequence of appropriate and responsible behavior. When a child follows the family rules, these privileges may be given in order to reinforce the continuation of the positive behavior. However, if the child behaves in an inappropriate manner for which there may be no true logical consequence; the parents can deny these special considerations.

The effectiveness of such a consequence increases when the privilege is relevant to the child's interest. For example, if the consequence for the misbehavior of a shy, introverted child would be to lose the privilege of attending a birthday party, it may not be effective. On the other hand, not allowing him to participate in an activity of personal interest, such as losing the privilege of watching a favorite DVD, probably would have an impact.

If At First You Don't Succeed

In making the transition to more effective discipline through the use of consequences, parents are often concerned that they are not always acting quickly enough, that there is a delay between their child's misbehavior and the consequences. Instant action, however, is often not the most effective discipline. In fact, feeling the need to act immediately is usually only for the purpose of reducing your own tension and anger. And since, in an angry state, even the most enlightened disciplinarian may be tempted to become punitive, the instant response is often a serious obstruction to effective discipline.

A common roadblock to the consequences approach of discipline is the cleverness of your child. A child may try to sabotage the program by feigning not to care about the consequence a parent implements. For example, Marty has been riding his bike in the street and so his parents have taken away the privilege of using his bicycle for one week. Rather than protest, Marty shrugs and says he doesn't care, pretending that he doesn't like to ride his bike all that much anyway. After a couple of days his mother takes Marty at his word and returns the bike to Marty on the third day. From this experience, Marty may not think twice about misbehaving again since he has learned how to trick his mother.

If you, as a parent, feel confident that a privilege does have meaning to your child, continue to withhold it as a consequence, regardless of your child's expressed disinterest in the privilege. By and large parents know what would be a meaningful consequence for their child and can trust their feelings in this matter. Even if you are wrong in a particular instance, your firmness will be an effective teacher in regard to the consequences your child would really like to avoid.

Choose a Consequence That Can Be Reasonably Implemented

An appropriate consequence is not only one that is the natural or logical ramification of the behavior, but also one that parents can realistically enforce. After all, if you cannot ensure that a consequence is carried through, then there is no consequence. Following are two examples to illustrate this point.

- Several families have been invited over to join the Kirk's for a summer barbecue and swim. Nine-year-old Jeffrey, running around the wet pool deck, ignores his parent's instructions to slow down. Mom enforces a harsh consequence: "If you cannot follow the safety rules of a swimming pool, you'll have to spend the rest of the day inside the house."
- Sixteen-year-old Morgan attends an unchaperoned party and returns home two hours after her designated curfew. Her furious father grounds her from attending any social functions for the next four months.

In both of the above cases, while the use of consequences is warranted, the degree of severity makes each very difficult to ensure. For the rest of the day, Jeffrey badgers his parents to permit him to return to the pool with all the other children and finally his parents relent in order to avoid creating a scene with their guests. Jeffrey learns in this case to become a strong arguer and to wear down parental authority, thereby decreasing the effectiveness of the consequence.

A more appropriate consequence to Jeffrey's stubborn misbehavior might have been to restrict him from the pool for thirty minutes. If he continues to run around the deck when told not to, the period of time out could then be increased to an hour. The meaning of a consequence must be more than just verbal threats. In this case, a thirty-minute restriction can be as effective as an entire day and can be much more readily enforced.

Likewise, in the situation with Morgan, the parents will have a difficult burden in monitoring a four-month grounding period. If they end up not following through, the effectiveness of the consequence is clearly diminished. A more appropriate and realistic consequence would be the loss of privileges for the following weekend or so.

The length of the consequence does not increase its effectiveness. A short consequence, consistently enforced, can in fact be more effective than a longer one that is dropped before it was supposed to end. Time is not the critical element here. It is that action is taken.

A Discipline Checklist

Discipline is an important process in creating an emotionally healthy, self-confident, and responsible young adult. However, its effective application takes thought and planning. If misused, discipline may cause children to grow up frustrated and angry, having poor self-esteem and a psychological dependency upon the controlling, directive, authoritarian figures in their lives. The following summary can serve as a pocket reminder to help affluent parents in this ongoing challenge:

- The goal of discipline is to create a sense of self-discipline within your child, not unquestioned obedience to a dominating power.
- Be sure that your expectations are age-appropriate; children often misbehave because they are placed in situations that are too sophisticated for their developmental state.
- Always pursue a win-win situation.
- Replace the concept of authority with a sense of mutual respect and participation.
- Positives are far more effective than negatives; if you generously reinforce the behavior that pleases you, you will find fewer instances to criticize.

- Develop a unified discipline plan that both parents and any surrogate caregivers can support, so that you have a consistent manner of handling behavioral problems.
- Involve the child in the discipline process before he misbehaves by making clear his choices of action and the possible consequences.
- When misbehavior has occurred, make sure consequences are fair, consistent, and as relevant as possible.
- Follow through on what you say; actions speak much louder than words when it comes to discipline.

Children are untrained and inexperienced. They need parental leadership. Effective discipline will create the learning environment that fosters the development of socially responsible, conscientious adults who are able to exhibit constructive and healthy self-control. In such an environment, everyone is a winner.

Epilogue:
Final Pep Talk

Like many parents, you may feel somewhat overwhelmed or discouraged upon completing a parenting book of this nature. Perhaps you have recognized many of your own attitudes and behaviors and are now concerned with the possible damage that has already occurred to your family system and your child.

Perhaps you are asking yourself: Does my child feel like a valued and responsible member of the family? Did my busy life limit the amount of time I have been able to spend with my children? Do I often respond to those closest to me in an angry, impatient manner? Have the personal high standards that served as such a motivating force in my life become a demoralizing burden on my children? How much positive reinforcement have I contributed to my child? Am I recognizing the individual differences between my children and encouraging the development of their special skills? How consistent and democratic is my discipline approach? Have I given my children a practical understanding about the value of money?

If you are upset that a number of your answers to these questions are not what you want them to be, don't panic. Although the drive for perfection is probably an important part of your makeup, there is no such thing as a perfect parent, and change, learning, and growth are always possible for both you and your child.

Remember that as you love your children, your children want to love you and want to believe that they have the best possible parents. Remember too that they are generally responsive to any positive change you make in your relationship. When you embark on new ways of being and behaving, let them know what you are trying to do and enlist their active cooperation. This can be done by a simple statement such as, "I've realized how little time we have been able to spend together and I want to make a change. Each week let's arrange one special activity that we can do together," or "I realize that I probably have been making too much of an issue about your grades in school. I know that you have been a conscientious student and from now on, let's try to just talk about the school activities that you are enjoying the most."

As you have been reading the nine steps for effective parenting, many of the principles may seem self-evident. "Why didn't I think of that myself?" you might have wondered. You didn't think of these ideas yourself because your current parenting behavior is based on your own parenting background, personal attitudes, and value system, which are an integral part of your personality. Making significant changes in these areas takes time, effort, and practice. Secondly, you are too close to and involved in this issue to be able to step back and objectively evaluate the situation. Often we don't see the forest for the trees.

Many of the solutions to the problems of parenting within an affluent environment may sound easy, but I know that the consistent application is not. You have been accustomed to interacting with people, including your children, in a certain manner for a considerable period of time, and now it will take a reasonable amount of time to change these habitual responses. Although you may be accustomed to responding rapidly, efficiently, and successfully to problems you encounter outside your home, family dynamics cannot be rectified with a mere quick fix. You will need patience, humility, and humor.

The best way to deal with this nine-step program is to concentrate on one or two issues at a time and work out as specific a plan as possible to make the desired changes. When these new behaviors feel more natural, you can turn your attention to additional areas. Do not overwhelm yourself by trying to do everything at once.

Also remember that you are not in this alone. Don't be too proud or frightened to seek professional help if it is needed, just as you would seek out a doctor, lawyer, accountant, or tradesman. A trained mental-health professional may be of use to you from time to time, even if only for a consultation. A few sessions with a mental-health professional may save many angry sessions with your child.

Parents like yourselves, who are willing to spend time reading a parenting book, represent highly motivated, concerned individuals who are trying to provide the best possible environment for your children. I have worked with families like yours and I know of the sincerity of your love and devotion for your family, and how it is sometimes difficult to express this in the most effective manner. You have achieved the success you now enjoy because of your ability to apply your considerable talents, energy, and commitment toward specific goals. I feel confident that as you master the information in this nine-step program, you can utilize these same skills toward creating a psychologically nurturing and supportive family system in which each member can become the best that he or she can be. The joy you will receive from watching your children become successful, emotionally healthy young men and women will be well worth all the effort you devote to this important challenge.

Resources for Parents

In addition to references in the text, the following books and articles may be of interest in elaborating issues presented in this book.

Albert, Linda and Michael Popkin, *Quality Parenting* (New York: Random House, 1987). Excellent information on how to implement quality time in a variety of situations.

Aldrich, Nelson W. Jr., *Old Money* (New York: Knopf, 1988). Observations on the life styles and value of individuals who have experienced several generations of influence.

Ames, Louis Bates and Joan Ames chase, *Don't Push Your Preschooler* (New York: Harper & Row, 1974). Discussions of the detrimental consequences of unreasonable expectations for the young child.

Ames, Louis Bates, *The Gesell Institute's Child from One to Six: Evaluating the Behavior of the Preschool Child* (New York: Harper & Row, 1979). Outlines developmental stages of young children and appropriate expectations for these various states.

Briggs, Dorothy Corkille, *Your Child's Self-Esteem* (New York: Doubleday, 1975). Classic book in the field of developing self-esteem in children.

Branden, Nathaniel, *How to Raise Your Self-Esteem* (New York: Bantam Books, 1987). Techniques for enhancing self-esteem.

Brazelton, T. Berry, *The Earliest Relationship: Parents, Infants and the Drama of Early Attachment* (Reading, MA: Addison-Wesley, 1990). A thorough presentation focusing on the importance of the parent-child bonding experience.

Canter, L. and L. Hausner, *Homework without Tears* (New York: Harper & Row, 1987). An action plan parents can utilize to assist their child in handling school obligations.

Coles, Robert, *Privileged Ones*. Children of Crisis, vol. 5. (Boston: Little, Brown & Company, 1977). A lengthy research study on the implications of affluence and child rearing.

Dreikurs, Rudolf, *Children the Challenge* (New York: Meridith Press, 1964). Classic general parenting guidebook.

Dreikurs, Rudolf and Pearl Cassel, *Discipline without Tears* (New York: Dutton, 1972). A more detailed discussion of the application of natural and logical consequences.

Dinkmeyer, Don and Gary D. McKay, *The Parent's Handbook for the Systematic Training for Effective Parenting* (American Guidance Service, 1982). The information contained in *Children the Challenge* has been condensed into an effective handbook format to accompany the Systematic Training for Effective Parenting program.

Elkind, David, *The Hurried Child* (Reading, MA: Addison-Wesley, Inc., 1981). Discusses the harmful consequences of hurrying children through their childhood at an accelerated pace.

Elkind, David, *Miseducation* (New York: Alfred Knopf, 1989). Evaluates the consequences of inappropriate educational approaches.

Gordon, Thomas, P.E.T. (*Parent Effectiveness Training*) (Wydan Books, 1976). Sound, basic parenting book.

Ginott, Haim, *Between Parent and Child* (New York: Macmillan, 1965). Highly popular general parenting book.

Holt, John, *How Children Learn* (New York: Delta/Seymour Lawrence, 1983). Presentation of the varied manners in which children can learn.

Levy, John L., *Coping with Inherited Wealth* (San Francisco: C. G. Jung Institute).

Results of a private research study into the influence of inherited wealth on heirs. Available through C.G. Jung Institute, 2040 Gough Street, San Francisco, CA 94109

Sedgwich, John, *Rich Kids* (New York: William Morrow, 1972). Series of interviews with numerous heirs and heiresses.

Stone, Michael H., "Upbringing in the Super-Rich," in *Modern Perspectives in the Psychiatry of Infancy* (New York: Brunner/Mazel, 1979). One of the few researchers in the field, the following papers discuss various research results obtained from studies of wealthy and celebrity parents.

The Child of a Famous Father or Mother," *Basic Handbook of Child Psychiatry*, vol. 1. (New York: Basic Books, 1979).

Stone, Michael H. and Clarice J. Kestenbaum, "Maternal Deprivation in Children of the Wealthy." *History of Childhood Quarterly*, vol. 1. no. 1. (Summer 1974).

Weinstein, Grace, *Children and Money* (New York: Charterhouse, 1975). A comprehensive presentation of children's understanding of money as well as methods for increasing their competency in dealing with financial issues.

Wixen, Burton N, *Children of the Rich* (New York: Crown, 1973). Psychiatric case studies.

Youngs, Bettie B, *Stress in Children* (New York: Arbor House, 1985). Identifies various stressors for children as well as suggesting interventions to reduce negative stress.